A PLUM

WRITERS BETWEEN THE COVERS

Brian Schmidt

Steven Rendon

SHANNON MCKENNA SCHMIDT and JONI RENDON are the authors of *Novel Destinations: Literary Landmarks from Jane Austen's Bath to Ernest Hemingway's Key West*.

Shannon has written for *Arrive*, *National Geographic Traveler*, *Shelf Awareness*, and other publications. A former New Jersey resident, she is traveling full-time in the United States and abroad.

Joni's work has appeared in *National Geographic Traveler*, *Travel + Leisure*, *BookPage*, *The Writer*, and on Bookreporter.com. Currently, she resides in London, England.

Writers Between the Covers

The Scandalous Romantic Lives of Legendary Literary Casanovas, Coquettes, and Cads

SHANNON MCKENNA SCHMIDT
AND JONI RENDON

A PLUME BOOK

PLUME
Published by the Penguin Group
Penguin Group (USA), 375 Hudson Street,
New York, New York 10014, USA

USA | Canada | UK | Ireland | Australia | New Zealand | India | South Africa | China
Penguin Books Ltd, Registered Offices: 80 Strand, London WC2R 0RL, England
For more information about the Penguin Group visit penguin.com

First published by Plume, a member of Penguin Group (USA), 2013

P REGISTERED TRADEMARK—MARCA REGISTRADA

LIBRARY OF CONGRESS CATALOGING-IN-PUBLICATION DATA
Schmidt, Shannon McKenna, 1971–
    Writers between the covers : the scandalous romantic lives of legendary literary
casanovas, coquettes, and cads / Shannon McKenna Schmidt and Joni Rendon.
      pages cm
    Includes bibliographical references.
    ISBN 978-0-452-29846-0 (pbk.)
    1. Authors—Relations with women.   2. Authors—Relations with men.   I. Rendon,
Joni, 1972–   II. Title.
    PN481.S36 2013
    700.92'2—dc23
    [B]   2013015840

Printed in the United States of America
10 9 8 7 6 5 4 3 2 1

Set in Perpetua Std.
Designed by Eve L. Kirch

To Brian and Steve

CONTENTS

Part Three: The Joy of Sex

Part Four: Unlucky in Love

Part Five: Your Cheating Heart

Part Six: Paradise Lost

Part Seven: This Side of Paradise

INTRODUCTION

What went on behind the doors of great writers' lairs? It's easy to envision solitary geniuses deep in contemplation, with only ink-stained manuscripts for company. What you'll actually find are sex symbols enjoying bacchanal romps and soul mates in the throes of passionate affairs of the heart.

We first became intrigued by the subject of writers' romantic lives while researching our previous book, *Novel Destinations*. Visiting the homes and haunts where famed writers lived, loved, and found inspiration, we repeatedly found ourselves sidetracked by the "love" aspect. Intriguing and surprising details emerged about their unorthodox and salacious behavior, inspiring us to delve deeper into their amorous entanglements.

Where exactly was the secret door that Victor Hugo used as an escape route for his mistress? Was it true that Charles Dickens had a thing for his sister-in-law? Like the nosy tourists who rented telescopes to spy on Lord Byron and the Shelleys during their summer on Lake Geneva, we wanted the inside scoop on the famous (and not so famous) hookups, makeups, and breakups of our literary idols.

Initially, we had glamorous notions of what hitching yourself to a writer was like—the fame! the glory! the romance!—but as we came to discover, love could be a dangerous game for the other half of a creative coupling. You could wind up stabbed in the back (Adele Mailer), alcoholic (Caitlin Thomas), institutionalized (Vivienne Eliot), alcoholic *and* institutionalized (Zelda Fitzgerald), or relegated to the role of caretaker (Leonard Woolf).

Some writers should come with a warning label. The same qualities that enabled many a successful wordsmith to bare his soul to the world—egotism, self-absorption, or plain old emotional intensity—often made him a lousy romantic partner. What's more, the world is uniquely forgiving of artistic types. Some, like Norman Mailer—whose violence, his editor claimed, was necessary to work up the courage to write—didn't even need to come to their own defense. They got away with unsavory behavior because, after all, they were *artists*. And aren't artists supposed to be bohemian, mysterious, and unpredictable?

It's practically a job requirement that writers live with greater intensity than the average joe. It shouldn't surprise us, then, that someone unshackled from the confines of traditional morality is more likely to turn out innovative, courageous prose than a kindly Ward Cleaver with a standing Saturday "date night." After all, Lord Byron didn't worry about a few shocking lines in his poem *Don Juan*, having bedded his sibling and been publicly dumped by his wife. On the contrary, he got a rush from scandalizing society with his prose as much as with his libidinous activities.

One wonders, would *Tender Is the Night* have been written if the Fitzgeralds' own marriage hadn't come undone in the south of France? Could T. S. Eliot have imagined the bleak world of *The Waste Land* without being driven to the brink of madness by his bipolar wife?

For other writers, a stalwart better half was the secret weapon that cemented their fame. Sophia Tolstoy hand transcribed the epic *War and Peace* seven times. Virginia Woolf's oeuvre largely owes its existence to her husband, Leonard, who for years kept her from heeding the call of the river Ouse. Gertrude Stein only became famous after channeling the voice of her longtime love Alice B. Toklas.

What makes literary romances so engrossing is that they are often documented in titillating detail in the writer's own hand. The most well-known epistolary lovebirds, Robert and Elizabeth Barrett Browning, exchanged nearly six hundred missives while courting. Others used the humble letter to fill the void in the days before phone sex and Internet porn. James Joyce's blushworthy correspondence waxed poetic about the eroticism of his wife's flatulence, while Henry Miller used letters to prime Anaïs Nin for an upcoming "literary fuck fest." She, by turn, used her sexcapades as fodder for her famed erotic diaries.

The jaw-dropping pairing of nerdy playwright Arthur Miller and sex symbol Marilyn Monroe showed that opposites can indeed attract, at least initially. But it appeared far more common for writers to choose partners similar to them, although even then a happy outcome was far from guaranteed. Enlightenment philosopher Voltaire and his brainy mistress bonded in the science lab *and* in the bedroom. Simone de Beauvoir and Jean-Paul Sartre shared a café table, a passion for philosophy, and a fondness for seducing their students. The very thing Ernest Hemingway and Martha Gellhorn had in common, war reporting, is what eventually led them to draw their own personal battle lines.

Our constant refrain while researching *Writers Between the Covers* was, "You can't make this stuff up." And you can't. Nor would you want to. When it comes to literary love lives, truth usually proves to be stranger (and more scandalous) than fiction.

PART ONE

Folie à Deux

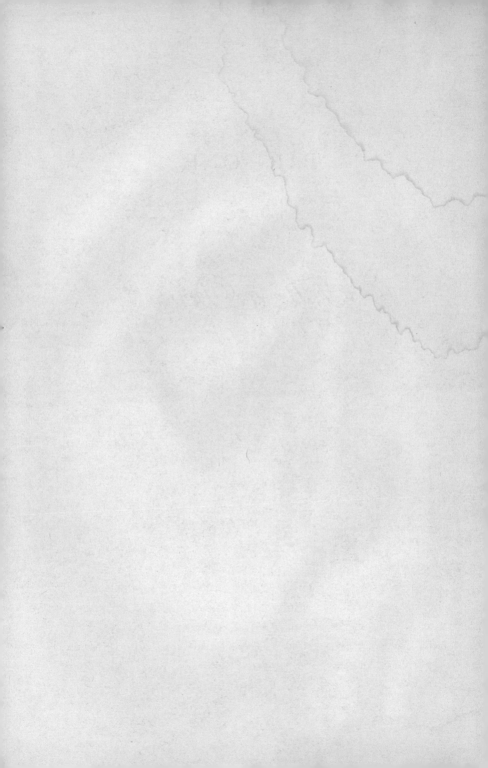

Some Like It Hot

ARTHUR MILLER

❧

A suicide kills two people, Maggie, that's what it's for!
—Arthur Miller, *After the Fall*

He was America's greatest living playwright; she was its most celebrated sex symbol. When Arthur Miller wed Marilyn Monroe, it was the start of a volatile, tempestuous relationship that lasted less than five years but haunted him for decades.

❧

"It was like running into a tree! You know—like a cool drink when you've got a fever," gushed blonde bombshell Marilyn Monroe after her first encounter with bespectacled playwright Arthur Miller, eleven years her senior. The unlikely pair had spent hours dancing and flirting at a Hollywood party, where the married father of two sensually rubbed Marilyn's toe as they gazed into each other's eyes. With only minor film roles under her belt, the twenty-five-year-old starlet was not yet famous when she met Miller in 1951. The playwright, on the other hand, had recently been crowned the titan of American theater after his dramatic masterpiece *Death of a Salesman* garnered both a Pulitzer and a Tony.

As Miller's career exploded, his marriage to college sweetheart Mary Slattery began foundering. By the time he met Monroe, "he was starved for sexual relief," said friend and film director Elia Kazan. Like most men, Miller was mesmerized by Marilyn's sensuality, while she was instantly smitten with his gentlemanly manners, intellectualism, and respect for her acting abilities. He insisted she had the chops to make it on Broadway at a time when no one was taking her ambition seriously.

Despite their mutual infatuation, the principled playwright was reluctant to begin an affair on the heels of a previous dalliance that had left him racked with guilt. Attempting to bury his feelings for Marilyn, he dutifully returned home to Brooklyn and didn't see the actress again for four years.

As her career skyrocketed, Marilyn dated many men and famously wed Joe DiMaggio, yet she continued to carry a torch for Miller. He was the first man to treat her as something more than a sex object, and she saw in him a protector and father figure whom she would eventually take to calling "Papa." When her whirlwind marriage to the Hall of Fame slugger ended after just nine months, the ambitious actress left Hollywood to hone her craft in New York. Once there, she didn't spend long licking her wounds and soon embarked on a clandestine courtship with the unhappily married playwright.

"She was a whirling light to me then, all paradox and enticing mystery," Miller wrote of the radiant, complex blonde whose glamorous, ditzy image belied her hidden depths and internal anguish. His fierce attraction to her was a combination of lust mingled with pity inspired by her troubled childhood. Born fatherless and unwanted, Marilyn was initially raised by her schizophrenic mother before being placed in foster care. The sensitive playwright was deeply moved by her tragic story and thought he could rescue Marilyn from her demons.

Despite the couple's vast differences, each found unmet needs fulfilled by the other. While Marilyn's deep-rooted insecurity and low self-esteem were buoyed by the brainy playwright, Miller's ego received a boost from having the most desirable woman in America on his arm. Like any ordinary couple, they enjoyed simple pleasures like bike riding, swimming, taking long walks, and listening to jazz records.

In the summer of 1956, Miller took the anguished step of divorcing his wife to marry the movie star. Even before the marriage took place, he found himself unprepared for the aggressive media attention that accompanied Marilyn's celebrity and engulfed everyone in her orbit. Once their engagement was announced, "the Great American Brain" and "the Great American Body" were dogged by paparazzi until the time of their divorce.

The sheer unlikelihood of their coupling—"Egghead Weds Hourglass" screamed newspaper headlines—brought their union much unwanted attention. Negative predictions and snap judgments were doled out by pundits like Truman Capote, who quipped the marriage could be called "Death of a Playwright." Marilyn's camp also discouraged the nuptials, concerned that her all-American image would be tarnished by Miller's "unpatriotic" leftist politics.

Despite Marilyn's prewedding declaration that she wanted to make fewer movies and cultivate her domestic side, it appeared domesticity would have to wait. Two weeks into the marriage, the world's most famous newlyweds touched down in England. The actress was due to star with Laurence Olivier in *The Prince and the Showgirl*, which thrust Miller into his own unexpected role as her caretaker, psychiatrist, parent, and chief apologist. He was shocked by his bride's Jekyll-and-Hyde transformation on the movie set, where the intense pressure she placed on herself to perform opened a Pandora's box of anxieties and insecurities.

In order to cope, Marilyn self-medicated with an arsenal of

prescription drugs, a predilection that came as yet another nasty surprise to Miller. He recorded his frustrations and doubts about her in a notebook, which Marilyn had the misfortune to discover. The contents of the journal sent her reeling, and the incident (later incorporated into Miller's play *After the Fall*) fueled her explosive temper and paranoia. To soothe her frayed nerves, she began hitting the bottle before filming, a volatile combination with her uppers and downers. Miller bore the brunt of her erratic mood swings and likened her to a smashed vase: "It is a beautiful thing when it is intact, but the broken pieces are murderous and they can cut you."

Some of Marilyn's emotional difficulties during the making of the movie could be blamed on an unexpected pregnancy, the first of three with Miller that she was unable to carry to term. The actress yearned to have a child, and each miscarriage sent her into a fresh spiral of depression, contributing to her multiple suicide attempts.

Although the couple's relationship never recovered from the battering it took on the movie set, there were occasional happy times, particularly when Marilyn was away from the stress of performing. She did take a stab at domesticity (once humorously drying homemade pasta with a hair dryer), and together they frolicked on the beach in the Hamptons and oversaw the restoration of their nineteenth-century Connecticut farmhouse.

But even at home, their glaring differences became impossible to ignore. Miller's work depended on privacy and quiet, while Marilyn, like an exotic hothouse flower, required constant attention. She had no hobbies and few close friends; according to their maid, most of her time was spent sleeping, seeing her psychiatrist, attending acting lessons, and looking at herself in the mirror. Marilyn hated being alone and resented the time her husband spent trying to write, at one point raging, "I'm in a fucking prison and my jailer is named Arthur Miller. . . . Every morning he goes into that goddamn study of his, and I don't see him for hours and hours. . . . And here I am, just sitting around; I haven't a goddamn thing to do."

Selfishly, she failed to recognize that the enormity of her needs smothered her husband's creativity. For the duration of their marriage, Miller wrote no new plays as he gave himself over to being Marilyn's protector and go-between with unhappy directors and studio executives. Such self-sacrificing devotion led Norman Mailer to deride him as "the most talented slave in the world."

In the summer of 1958, the actress flew to Los Angeles to film *Some Like It Hot*. Miller stayed behind to work but was soon forced to uproot himself after she was hospitalized for an overdose. Her unprofessionalism on the set—consistently being hours late, failing to memorize her lines (just saying "Where's the bourbon?" required fifty-nine takes), and being rude to coworkers—caused the usual problems, requiring Miller to stay and attempt to glue her back together.

After filming wrapped, Marilyn suffered another miscarriage. While she recuperated, her despairing husband hit on the idea of turning his short story "The Misfits" into a film for her. The movie would give Marilyn the type of serious role she craved, which Miller hoped would rouse her out of her depression and bring them closer together. Bizarrely, Marilyn seemed less than enthusiastic about the project, only reluctantly signing on after John Huston was secured as the director. Miller's feelings—and ego—were crushed by her reaction.

While the screenplay and casting were in the works, Marilyn starred in *Let's Make Love* and had a highly publicized fling with her costar, Yves Montand. Although the married actor fled to France as soon as filming was over, the groundwork was laid for disastrous conditions on the set of *The Misfits*. "By the time we got to make the film . . . we were no longer man and wife," said the defeated playwright.

Over the next four months, as they filmed on location in Nevada, the two were barely on speaking terms. Marilyn heaped scorn and hostility on her husband, refusing to pose together in photos and often screaming insults at him. She once drove off without him after a day of filming, forcing him to trek through the desert until he was spotted alongside the road and rescued by John Huston. Miller stoically ignored the ill-treatment so the production wouldn't face further delays and disruption.

Meanwhile, Marilyn's chaotic, drug-fueled behavior reached new extremes. In addition to her chronic tardiness and ill-preparedness, she would often appear dazed and disoriented and was even spotted riding a hotel elevator in the nude. In the midst of filming, she was hospitalized for "exhaustion," which in actuality was the director's attempt to lessen her dependence on barbiturates.

Miller later said of the doomed movie, "What's very sad is that I had written it to make Marilyn feel good. And for her, it resulted in complete collapse." In the semiautobiographical role he wrote for her, Marilyn played a beautiful, sensitive divorcée who is disappointed with marriage but arouses the interest of three very different men. The rawness of the role, which stripped the movie star of her trademark glamour and glitz, gave her talent the chance to shine.

Rather than being grateful, Marilyn became convinced, as she did on every movie set, that she was being victimized. By the time filming wrapped, in the fall of 1960, she had announced her separation from Miller. In the end, each had married an idea of the other that could not be sustained. "I think we believed we'd complement each other. Of course that was a mistake," rued Miller.

Although *The Misfits* signaled the death of his marriage, it opened a surprising new door. Once back in New York, Miller was viewing movie stills when chemistry sparked with Inge Morath, one of the photographers who documented the making of the film.

Inge reluctantly accepted the playwright's lunch invitation, bringing along a coworker as a buffer. "I thought Arthur would be a sad person," she said, "but he turned out to be a very funny man."

The globe-trotting photographer, whose high-powered career meant she was rarely in one place for more than a few days, was the polar opposite of Marilyn. "Inge was a great relief, because she didn't need anybody nursing her along," admitted Miller. Soon into their relationship, he was inspired to write his play *After the Fall*, which centers on a twice-married man redeemed through the love of a third woman. When it opened on Broadway in 1964, audiences reacted angrily to its thinly veiled portrayal of Marilyn as a self-destructive singer who dies of an overdose, just as the star herself had died eighteen months earlier. Although Miller had begun working on the play well before Marilyn's death, he was accused of exploiting the martyred actress for his own dramatic purposes.

Insisting the work was "neither more nor less autobiographical" than his other plays, Miller penned an elaborate protestation of his innocence for *Life* magazine. What the public didn't know was that the playwright was using the stage to examine his conflicted feelings about proposing to Inge. His dismal track record had made him gun-shy about marriage, but the third time proved a charm. He later described his forty years with Inge as "the best of my life."

Despite Miller's unexpected happiness and salvation, it was never enough to absolve his guilt over Marilyn. His failure to save her—and salvage their marriage—continued to haunt him until his death. At the age of eighty-seven he wrote his last play, *Finishing the Picture*, about their experience working together on *The Misfits*. Perhaps by exhuming Marilyn one last time on the stage, he was able to bury her ghost along with his own personal demons.

ɾ THREE'S A CROWD ɚ

Playboy poet Ezra Pound slyly justified his infidelity by claiming a correlation between his ability to seduce and his creativeness. For him and other writers, love triangles endured for decades, often turned out badly, and occasionally led to unusual friendships.

~ **Too close for comfort.** Ezra Pound and his wife moved in with his mistress after German troops took over the Italian town where they lived during World War II. For nearly two years, he was "pent up with two women who loved him, whom he loved, and who coldly hated each other," said his daughter of the strained living arrangements. Pound maintained relationships with both women simultaneously for an astounding fifty years.

~ **Master of two mistresses.** Victorian novelist Wilkie Collins's aversion to marriage didn't stop him from setting up households with two different women. One moved into his London abode, pretending to be his housekeeper, while his second paramour and their three children lived in another part of town under an assumed name.

~ **Share and share alike.** E. M. Forster was a witness at the registry-office ceremony when his lover, policeman Bob Buckingham, married nurse May Hockey. For decades, the energetic lawman divided his time between his wife and the writer. The two competitors started out as adversaries but eventually became such close friends that May nursed Forster in his final days.

~ **Put it in writing.** Serial philanderer Kingsley Amis always went back to his wife—until he fell for fellow novelist Elizabeth Jane Howard. On a last getaway together, his spurned spouse aired her grievances. As Amis snoozed poolside, she scrawled on his back in lipstick, "1 fat Englishman. I fuck anything."

~ **Crime of passion.** One mistress wasn't enough for Victor Hugo, whose insatiable sexual appetite got him arrested after he was caught with Léonie Biard, an artist's wife. Tipped off by Léonie's jealous husband, a detective found the amorous pair in flagrante delicto in a Parisian love nest Hugo kept just for such purposes. While the writer was ultimately freed, under the sexist French legal system, Léonie was sent to jail. Hugo's wife took up the shamed woman's cause, pleased that his beloved, longtime mistress Juliette Drouet had a rival.

The Love Song of T. S. Eliot

T. S. ELIOT

What we call the beginning is often the end. And to make an end is to make a beginning. The end is where we start from.

—T. S. Eliot, *Little Gidding*

During his disastrous honeymoon, T. S. Eliot reportedly spent the night in a deck chair while his bride barricaded herself inside their hotel room. The neurotic pair's eighteen-year partnership produced numerous nervous breakdowns and some of the twentieth century's finest poetry.

"The truth will all come out, if not in *our* life—*then after it*," promised Vivienne Eliot, wife of famed modernist poet T. S. (Thomas Stearns) Eliot, from the asylum where she had been committed against her will in 1938. She blamed Eliot's cruelty for causing her breakdown and longed for the world to know her side of the story.

Although she was eccentric and plagued by a nervous disposition, Vivienne may not have been the "mad" Ophelia that history has made her out to be. Decades after her death in 1947, her brother, who signed her incarceration papers, admitted, "It was only when I saw Vivie in the asylum for the last time I realised I had done something very wrong. . . . She was as sane as I was." Like Zelda Fitzgerald, the neurotic wife of another famous writer, Vivienne died while institutionalized.

She had spent her last hours of freedom wandering the streets of London in a delusional state, not unlike the tortured wife in Eliot's poem *The Waste Land*, who proclaims in desperation, "I shall rush out as I am, and walk the street." When her brother was summoned to collect her, he wrote alarmingly to the vacationing poet that Vivienne was "full of the most fantastic suspicions. She asked me if it was true that you had been beheaded."

Vivienne's grip on reality had steadily loosened after Eliot deserted her five years earlier. Coldly, he had informed her of his desire to separate in a letter from his solicitor, sent while he was abroad teaching. His cowardly action avoided a painful confrontation, which he continued to forestall after his return to England by going into hiding.

Denied even the chance to meet with her husband, Vivienne refused to accept their breakup and became convinced she could change his mind if she could only speak to him again in person. Eliot refused, insisting through his lawyers that further discussions were "fruitless and unnecessary." His abrupt and inexplicable withdrawal would have driven even the sanest of wives to the brink, but for a woman already plagued by abandonment issues, it spelled disaster. Overcome with a growing sense of helplessness and hysteria, Vivienne began to stalk him.

Her attempts to track him down through the passport office and their dentist were foiled by his frequent moves, and she took to haunting his workplace. Embarrassingly, she would sit weeping in the waiting room while Eliot slipped out the back door, alerted by a special ring from his secretary. Evenings would find her canvassing performances of his plays, hoping for a sighting.

Out of options, she attempted to place an advertisement in the *Times* personals, which the newspaper withheld from publication. The ad pleaded: "Will T. S. Eliot please return to his home 68 Clarence Gate Gardens which he abandoned Sept. 17th, 1932." Even after bailiffs raided her apartment to repossess her estranged husband's belongings, she clung to the hope that he might return and would often leave the door ajar.

After three long years, Vivienne's perseverance was briefly rewarded when she tracked Eliot down at a book signing. She approached him but was swiftly rebuffed: "I cannot talk to you now," Eliot said dismissively, before rushing off. He never again made an effort to see her, either before or during her nine-year incarceration. Although he was said to be acting on the advice of her doctors, his complete disengagement seems unfeeling and inhumane.

When Vivienne's brother rang in 1947 to tell him she had unexpectedly died (possibly from a deliberate overdose), the poet is said to have become profoundly distressed, crying out, "Oh God, oh God." Despite his conviction that leaving had been a necessary act of self-preservation, he was nonetheless tormented by his decision. His autobiographical play *The Family Reunion*, about a tortured man who may or may not have killed his wife, is thought to have been an attempt to grapple with his conflicted feelings.

For a repressed man who spent a lifetime fleeing emotion, Eliot's choice of a flamboyant, high-strung bride like Vivienne is puzzling. The mismatched pair had wed after a whirlwind courtship while the shy American poet was a student at Oxford. Cracks in their marriage began showing immediately, when Vivienne's unpredictable menstrual period arrived on their honeymoon.

It's hard to say who was more distressed, the nervous bride or the inexperienced poet, who was still a virgin and squeamish about female sexuality. The reluctant Romeo was also hamstrung by embarrassment over his hernia, and the abortive first night of passion did little to boost his confidence. Vivienne's insistence on bringing home the soiled sheets for laundering only prolonged the painful ordeal.

Flummoxed by her husband's disinterest in sex, Vivienne consoled herself in the arms of his former teacher, the philosopher Bertrand Russell. Eliot may have tacitly condoned the affair, happy to be off the hook in the bedroom. At the time, he was preoccupied with his dawning awareness of Vivienne's many maladies. In addition to suffering from manic depression and a hormonal imbalance, she had debilitating migraines, neuralgia, rheumatism, and later developed an eating disorder and addiction to pain medication.

Vivienne's illnesses blighted every aspect of their existence, but Eliot stuck it out for more than a decade. He bore her difficulties with saintly patience, even giving up teaching for a higher-paid job in a bank so he could afford her mounting medical expenses. His round-the-clock ministrations brought on his own collapses, which would render him bedridden for weeks at a time.

Still, there were unexpected compensations. "Vivienne ruined him as a man but she made him as a poet," claimed an acquaintance. Eliot himself later admitted, "To her the marriage brought no happiness . . . to me, it brought the state of mind out of which came *The Waste Land*." The 434-line confessional poem, considered one of the greatest of the twentieth century, was largely composed in a Swiss sanitarium while he was being treated for his own breakdown.

Eliot's illnesses and heavy drinking offered him a refuge from his marriage as his wife's bizarre behavior intensified. Among other eccentricities, she took to carrying a toy knife in her handbag, once using it to threaten Virginia Woolf, whom she accused of being Eliot's mistress. Sympathetic to the poet, Woolf spoke of Vivienne as a "bag of ferrets" around his neck, forever "biting, wriggling, raving, scratching." Vivienne's erratic actions, Eliot's compensatory drinking, and their constant mutual sniping hampered their social life. Friends described being sucked dry by their presence, and many refused to see the dysfunctional pair together anymore.

As the marriage reached its inexorable conclusion, Eliot laid the foundations for a separate life by joining the Church of England and taking a vow of chastity, an insurance policy against any more bad sex. He also began a secret correspondence with Bostonian Emily Hale, who had been his first love while he was a student at Harvard. Both of their families had assumed the sweethearts would marry, until Eliot's move to Europe and his impulsive decision to wed Vivienne. Twelve years after being thrown over, Emily wrote to her former flame, instigating a furtive but chaste cross-Atlantic friendship.

Over the next three decades, the poet penned her more than a thousand letters, and she frequently visited him in England. When Vivienne was found wandering the streets and committed to an asylum, Emily and Eliot were away together. Despite their closeness, Eliot imposed a wall of secrecy around their relationship and few in his circle knew of Emily's existence.

Emily acquiesced to remaining in the shadows, believing her virtuous silence would be rewarded with a walk down the aisle. But after Vivienne passed away, she was dismayed to find Eliot unwilling to make a commitment. Instead he claimed he felt incapable of ever sharing a life with anyone again. Their friendship continued in spite of the crushing rejection, perhaps because Emily, like Vivienne before her, did not give up hope that he might reconsider.

She might have reacted differently if she had known that the unlikely playboy had another gal pal in the wings. Englishwoman Mary Trevelyan had been Eliot's confidante and frequent escort to social events since the year of Vivienne's confinement. Although he gave off mixed signals by sending her presents and sometimes holding her hand, he also discouraged intimacy by limiting their contact to once every two weeks. Undeterred by Eliot's standoffishness, Mary proposed to him three times. Each time the poet demurred, claiming he thought they were just friends and that the idea of re-marrying was like a nightmare.

Despite his seemingly implacable stance on marriage, at the age of sixty-eight Eliot stunned everyone by tying the knot with his thirty-year-old secretary, Valerie Fletcher. The couple exchanged vows in a secret ceremony that took place at 7:00 a.m. to avoid publicity, and was witnessed only by the bride's parents and a single friend. Not a soul had known of this covert office romance. After hearing the shocking news, Mary Trevelyan stopped speaking to him, while Emily Hale had a nervous breakdown.

Eliot's second marriage brought him immense happiness. He and Valerie were inseparable, and those who knew him marveled at his profound contentment. Not known for sentimentality or romanti-cism, he broke the stereotype by publishing a love poem called "A Dedication to My Wife." The verse describes an ideal union between two people "Who think the same thoughts without need of speech / And babble the same speech without need of meaning."

The second Mrs. Eliot was equally besotted, having been a dev-otee of the poet since age fourteen when she heard a recording of his poem "Journey of the Magi." Fate was on her side when, after train-ing as a secretary, she learned of an opening working for Eliot at the publishing firm Faber and Faber. During Valerie's seven years as his devoted employee, the couple's feelings quietly blossomed until she received Eliot's coy handwritten proposal in a batch of typing.

Cynics claim the ailing poet, who suffered from emphysema and heart problems, had married to secure a trustworthy nurse-maid and literary executor, though Valerie disputed this interpreta-tion. "He obviously needed to have a happy marriage. He wouldn't die until he'd had it," she said. "There was a little boy in him that needed to be released."

❧ BREAKING UP IS HARD TO DO ❧

Before social media made saying sayonara as easy as changing your Facebook status, the time-honored tradition of the breakup letter did the dirty work.

~ To have and have not. Prior to earning his macho reputation as a love 'em and leave 'em ladies man, eighteen-year-old Ernest Hemingway had his heart broken by an older woman during World War I. While serving as an ambulance driver on the Italian front, the writer was injured by exploding shrapnel and tended to by Agnes von Kurowsky, a pretty American Red Cross nurse. A heady romance ensued, but their plans to marry were dashed when Agnes (the model for Catherine Barkley in *A Farewell to Arms*) fell for someone else and crushed him with a Dear John letter:

> *For quite awhile before you left, I was trying to convince myself it was a real love-affair. . . . Now, after a couple of months away from you, I know that I am still very fond of you, but, it is more as a mother than as a sweetheart.*

~ Valley girl. Before Jacqueline Susann found stardom with her tale of bed-hopping, pill-popping starlets, *Valley of the Dolls*, the struggling actress funded her glamorous lifestyle by marrying wealthy publicist Irving Mansfield. The two sybarites enjoyed the good life, living in a posh New York City hotel and dining on steak and Dom Pérignon. But after Irving was drafted into the army, Susann fell for someone else. She composed a heartlessly humorous kiss-off letter and read it aloud to her shocked cast mates before mailing it to Mansfield:

Irving, when we were at the Essex House and I had room service and I could buy all my Florence Lustig dresses, I found that I loved you very much, but now that you're in the army and getting $56 a month, I feel that my love has waned.

~ **It's not you; it's me.** Like her famous character Jane Eyre, who turned down a marriage proposal from a man she didn't love, Charlotte Brontë did the same when her best friend's brother popped the question. Although the twenty-three-year-old novelist thought herself unattractive and doubted other offers would come her way, she refused to make a passionless match simply for the sake of security. Rebuffing her dull clergyman-suitor, she gently explained that she was not the right wife for him:

My answer to your proposal must be a <u>decided negative</u>. . . . I have no personal repugnance to the idea of a union with you—but I feel convinced that mine is not the sort of disposition calculated to form the happiness of a man like you. . . . I am not the serious, grave, cool-headed individual you suppose.

~ **Exile on Main Street.** The marriage between Nobel laureate Sinclair Lewis and foreign correspondent Dorothy Thompson was troubled from the start. Thompson mistakenly thought she could reform the notorious alcoholic, while the insecure author of classics like *Babbitt* and *Main Street* was jealous of his wife's political clout. (Once, while they were in bed together, President Roosevelt rang for Dorothy.) After more than a decade of marriage, Lewis stormed out, claiming his wife's success had robbed him of his creativity. While

Dorothy was reluctant to part ways, she finally agreed to call it quits four years later:

> Go ahead and get a divorce. I won't oppose it. I also won't get it. For God's sake, let's be honest. You left me, I didn't leave you. You want it. I don't. You get it. On any ground your lawyers can fake up. Say I "deserted" you. Make a case for mental cruelty. You can make a case. Go and get it.

Beautiful and Damned

F. Scott and Zelda Fitzgerald

Nobody has ever measured, even the poets, how much a heart can hold.

—Zelda Fitzgerald, "The Big Top"

During one unforgettable week in 1920, F. Scott Fitzgerald published his debut novel, *This Side of Paradise*, and married his dream girl, Zelda Sayre. Their charmed life cracked up within a decade, heartbreakingly mired in alcoholism, mental illness, infidelity, and artistic rivalry—leading Fitzgerald to bitterly lament that his capacity for hope was left on the road to Zelda's sanitarium.

In the summer of 1918, at a country club dance in Montgomery, Alabama, dashing young army lieutenant F. Scott Fitzgerald met free-spirited, flirtatious Zelda Sayre, who had a reputation for speaking her mind and engaging in wild behavior like smoking in public. A stormy courtship ensued, with endearing, passionate, and angry letters exchanged between the southern belle and her beau, who worked as a poorly paid advertising copywriter in New York City after leaving the military.

While eager to escape her parents' home and start a new life, Zelda nonetheless took a hard line with Fitzgerald. She broke off their relationship and refused to marry him until he made something of himself and could support them in high style. Zelda's declaration, along with steep competition for her affections, spurred the aspiring novelist to take a leap of faith. He jettisoned his job and sequestered himself in his parents' attic in Saint Paul, Minnesota, to work on his writing.

Within months of being given this ultimatum, Fitzgerald jubilantly ran up and down the streets of his hometown as he shouted out the news that his first novel, *This Side of Paradise*, was going to appear in print. Picked up by a renowned publisher, the book brought him instant fame, considerable cash, and a new bride. A week after it debuted in April 1920, selling out the initial printing within days, he and Zelda tied the knot at St. Patrick's Cathedral in New York City. The twenty-three-year-old groom and his nineteen-year-old bride honeymooned at the Biltmore Hotel, where their drunken revels got so out of hand that they were asked to check out and take the festivities elsewhere.

The public was fascinated by the striking pair, who epitomized the glamour and lavishness of the postwar 1920s, a period Scott famously dubbed the Jazz Age. The fashionable, vivacious Zelda shared the limelight with her spouse and even gave joint interviews with him. She represented a new generation of liberated women who emerged in the Roaring Twenties, as young people disillusioned by the devastation of World War I rebelled against old-fashioned conventions and attitudes. Determined to be recognized as men's equals, flappers like Zelda boldly cut their hair into boyish bobs, abandoned corsets for shift dresses with shortened hemlines, drove motorcars, defied Prohibition at speakeasies, and treated sex in a newly casual manner.

"I married the heroine of my stories," boasted the novelist. He was already writing about flappers when he met Zelda, the flesh-and-blood embodiment of his fictional creations. Scott infused the character of Rosalind Connage in *This Side of Paradise* with aspects of his love interest's personality, mannerisms, and witticisms (often verbatim). He gave Zelda chapters of the novel to read, courting her in a unique way that both charmed her and appealed to her vanity.

Despite flattering Zelda by immortalizing her in print, Scott was still smarting over being dumped by her until his coffers increased. He denied the novel's lovesick Princeton University student Amory Blaine a walk down the aisle with the debutante Rosalind. "Marrying you would be a failure and I never fail," she blithely informs her smitten suitor before running off with a wealthier man. The fictional heartbreaker's callous treatment of Amory, however, didn't dissuade Zelda from identifying with her. "I like the ones that are like me! That's why I love Rosalind in *This Side of Paradise*," she proclaimed. "I like their courage, their recklessness and spendthriftness."

Before Fitzgerald published any additional novels, he and Zelda produced their only child. Following a two-month trip to England, France, and Italy, they retreated to Saint Paul to await the arrival of their daughter, Scottie, in October 1921. Becoming parents didn't slow down their hard-partying ways. They headed east, baby in tow, resuming their life of excess in Manhattan and Great Neck, the suburban Long Island town that provided a model for West Egg in *The Great Gatsby*.

The couple regularly showed up in gossip columns because of outrageous escapades like riding atop a taxi down Fifth Avenue, jumping into a public fountain (Zelda), and undressing at a theater (Scott). Their turbulent, hedonistic lifestyle and alcohol-fueled fights offered fodder for Scott's second novel, *The Beautiful and Damned*. The story follows New York City socialites Anthony and Gloria Patch from heady days of extravagance and nonstop revelry to a

sobering new reality when an anticipated inheritance doesn't mate-
rialize.

Zelda penned a cheeky review of *The Beautiful and Damned* in
which she implored readers to buy the book as she had her eye on a
pricey gold dress and a platinum ring. But underlying the seemingly
irreverent piece is a serious admission. "On one page I recognized a
portion of an old diary of mine which mysteriously disappeared
shortly after my marriage, and also scraps of letters which, though
considerably edited, sound to me vaguely familiar," revealed Zelda.
"In fact, Mr. Fitzgerald . . . seems to believe that plagiarism begins
at home."

Not only did Fitzgerald attribute some of Zelda's physical char-
acteristics and personality traits to his characters, with her consent
he lifted passages from her journals and letters to use in his fiction.
At the time this "plagiarism" was something of a lark to Zelda and
a way for her to support the breadwinner who funded their swanky
lifestyle. When a well-known drama critic happened upon her
lively diaries during one of the couple's soirées and expressed interest in publishing them, Scott opposed the idea because he wanted
dibs on the material for his novels and short stories.

The Fitzgeralds' finances were perpetually shaky, with the royalty checks spent almost as soon as they were cashed. In 1924, after
the failure of a play they were counting on to boost their bank account, the couple and their daughter set sail for Europe, where a
favorable exchange rate meant they could afford a grander lifestyle.

After a brief stay in Paris, Scott and Zelda headed to the French
Riviera in search of the solitude he needed to write. At a seaside villa,
he shut himself away for long periods and forbade any interruptions
while he worked on *The Great Gatsby*. Lonely and resentful at being
abandoned, Zelda struck up an intimate friendship with French aviator Edouard Jozan. "I must say everyone knew about it but Scott,"
remarked an acquaintance who witnessed the budding affair.

A histrionic scene ensued when Zelda confessed to Scott that she was in love with Jozan and asked for a divorce. He furiously responded that her lover would have to confront him in her presence. Zelda backed down and ultimately decided to stay with Scott, having regained his attention with the illicit fling but still desperately unhappy. The incident further damaged their already strained relationship, and shortly afterward she tried to commit suicide by taking an overdose of sleeping pills.

"That September 1924 I knew something had happened that could never be repaired," Fitzgerald said of the unhappy period. He admitted having encouraged his wife to spend time with Jozan as a distraction while he worked. Although other men routinely fell in love with Zelda, "it never occurred to me that the friendship could turn into an affair," he said. And yet he acknowledged that he may have unconsciously encouraged the situation to stimulate his fiction. An affair with tragic consequences is integral to *The Great Gatsby*'s storyline. Infidelity is also a pivotal plot point in a later work, *Tender Is the Night*, in which Nicole Diver leaves her psychiatrist husband for a mercenary soldier.

The couple's incessant love of drama found expression in the various embellished accounts of the love triangle they shared with friends and acquaintances, including the claim that Scott locked Zelda in the villa for a month after finding out about her romance. She falsely reported that a despondent Jozan killed himself, while her husband boasted that he had challenged her admirer to a duel. According to Scott's fantasized account, both men fired and missed— an episode that appears in *Tender Is the Night*.

Back in Paris, the Fitzgeralds fell in with other expatriate writers, including Ernest Hemingway, who made some sharp observations about the couple's relationship in the memoir *A Moveable Feast*. He believed his fellow writer was talented enough that he might have surpassed his masterwork, *The Great Gatsby*, if not for a critical factor. "I did not know Zelda yet," Hemingway wrote, "and so I did not know the terrible odds that were against him."

In Hemingway's opinion, Zelda was jealous of Scott's work and encouraged him to drink to excess so he wouldn't be able to write. "As soon as he was working well Zelda would begin complaining about how bored she was and get him off on another drunken party," he recalled. "They would quarrel and then make up and he would sweat out the alcohol on long walks with me, and make up his mind that this time he would really work, and would start off well. Then it would start all over again."

According to the gossipy Hemingway, who had a notoriously contentious acquaintance with Zelda, she verbally emasculated her husband by telling him he could never make a woman happy in bed. "She said it was a matter of measurements," confided Fitzgerald, who hadn't slept with anyone expect his wife. In the bathroom of a Paris restaurant, Hemingway assessed his writer pal's implement, deemed it acceptable, and called Zelda crazy.

On subsequent trips to the Riviera following Zelda's affair, both Fitzgeralds began drinking more heavily. They became increasingly and deliberately reckless, daring each other to cliff dive into the sea at night and driving dangerously on winding mountain roads. While dining out one evening, Scott flirted with dancer Isadora Duncan, who was seated at a nearby table. As she stroked his hair and called him her centurion, Zelda launched herself down a set of stone stairs.

After two and a half tumultuous years abroad, the Fitzgeralds returned stateside but found little respite from their marital woes. During a stay in Hollywood, Zelda was distressed by Scott's blatant infatuation with seventeen-year-old actress Lois Moran. He would often take the young girl and her mother out on the town, leaving his wife behind. Scott further upset Zelda with his effusive praise of Moran's initiative in forging a career, something she desired for

herself. (When she had expressed an interest in acting, years earlier, he derided her ambition and ultimately persuaded her against
it.) During one desolate evening alone, she made a bonfire in the
hotel bathtub and destroyed clothes she had designed herself.

On their way back east by train, Scott informed his wife that
he had invited Moran to visit them once they found a home. Zelda
responded to this malicious pronouncement by tossing out the window a platinum and diamond wristwatch Scott had bought her as an
engagement gift.

It's not known for certain if Fitzgerald's involvement with
Moran—whose short blonde hair and facial features were strikingly
similar to his wife's—was merely emotional or turned physical. She
did, at any rate, leave enough of an impression to inspire Rosemary
Hoyt, the beautiful teenaged actress with whom Dick Diver, a married man twice her age, has an affair in *Tender Is the Night*. Even the
name Rosemary is a not-so-subtle reference to Moran, taken from
the character she played in the film *The Road to Mandalay*.

When introducing readers to Rosemary, Fitzgerald waxed poetic about the character's youth and looks. "Her fine forehead sloped
gently up to where her hair, bordering it like an armorial shield,
burst into lovelocks and waves and curlicues of ash blonde and
gold," he wrote. "Her body hovered delicately on the last edge of
childhood—she was almost eighteen, nearly complete, but the dew
was still on her."

Fitzgerald toiled for years on *Tender Is the Night*, which appeared
nine years after *The Great Gatsby*. Zelda meanwhile had a creative
awakening of her own and began painting, writing, and taking ballet lessons, a youthful interest revived during her time in Paris. She
penned articles and short stories that appeared under a dual byline
with her husband, who was seen as the top draw by magazine editors. In at least one instance, a tale she wrote appeared solely as his
creation.

The couple crossed the Atlantic two more times for extended stays. While living in Paris, thirty-year-old Zelda suffered her first mental breakdown, triggered in part by obsessive and strenuous ballet practice. In 1930, less than a month after the couple's tenth wedding anniversary, she entered a clinic for a short time. When hallucinations recurred and she again attempted suicide, Fitzgerald took her to a sanatorium in Switzerland. Zelda spent the rest of her life in and out of institutions in Europe and the United States, with Scott standing by her and often taking lodgings nearby.

The deck may have been stacked against the couple from the start. It's possible that Zelda, whose family had a history of mental illness, suffered from manic depression or schizophrenia, or perhaps both. Not much was known about either disease at the time. Likewise, the alcoholism that afflicted Scott was not yet recognized as an addiction but instead seen as a moral failing or a character flaw. Others speculate that Zelda's maladies had a far simpler cause: stifled artistic creativity.

During a stay at a Baltimore clinic in 1932, Zelda turned out, in less than two months, the autobiographical novel *Save Me the Waltz*. She incorporated elements of her life with Scott, which infuriated him because it overlapped with material he was using in *Tender Is the Night*. He became even more enraged when he learned that Zelda had sent her novel to his editor, who wanted to publish it. Along with demanding that half the royalties be applied to debts he owed the publisher, Scott took a heavy hand in editing the story, including reworking the portrayal of the fictional husband to make him more sympathetic.

When Hollywood beckoned again, Fitzgerald heeded the call and signed on as a scriptwriter with a movie studio. He took up romantically with gossip columnist Sheilah Graham and started working on a novel, *The Love of the Last Tycoon*. Living a fairly quiet life, he altered some of his self-destructive behavior, even giving up drinking in his last year. But it was too little too late, and the forty-four-year-old writer died of a heart attack at Graham's apartment in December 1940.

A year and a half before Scott's death, he and Zelda saw each other for the last time during a drama-filled holiday in Cuba. After Scott became drunk and was severely beaten while trying to break up a cockfight, Zelda took charge and got them back to the States. Upon their return, he wrote to her of the affection he still had for her: "You are the finest, loveliest, tenderest, most beautiful person I have ever known."

Seven years after Scott's death, Zelda too met an untimely and tragic end. While she was locked in a North Carolina hospital room awaiting electroshock treatment, a nighttime fire broke out, killing her and eight other women. The Jazz Age chronicler and his muse are laid to rest in a Maryland cemetery, where their shared tomb is etched with *The Great Gatsby*'s concluding line: "So we beat on, boats against the current, borne back ceaselessly into the past."

❧ COUGARS AND CRADLE ROBBERS ❧

These May-December romantics were undeterred by their vast differences in age.

Fourteen years. Cradle robber Edgar Allan Poe wed his thirteen-year-old cousin, Virginia Clemm, though he respectfully waited until his bride turned sixteen before consummating their union.

Sixteen years. With a failed heterosexual marriage behind her, venerated 1960s essayist Susan Sontag found her soul mate in celebrity photographer Annie Leibovitz, sixteen years her junior.

Seventeen years. Nineteen-year-old Rebecca West captured H. G. Wells's attention when she panned his novel *Marriage* in a feminist journal. The married, middle-aged writer's subsequent invitation to dine morphed into a decade-long affair that produced a son.

Eighteen years. Thomas Wolfe's long-term affair with MILF Aline Bernstein began on the last night of a transatlantic voyage, when the two jumped in the sack just hours after meeting.

Twenty-four years. Under pressure to write a novel in one month or face losing all of his copyrights, debt-ridden Fyodor Dostoyevsky hired stenographer Anna Snitkina. Impressed by more than just her shorthand skills, he proposed within nine days of dictating *The Gambler*.

Thirty years. Arguably the world's first cougar, French writer Colette managed to shock even laissez-faire Paris by embarking on an affair with her sixteen-year-old stepson in the 1920s.

Thirty-eight years. Modernist poet T. S. Eliot, who once took a vow of chastity, left a trail of broken hearts in his wake before secretly tying the knot with his young secretary.

Thirty-nine years. Although unhappy in his first marriage, Victorian novelist Thomas Hardy tormented his next bride, Florence, with tender poetic tributes to her predecessor. She exacted revenge after Hardy's death by editing her long-deceased rival out of his papers.

Fifty-five years. "I honestly didn't know Arthur Miller was still living!" said artist Agnes Barley when she was introduced to the playwright, who was old enough to be her grandfather.

All War, No Peace

LEO TOLSTOY

Nobody will ever understand me. —Leo Tolstoy

He has never taken the trouble to understand me, and he simply doesn't know me. —Sophia Tolstoy

When Leo Tolstoy penned the famous first line of *Anna Karenina*, "Happy families are all alike; each unhappy family is unhappy in its own way," he never imagined his own marriage would become one of the unhappiest in literary history.

"They wouldn't let me take leave of my husband. Cruel people," Sophia Tolstoy said bitterly of her husband's zealous disciples, who prevented her from visiting the writer on his deathbed until he had lapsed into unconsciousness. The heartbreaking photo of her tapping at the window outside the remote railway station where he died in 1910 has become an indelible symbol of the disastrous final chapter of their forty-eight-year marriage.

It was a tragic end to a partnership that had started out promisingly. "I've lived to the age of thirty-four, and I didn't know it was possible to be so much in love and so happy," Tolstoy exclaimed shortly after he wed. Still, an impending sense of doom had over-shadowed his trip to the altar, and he fought a last-minute urge to back out, as does his alter ego, Levin, in *Anna Karenina*. Similarly, he had Levin misguidedly show his bachelor diaries to his fiancée, just as Tolstoy insisted that eighteen-year-old Sophia read of his own history of womanizing, drinking, gambling, and the illegiti-mate child he fathered with a serf on his estate.

"I wept when I saw what his past had been," confessed Sophia. Despite her shock at the revelations, within three days they had ex-changed vows and were on their way to the Tolstoy family estate, Yasnaya Polyana, in the Russian countryside. During the overnight carriage ride, Tolstoy deflowered his bride, who afterward confided in her diary, "How torturesome it was and unbearably shameful!"

Despite Sophia's initial qualms about her husband's past and the frequent arguments that erupted between the strong-willed pair, their first decades together were largely contented ones. "Could any marriage be more happy and harmonious than ours?" Sophia pondered blissfully. Tolstoy, meanwhile, wrote in his diary, "There probably isn't more than one person in a million as happy as the two of us are together."

Tolstoy's literary star was on the rise, and their marriage pro-vided ample fodder for the meditations on matrimony in *War and Peace* and *Anna Karenina*. Sophia transcribed several drafts of both novels in longhand—totaling tens of thousands of manuscript pages—often straining her eyes to the point of near blindness while deciphering her husband's illegible handwriting. She also offered valuable editorial suggestions, such as advising Tolstoy to curtail the historical digressions in *War and Peace* and focus more on the characters.

In addition to serving as Tolstoy's muse and personal secretary, Sophia was an ideal helpmate on the domestic front. Like most

women of her era, she channeled her energy into her family, almost
singlehandedly raising and educating their brood of thirteen children (nine of whom survived into adulthood) while Tolstoy focused
on his writing. Tirelessly, she cooked, sewed, nursed sick peasants,
negotiated with Tolstoy's publishers, and even met with the czar
when one of her husband's works was banned.

Along with the physical demands of her role, the saintlike Sophia also had to endure emotional hardship. Ironically, the man
who showed such insight and compassion toward his heroines on
the page was in reality cruel, self-absorbed, and harshly critical of
his own wife. He was also highly temperamental and prone to violent outbursts and bouts of depression. Sophia's diary often describes the crippling loneliness she experienced as a result of
her husband's moody withdrawals and their isolation in the countryside.

Loneliness, though, would be the least of her problems. At the
height of his career, after the completion of *Anna Karenina*, the forty-
nine-year-old writer experienced the mother of all midlife crises.
Announcing to the world that he was abandoning fiction, the former atheist began churning out ideological and religious tracts about
how men could save their souls.

Tolstoy took to working in the fields and preaching his own
zealous form of religion, extolling the virtues of poverty, vegetari-
anism, and sexual abstinence. Proclaiming his desire to live as a
peasant, he spoke of his intention to give away his estate and put his
copyrights into the public domain. But the writer's family was loath
to follow in his monastic footsteps and shed their upper-class existence, which Tolstoy bitterly resented. He wrote indignantly that
he found his children "repulsive, pathetic and degrading to listen
to" and that "it would have been better for me to have no children
at all."

Tolstoy's radical new beliefs and the practicalities of supporting

a large family were irreconcilable, but he convinced himself otherwise by ceding his responsibilities to Sophia. Though overtaxed already, she suddenly found herself in charge of the huge estate and a
strained family budget that had to be stretched to accommodate the
hundreds of disciples flocking to Yasnaya Polyana. Followers from
as far away as America and India (Gandhi was a proponent) were
attracted to Tolstoy's teachings and came to visit.

The steady stream of disciples only added to Sophia's anguish because they diverted Tolstoy's scarce attention away from her and their
family. All but abandoned by her husband while he served humanity,
Sophia exclaimed, "He disgusts me with his talk of the 'people.' I feel
it is either me . . . or the people." Throughout the latter years of their
marriage, Tolstoy consistently chose "the people."

What disturbed Sophia most was her husband's hypocrisy. She
noted in her diary that he not only lived in the luxury he claimed to
deplore but also continued to make her pregnant despite advocating
celibacy. (For his part, Tolstoy blamed Sophia for tempting him away
from his ideal of chastity). She couldn't fathom his intention to give
away his copyrights, which, far from benefiting the people, would
only enrich the publishers. In her eyes, it was a gross betrayal of their
family. His works were their primary source of income, and she worried that their children would be left with nothing after his death.

Another heartbreak for Sophia came with the publication of
Tolstoy's searing diatribe against marriage, *The Kreutzer Sonata*, in
which a fictional character murders the wife he has come to hate.
The book describes matrimony as a prison and maintains that happy
marriages don't exist. Embarrassingly for Sophia, the public immediately perceived *The Kreutzer Sonata* as being based on the Tolstoys' stormy marriage and the humiliation drove a further wedge
between the couple.

Tolstoy's shrewd and manipulative disciple Vladimir Chertkov
exploited their discord to his advantage. The writer had fallen

under the spell of the scheming young man in the early years of his midlife crisis, and the two formed an immediate bond. "He and I are amazingly one," Tolstoy enthused in his diary.

Others found Chertkov arrogant and underhanded and were deeply concerned about his pernicious influence on the aging writer. Chief among his detractors was Sophia, who suspected the despotic disciple of plotting to gain custodianship of her husband's works after his death. Chertkov recognized Sophia as a formidable rival and did everything in his power to poison Tolstoy's mind against her.

Increasingly excluded from her husband's life, Sophia took to eavesdropping on his conversations, rummaging through his papers, and following him when he left the house. She rightly feared that Tolstoy and Chertkov were conspiring to draw up a secret will disinheriting the family. Shortly before her husband's death, a new will was indeed covertly signed, ceding the rights to Tolstoy's works to his daughter Alexandra, a Tolstoyan disciple. She in turn agreed to surrender control to Chertkov, who could edit and release the works as he saw fit.

Although Sophia remained unaware of the devious arrangement, she was pushed over the edge of reason upon discovering that Chertkov possessed several of her husband's diaries. She worried that he would use them to present an unflattering portrayal of her and their marriage after Tolstoy's death. (Indeed, in his memoir, Chertkov compared Sophia's treatment of her husband to torture methods practiced by the Spanish Inquisition.) She also believed that such personal documents did not belong in the hands of an outsider.

Sophia became obsessed with retrieving the diaries, but her endless pleadings were met with stony refusals. A dance of resistance ensued between her, Chertkov, and Tolstoy, which the writer ominously described as "a struggle to the death." Sophia's increasing hysteria and paranoia spurred her worried family to call in a psychiatrist from Moscow. The doctor advised the Tolstoys to separate until her mental condition improved, but Sophia wouldn't hear of it.

In increasingly desperate bids for attention, she brandished vials of opium and threatened to commit suicide by poisoning herself, drowning herself in a pond, or following in Anna Karenina's footsteps and throwing herself under a train. At the same time, Tolstoy frequently threatened to leave and occasionally did depart in anger, once when Sophia was going into labor with their twelfth child. After weeks of explosive scenes over the diaries, Tolstoy finally interceded and sent an assistant to collect them. However, this did little to appease Sophia, since he had the journals deposited in a bank vault before she had a chance to see them.

The poisonous atmosphere in the Tolstoy house was punctuated by the couple's brief and increasingly rare reconciliations. Two months before their final parting, Sophia recorded a particularly tender scene in her diary: "I burst out crying, embracing him, and said that I was afraid of losing him . . . I had never for one moment ceased to love him more than anyone on earth." Tolstoy reciprocated with his own avowals of love, promising that he would never leave her. A short time later, soon after their forty-eighth wedding anniversary, Tolstoy broke his promise after hearing Sophia rifling through his papers in the middle of the night. Her constant spying and theatrics had become unbearable to him.

On the night of October 28, 1910, Tolstoy snuck away from Yasnaya Polyana, writing in his farewell letter: "I cannot go on living in the luxury by which I have always been surrounded, and am . . . giving up the world in order to spend my last days alone and in silence." When Sophia awoke and read his words, she rushed to drown herself in a pond but was rescued before her body sank. After being fished out, she pleaded histrionically to her daughter, "Telegraph Father at once that I am going to drown myself."

Tolstoy never received her message, having fallen ill soon into his journey. He was discovered in the railway stationmaster's house in the small town of Astapovo, where he succumbed to pneumonia. The giant of Russian literature was never able to find the peace he craved, dying within ten days of leaving home and crying fitfully on his deathbed, "To escape. . . . It is necessary to escape!"

❧ FIGHT CLUB ❧

For these couples, love was less a game of hearts than it was a blood sport.

~ **Armed and dangerous.** Paul Verlaine left his family for fellow poet Arthur Rimbaud, fleeing Paris in 1872 and carrying on a violent, absinthe-fueled affair in London and Belgium. "We love each other like tigers!" Verlaine told his spurned wife, who had followed them in hot pursuit. Shamelessly, he bared his chest, revealing the wounds inflicted by his seventeen-year-old lover. The liaison ended a year later when Verlaine shot Rimbaud in the wrist during a drunken argument and was imprisoned for assault and sodomy.

~ **Love in a bottle.** "Ours was a drink story, not a love story," Caitlin Macnamara said of her marriage to Welsh poet Dylan Thomas. The pair met in a pub, where Thomas announced they would wed the moment he saw her. Their alcoholism and his rampant infidelities fueled Caitlin's epic rages, sometimes leading her to bang her husband's head against the floor so hard that he would pass out. When Thomas died at age thirty-nine, after consuming a reported eighteen whiskies, Caitlin pulled a four-foot crucifix from the hospital wall before being hustled off in a straitjacket.

~ **Domestic disturbance.** Violent, often public battles were a hallmark of D. H. Lawrence and Frieda Weekley's fifteen-year marriage. In addition to pummeling his wife, Lawrence threw a glass of Chianti at her in a restaurant and another time choked her, shrieking, "I am the master!" Strong-willed Frieda retaliated by hurling dishes at his head.

Perversely, the vicious exchanges seemed to strengthen the couple's bond. An acquaintance once saw Lawrence pull Frieda's hair and threaten to cut her throat, only to find them amicably discussing macaroni and cheese an hour later.

~ **Backstage theatrics.** Eugene O'Neill's relationship with former actress Carlotta Monterey rivaled the dysfunctional family sagas he created for the stage. One particularly bitter argument left them both hospitalized: O'Neill slipped in the snow and broke his leg after being locked out of the house, while Carlotta was found wandering the streets in a drug-induced psychosis. The playwright tried to have her certified, and the couple initiated divorce proceedings. But O'Neill, debilitated by alcoholism and a severe palsy, couldn't live without his bossy, overprotective wife, and they reconciled shortly before his death.

~ **The spy who spanked me.** British intelligence officer and James Bond creator Ian Fleming was a notorious womanizer with a vigorous sex life. He and his future wife, Ann, enthusiastically participated in a sadomasochistic affair that began while both were with other partners. "I long for you to whip me because I love being hurt by you and kissed afterwards," Ann once told him of their fiery bouts of lovemaking.

PART TWO

Bad Boys, Scoundrels, and Rogues

Hell Hath No Fury

ERNEST HEMINGWAY

No matter how being in love comes out it's sure worth it all while it's going on.

—Ernest Hemingway

Serial monogamist Ernest Hemingway was eager to tie the knot each time he fell in love, and yet he always became disenchanted with the women he married. After walking out on his first two spouses, he had the tables turned on him the third time he took the plunge. Hemingway wed a globe-trotting journalist, Martha Gellhorn, but what he really wanted was a happy homemaker by his side.

M artha Gellhorn's willingness to venture into danger zones was one of the things that attracted Ernest Hemingway to the sassy blonde journalist when they met in 1936. During their first encounter at a bar in Key West, where the thirty-seven-year-old novelist resided with his family, conversation turned to the civil war under way in Spain. Martha, the author of an acclaimed story collection, *The Trouble I've Seen*, which portrayed the plight of

Americans during the Great Depression, planned to try her hand at war reporting. Hemingway, meanwhile, had already been hired by a newspaper to cover the bloody conflict. Ten years his junior, Martha avidly listened to what he had to say about both writing and the battlefield.

The pair met up in Spain on three separate occasions, navigating terrain rigged with explosives, sleeping on the side of the road, and enduring enemy fire. Hemingway, who served with the Italian Red Cross on the front lines during World War I, praised Martha's courage and pronounced her one of the bravest people he knew. He actively supported her quest to become a war correspondent, encouraging her to submit her first piece to *Collier's* magazine and teaching her essential survival skills. Although fond memories of their volatile, seven-year relationship were scarce for Martha after it ended, she acknowledged being obliged to Hemingway for one thing: teaching her to recognize the different sounds of gunfire and knowing when to take cover.

While they were lodging at a Madrid hotel, Hemingway got a taste of Martha's temper. After the place was bombarded, she tried to leave her room and found the door was locked from the outside. When Hemingway finally turned up, he admitted he had done it to protect her from the pimps and drunks milling around, thinking they might mistake her for a prostitute. Instead of seeing Hemingway's overprotective behavior as a sign she should flee, Martha slept with him for the first time two weeks later, her feelings driven more by hero worship than love or lust. She later claimed he was a ghastly lover and sometimes greeted her at the door with his pants down and ready for a romp.

As Hemingway zealously pursued Martha in Spain and later stateside, he was maneuvering to get rid of the woman standing in the way of his happiness—his wife of ten years, Pauline Pfeiffer. But she was not as amenable to letting the philanderer off the hook as his first wife, Hadley Richardson, had been. Hemingway grew resentful at Pauline's refusal to step aside, resulting in a several-year standoff. The writer's increasingly callous behavior toward his wife included spending long stretches away on fishing expeditions and in Cuba, where he set up house with Martha. When Pauline joined him on holiday at a Wyoming ranch, he made it clear that he wanted her to leave and then called Martha to extend an invite. Hemingway rationalized that Pauline deserved the harsh treatment for having stolen him away from Hadley.

At the time Hemingway's marriage to Pauline was unraveling and his affair with Martha heating up, he finished his novel *To Have and Have Not*, in which a female character tellingly hypothesizes that men can't be expected to be monogamous. "They aren't built that way. They want some one new, or some one younger, or some one that they shouldn't have. . . . You can't blame them if that's the way they are," she reasons. "Women have a bad time really. The better you treat a man and the more you show him you love him the quicker he gets tired of you."

Unlike Hemingway, Martha was in no hurry to tie the knot. "I think living in sin is wonderful (we are now on our fourth contented year)," she confided to a friend less than three months before she became the latest Mrs. Hemingway. A fed-up Pauline had finally acquiesced to a divorce, thrusting the now-famous writer's love life into the national news. His split from Pauline in November 1940 was announced over the AP wire, and his marriage to Martha, which took place that same month, was splashed across the pages of *Life* magazine.

Along with photos of the newlyweds, the article highlighted Hemingway's just-published novel *For Whom the Bell Tolls*. Set during the Spanish Civil War, the tale is dedicated to Martha and features a character that resembles her in appearance. A resounding success, it cemented Hemingway's place as one of America's greatest living writers and gave credence to F. Scott Fitzgerald's theory that he required romantic drama to stimulate his pen. "Ernest needs a new woman for each big book," Fitzgerald mused after Hemingway walked out on his first wife, Hadley. "There was one for the stories and *The Sun Also Rises*. Now there's Pauline. *A Farewell to Arms* is a big book. If there's another big book I think we'll find Ernest has another wife."

Pauline would have done well to heed Fitzgerald's observation, especially since she had played a part in the destructive pattern. Love triangles were well-trodden territory for Hemingway, who began romancing her while still married to Hadley. When Hadley found out about the affair and confronted him, the unapologetic writer berated her for having the bad taste to bring it out in the open. Reluctant to give up either woman, or even to make a definitive decision, he vowed to commit suicide if the situation wasn't resolved soon. When the good-natured Hadley decided to let him out of their marriage, Hemingway praised the breakup letter she penned him as brave and generous.

While Hemingway's first two weddings took place in churches (Methodist with Hadley and Catholic with Pauline), his and Martha's nuptials were performed by a justice of the peace in Cheyenne, Wyoming. A month after they married, the happy groom expressed his satisfaction that they had finally made it legal. Still in the honeymoon phase, he accompanied his wife to the Far East, where she reported on the Japanese invasion of China. While Martha envisioned a future in which the intrepid pair continued to travel and work together, Hemingway sought to change the rules after they swapped vows. He wanted her by his side in Cuba, where he was content to remain working on his fiction.

Unlike Hemingway's previous helpmates, Martha had no interest in devoting herself to running a household or putting her husband's needs above her own. Giving up the career he had helped nurture was not something she was willing to do. She also needed to work to support herself and pay her share of the couple's living expenses. Hemingway, who frequently claimed to be cash-strapped and groused about alimony payments to the well-to-do Pauline, wasn't exactly a generous breadwinner.

For two years, Martha pleaded with Hemingway to travel to Europe with her and report on the events unfolding as Hitler's army marched across the continent. Not inclined to leave their lush Cuban estate, he resisted going abroad, claiming he was doing his part for the war effort by patrolling Caribbean waters for German U-boats. While Martha risked her life to report on the growing atrocities taking place abroad, his focus was on his libido. "Are you a war correspondent or wife in my bed?" he petulantly cabled.

His wife's career was Hemingway's bitter rival, and the more she traveled on assignment, the more acrimonious their relationship became. When an exhausted Martha returned to Cuba after reporting in England, Italy, and North Africa, Hemingway woke her from a sound sleep and launched into a tirade. "My crime really was to have been at war when he had not, but that was not how he put it," she explained. "I was supposedly insane, I only wanted excitement and danger, I had no responsibility to anyone, I was selfish beyond belief. . . . It never stopped and believe me, it was fierce and ugly."

No longer content with doling out mere insults and complaints, Hemingway attempted to put Martha in her place by deliberately trying to sabotage her career. In 1944 he approached *Collier's*, his wife's longtime employer, and offered to head to Europe and write war dispatches for them. Capitalizing on his illustrious name was an offer too good for the magazine to refuse. With that malicious move, he destroyed Martha's chances of covering the war in an official capacity since publications were allowed only one frontline correspondent.

In a further fit of pique, Hemingway refused to secure passage for Martha on the government plane he was taking to London. Determined to go anyway, his fearless wife crossed the treacherous waters of the Atlantic on a cargo vessel loaded with explosives and carrying no lifeboats. On arriving in England, Martha learned that her husband had suffered a concussion during a car accident several days earlier. Other than a bandage wrapped turban-style around his head, the writer appeared little the worse for wear, downing champagne and whiskey and entertaining well-wishers from his hospital bed. Instead of offering the sympathy the patient expected, Martha bid him a not-so-fond farewell. She was the only one of Hemingway's wives to leave him, an offense for which he never forgave her. "Hell hath no fury like E.H. scorned," Martha claimed.

His anger was all the more ironic given that he had already begun romancing someone else. In between his arrival in the English capital and the time Martha's ship docked, he had set his sights on Mary Welsh, a married American writer covering the war for *Time* magazine. Once again he was quick to jump the gun and within days of meeting his new flame professed, "I don't know you, Mary. But I want to marry you. You are very alive. You're beautiful, like a May fly."

Of Hemingway's four wives, Mary had the clearest idea of the challenging road that lay ahead if she divorced her husband and wed the demanding writer. Unlike her willful predecessor, Martha, she understood it was expected that she give up her much-loved career to tend to the Hemingway household. In addition, she experienced both the writer's devotion and his dark side while she still had the chance to walk away.

Hemingway penned love poems for Mary during a stay in Paris, where they rendezvoused after the city was liberated, and wrote her heartfelt letters from the French countryside when he left to meet up with a military regiment. Then came "an unexpected slap in the face." Vexed that Mary hadn't helped him out during an awkward social situation, Hemingway berated her as "a goddamn, smirking, useless female war correspondent." She had never before been cast in the role of whipping boy, "a part which I would play, unexpectedly, from time to time for years," admitted Mary. "I never learned to play it as gracefully and dispassionately as I should have liked." An actual slap in the face was delivered a short time later during another altercation. The next morning the perpetrator sent several emissaries, including actress Marlene Dietrich, to plead his case with Mary.

"Although I was entirely enthralled by him, especially when we were alone, I felt dubious about the wisdom of any formal commitment between us," confessed Mary. Not only troubled about giving up her career, she was concerned Hemingway's larger-than-life personality would strip away her own identity. Suppressing any lingering doubts about aligning herself with "such a complicated and contradictory piece of machinery as Ernest," Mary agreed to a trial run with him in Cuba and ended up a bride.

Despite a blowout on their wedding day—during which she went so far as to pack her bags—their union was the most enduring of Hemingway's four marriages. For fifteen years, Mary remained intensely loyal to her husband, even sticking it out when the middle-aged writer became besotted with Adriana Ivancich, an eighteen-year-old Italian girl. The May-December pair met on a duck-hunting weekend and began overtly displaying their affection in public. They saw each other in Venice and later in Cuba, after Hemingway invited Adriana and her mother for a visit.

He went on to use their relationship as fodder for *Across the River and into the Trees*, which features Adriana in the guise of Renata, a Venetian countess madly in love with an American colonel stationed in Italy. Ironically, Hemingway dedicated the novel "To Mary with Love." With good reason, she claimed the book was her least favorite of all his works. (Hemingway also used the novel to take potshots at Martha: the colonel's comments about his estranged third wife were so vitriolic the publisher feared they might incite a libel suit.)

As Hemingway's infatuation with Adriana intensified, his treatment of Mary grew worse, calling her names and humiliating her in public by bragging about his sexual conquests. One reason Mary stayed with him in spite of his abhorrent behavior was because early in their marriage he had saved her life. Complications during pregnancy caused her to hemorrhage, and her veins collapsed while she was being prepped for surgery. When the doctor stripped off his gloves and advised Hemingway to say good-bye to his wife, the writer refused to accept the grim diagnosis and took charge. After ordering a physician's assistant to cut for a vein in Mary's arm and insert an IV, he took over the administration of the plasma needed to stabilize her—even clearing the line by tilting the tube up and down until he got the liquid flowing. Once she responded to the treatment, he insisted the medics operate.

Mary returned the favor by devotedly caring for Hemingway at their Idaho home, where they relocated after leaving Cuba, as his physical and mental health severely declined. Depressed and having trouble writing, he became reclusive and paranoid and was institutionalized several times. Then, early one morning, Mary was awakened by a gunshot that reverberated through the house as the sixty-year-old writer took his own life. The night before Hemingway died, she spoke her last words to him: "Good night, my lamb. Sleep well."

BEHIND EVERY SUCCESSFUL MAN

These wordsmiths didn't make it solely under their own steam, but rather looked to the women in their lives for money, moral support, and a whole lot more.

~ **The better half.** Beautiful, brilliant Vera Nabokov was not only her husband Vladimir's biggest cheerleader but also his typist, editor, agent, business manager, chauffeur, and university classroom assistant. No task was too big or too small for the enthusiastic helpmate, from rescuing the manuscript of *Lolita* after the writer tried to burn it to cutting up his food at mealtimes.

~ **Fraudulently ever after.** When Colette's opportunistic husband discovered her flair for storytelling, he locked her in a room and forced her to write, demanding that scenes be made more titillating. The villainous journalist claimed authorship of his wife's popular Claudine novels, which are based on her experiences as a naive country girl who winds up in Paris with a rakish spouse.

~ **Can't buy me love.** When Thomas Wolfe's mediocre plays failed to sell, his wealthy lover urged him to write a novel instead and bankrolled his living expenses. After making a name with *Look Homeward, Angel* and other works, he repaid her by acrimoniously ending their affair, accusing her of sleeping around and deriding her Jewish heritage. During a slur-filled altercation in her apartment building lobby, she punched him in the nose before having him tossed out on the street.

~ **What's in a name?** Austro-Hungarian poet Rilke's married lover, Lou Andreas-Salomé, suggested he man up by using the first name Rainer rather than his given name, René. The girlish moniker had been bestowed on him by his mother, who had lost an infant daughter a year before his birth and tried to atone for the loss by feminizing her son and dressing him up as a girl.

~ **Gender bending.** A century before "equal opportunity" became a buzzword, women novelists often fared better if they wrote anonymously or used a man's name to get their works noticed. George Eliot (Mary Ann Evans) and George Sand (Aurore Dupin) both used a lover's name to inspire their noms de plume, though in Sand's case the pen name stuck but the relationship didn't. After partnering with her lover Jules Sandeau to cowrite her debut novel, she dumped him but kept the moniker as a memento, achieving greater fame as a writer than he did.

The Alpha Mailer

NORMAN MAILER

You know nothing about a woman until you meet her in court.

—Norman Mailer

Known for fistfights, head butts, womanizing, and attacks on feminism, Norman Mailer's off-the-page antics often overshadowed his writing. After five ex-wives and a notoriously violent past—which included stabbing his second wife, literally, in the back—the philandering brawler believed he was finally ready to settle down when he wed teacher-turned-model Norris Church.

"Why had I been so consumed with this old, fat, bombastic, lying little dynamo?" Norris Church berated herself after discovering her randy sixty-nine-year-old husband had been unfaithful for eight years. Giving a whole new meaning to the term "immersive journalism," Mailer claimed he had started the subterfuge to research his novel about the double lives of CIA agents.

By the time of Norris's discovery, the couple's ten-year marriage had already defied skeptics. It appeared to disbelievers that Mailer's sixth wife had somehow tamed the horny hedonist who once described love as "the search for an orgasm more apocalyptic than the one which preceded it." When the two first met in 1975, the five-foot-ten redhead was a divorced single mom who taught high school art classes in Russellville, Arkansas. Her path crossed Mailer's when he came through the tiny backwater (population: twenty-eight thousand) to visit friends and she crashed a party to get a book signed by him.

At the time, romance was the last thing on her mind. The flame-haired siren had no shortage of admirers and had been dating another charismatic charmer, future president Bill Clinton. But unexpectedly, she found herself smitten with the writer—who was older than her father, still married to his fourth wife, and had a reputation as a violent misogynist. Like many women drawn to bad boys, Norris found his macho image a turn-on.

As for Mailer, he was so flustered by the statuesque beauty that for once he was at a loss for words. When she introduced herself, he turned on his heel and fled the room. He later mustered the nerve to talk to her, and the night ended back at Norris's apartment, where they shared a box of cheap apple wine and made love on the living room floor. Although she assumed rug burn would be the only reminder of their night of passion, Mailer kept in touch and came back to visit her one month later.

The writer believed he had found his soul mate, a notion seemingly confirmed by the fact that they shared the same birthday and their birth times were one minute apart. But lest the starry-eyed Norris be under any delusions that the famously abrasive narcissist had turned soft in middle age, he returned a love poem she'd sent him marked with corrections in red pencil and then mailed her a box of his own books.

Within three months, Norris was on a flight to visit him (her first plane ride). Although still married to his fourth wife and living in Connecticut with yet another woman, Mailer soon asked Norris to move into his Brooklyn brownstone. Enthusiastically, she accepted his offer, undaunted by the prospect of becoming stepmother to his seven children, born to five different women. (At twenty-six, his eldest daughter was the same age as Norris.)

The writer loved inducting the small-town girl into his jet-set lifestyle, teaching her about fine wines and introducing her to exotic foods like escargot. As Norris described it, Mailer played Henry Higgins to her Eliza Doolittle. They were soon gossip-column regulars, jetting off to Manila for the historic Ali-Frazier fight and throwing parties attended by the likes of Bob Dylan, Woody Allen, and Jackie Onassis.

Surprisingly, the hard-partying Mailer had a domestic side and relished being a father and family man. He adopted Norris's young son, and the couple went on to have a child of their own before tying the knot four years later. In the course of two whirlwind months in 1980, Mailer divorced his fourth wife, married his fifth (for the purpose of legitimizing their daughter), divorced her, and married Norris. These convoluted machinations led newspapers to brand him a trigamist.

By the time of his marriage to Norris, Mailer had sowed most of his wild oats and was well established in his career, factors that contributed to their relative success as a couple. Thirty years earlier, the picture was starkly different: drugs and partying had taken their toll and his career seemed to be on the rocks. Although his first book, *The Naked and the Dead*, had exploded onto best-seller lists and turned the twenty-five-year-old into an overnight celebrity, unexpected success at a young age had its drawbacks.

With little chance to develop an identity before one was thrust upon him, a conflict developed between the two Mailers: the nice

Jewish kid who, five years earlier, had been a brainy engineering student at Harvard, and the feted celebrity whose testosterone-fueled war novel made him the poster child of American manhood. When his next two novels failed miserably, his self-confidence plummeted and he became terrified that he was a one-hit wonder. As a result, he didn't write another work of fiction for ten years, instead turning his hand to journalism and cofounding the alternative newspaper the *Village Voice.*

Along with Truman Capote and Tom Wolfe, he pioneered a hybrid literary form, dubbed the New Journalism, which applied the techniques of novel writing to nonfiction. Although Mailer later garnered two Pulitzer prizes and achieved great success with sprawling nonfiction epics like *The Executioner's Song*, before he realized his potential his career had stalled out. Alone, angry, and drifting after the breakdown of his first marriage, the washed-up writer should have come with a warning label. Unfortunately for Adele Morales, he did not.

The fiery Latin beauty, who became his second wife, ran with a fast crowd in New York City and compared herself to the plate-throwing operatic character Carmen. She had briefly dated Jack Kerouac and when a friend rang at 2:00 a.m. and told her to come meet Mailer, she was unimpressed. But when he got on the line and charmed her by quoting F. Scott Fitzgerald, she had a change of heart and hopped into a taxi to continue their conversation in person. In a further testament to Mailer's conversational prowess, the two were in the sack within hours of meeting. During the coming years, the bedroom would be the only place where the combative, sex-obsessed couple would see eye to eye.

Soon, they became codependent alcoholics living a life of spiraling tragedy. Mailer seemed hell-bent on self-destruction, spending most of the 1950s high on a cocktail of Seconal, Benzedrine, marijuana, and alcohol. Often he was so out of it that he could only write for an hour a day. His ham-handed attempts at self-medication couldn't mask his gnawing career frustrations, which manifested in outbursts of violence. Even an innocent stroll with his dogs could occasion a bust-up, and he once returned home bloodied and bruised after attacking a sailor who called his poodle a queer.

Mouthy drunken sailors were not the only targets of his wrath, as Adele discovered. Six years into their marriage, in November 1960, the confrontational writer undertook the improbable stunt of running for New York City mayor, throwing an all-night party to launch his campaign. Guests included beat poet Allen Ginsberg, journalists, boxers, actors, and an unsavory assortment of prostitutes, pimps, and winos he asked in from the street.

Throughout the evening, Mailer got into many drunken brawls and at 4:00 a.m., after throwing punches at a departing guest, he turned on Adele when she called him a faggot. Brandishing a rusty three-inch penknife he had found in the street, Mailer stabbed her first in the abdomen and then in the back. Close to death from loss of blood, Adele was rushed to the hospital, where she stayed for three weeks recuperating from a punctured cardiac sac.

Her knife-wielding husband, who once promised to "love, honor and cherish" her, was arraigned on charges of felonious assault and spent seventeen days in a psych ward, where he was diagnosed as a paranoid schizophrenic. Upon his release, Adele refused to press charges (writing later that she was too scared) and Mailer got off with just five years' probation for the violent crime.

Adele never fully recovered from the attack, developing pleurisy and hacking up phlegm several times a day. Although she eventually filed for divorce, she initially returned to Mailer because she had no money and nowhere else to go with their two small children. She also admitted she was drinking too much to think clearly. Later, she compared Mailer to O. J. Simpson and penned a memoir about their relationship revealing that years of domestic violence had preceded the assault. Mailer once punched her in the stomach when she was six months pregnant and in addition to physically abusing her subjected her to a constant stream of insults. "At different times, I had to deal with God, Svengali, Ivan the Terrible, Rocky Marciano, Jesse James . . . and Scott Fitzgerald the drunk," Adele wrote of his unpredictable personality.

The belligerent writer encouraged her to fight other women and frequently initiated group sex, becoming angry if Adele enjoyed herself. By the end of their relationship, he "needed a three ring circus to get it up," said Adele, who began taunting him with the word "faggot." This was the worst possible insult for a man who, in spite of his machismo, was never terribly secure in his masculinity. She chalked up Mailer's aggressive tendencies to his fear he might be gay, which she believed drove his need to exert his manhood.

Mailer's third wife and sparring partner, Lady Jeanne Campbell, didn't stick around long enough to test Adele's theory. The English aristocrat divorced him in little over a year, and he symbolically murdered her in his novel *An American Dream*. In the dark urban fantasy, the main character strangles his wife, throws her out a window, and then sodomizes the maid. In real life the pair's bickering was so fierce it was said they could empty a room quicker than anyone in New York. "We would arrive at a party, and even the hosts would put on their hats and coats and leave," joked Campbell. Although the marriage was short-lived, Mailer's metaphoric revenge novel had a permanent legacy. Combined with his other misogynistic works, it cemented his place on the feminist hit list.

Throughout the 1970s, Mailer missed no opportunity to taunt women's libbers with outrageous pronouncements that may or may not have been made in jest, like his declaration during a TV interview that women "should be kept in cages." Yet the man who in

print nicknamed his penis the Retaliator seemed genuinely per-
plexed about why feminists hated him and once asked Gloria
Steinem what women had against him. "You might try reading your
books someday," she replied dryly.

Norris Church Mailer argued that in spite of his inflammatory
remarks, her husband was no sexist. "Norman has never opposed
feminism, he's just fond of saying naughty things," she explained.
As his biggest defender, she was blindsided when in 1990 she came
across a drawer filled with letters, gifts, and photographs from various mistresses.

One mistress, journalist Carole Mallory, later wrote a tell-all
book about her eight-year affair with Mailer and jokingly referred
to herself as his "seventh wife." The remark would have affronted
Norris, who took pride in the fact that she had outlasted all chal-
lengers to his affections. When asked, "Which wife are you?" she
would quip, "The last one." In her own defense, Mallory claimed
the writer had told her he was in an open marriage. She asserted
that their affair wasn't just about sex but also a product of Norman's
excessive need for mothering.

Norris believed the reason she had been blind to Mailer's deception was that he really *had* changed during their early years together, before his old ways reasserted their grip. In the reeling
aftermath of her discovery, she went home to Arkansas and issued
her husband an ultimatum: stop seeing anyone else or she would
leave. Mailer agreed and, remarkably, their marriage survived.

They were still at each other's side as Mailer's health declined
and he underwent bypass surgery and endured several hospitaliza-
tions for lung problems. Although he became a shadow of his former self—sporting dentures and a hearing aid and using two canes
to walk—the pugilistic writer kept churning out ambitious books
and never lost his feistiness, even punching a hostile book reviewer
at the age of seventy-four.

Norris, too, suffered from her share of health problems and was diagnosed with cancer in 1999. Her husband became an unlikely Florence Nightingale, nursing her through multiple operations while often sick himself. When a collapsed lung and kidney failure rendered him bedridden, his family maintained a bedside vigil. The writer reportedly continued thumb wrestling and cracking jokes until the end.

Although Norris did not take the stage at Mailer's 2008 Carnegie Hall memorial service, a recording of her singing "You'll Come Back (You Always Do)" accompanied a slideshow commemorating their thirty-three years together. Before later losing her own battle with cancer, she told an interviewer, "In the end, I have no complaints. At all."

MAD ABOUT YOU:
EDGAR ALLAN POE

While Edgar Allan Poe's young wife, Virginia, was dying of consumption in 1845, his love life took a twisted turn. The master of the macabre became involved with two married women who bared their claws over him and took the catfight public.

Poe and the coquettish poet Fanny Osgood openly flirted with each other in poems and stories published in a magazine he was editing at the time. Joining in the literary seduction, fellow poet Elizabeth Ellet submitted a work revealing her own romantic feelings for the famed writer. When Fanny responded to her rival in verse, Poe added fuel to the fire by printing both works in the same issue.

His wife sanctioned his friendship with Fanny, under the impression that it was platonic (although the pair had at least one out-of-town rendezvous). Virginia Poe believed the other woman was a positive influence on her husband because he gave up drinking to impress her. Others in their New York circle weren't so high-minded and penned the ailing wife anonymous letters suggesting that Poe and Fanny were more than just pals.

Poe was convinced the jealous Elizabeth was behind the malicious missives, especially after she paid a call on his wife and hinted that he was the father of Fanny's newborn daughter. The disturbance worsened Virginia's precarious health, and on her deathbed she called the scandalmongering Elizabeth a murderer.

Although devastated by his wife's passing, Poe didn't slow down his romantic pursuits. After his love triangle foundered, he proposed in a cemetery to a widow who shared his fascination with the macabre, but the short-lived engagement was called off after he broke his promise not to drink. Poe quickly went on to woo other women, and at the time of his death in 1849, the forty-year-old writer was betrothed to his childhood sweetheart.

Mad, Bad, and Dangerous to Know

LORD BYRON

~

I have been all my life trying to make someone love me.

—Lord Byron

Two centuries before rock stars and celebrities were making headlines with their fast lives and wicked ways, the original playboy, Lord Byron, garnered enough notches on his bedpost to make a seasoned sex addiction counselor blush. "Mad, bad and dangerous to know" was one lover's famous assessment of the flamboyant poet, whose fickle attentions prompted two women to attempt suicide. Even in death, his manhood attracted undue attention, with one observer commenting on the sizeable proportions of his embalmed penis.

~

"Thus has perished, in the flower of his age . . . one of the greatest poets England ever produced," announced the *Morning Chronicle* as news spread throughout England of Lord Byron's death in April 1824. His obituary in the *Times* lauded him as "the most remarkable Englishman of his generation," a sentiment echoed by the hordes of spectators lining the London riverbanks as the undertaker's barge transported Byron's body up the Thames. The poet's lying-in-state, to which the public was admitted by ticket, attracted unprecedented crowds and an abundance of swooning females.

Despite this outpouring of grief, Byron's scandalous reputation remained a liability that haunted him to the grave. The dean of Westminster refused to inter his remains in Poet's Corner, the abbey's hallowed shrine for England's bards, and St. Paul's Cathedral quickly followed suit. Bryon's aristocratic peers faced the dilemma of paying their respects without tainting their own good names, and in lieu of attending his funeral themselves sent their empty carriages to trail behind the hearse.

The poet would have been unsurprised at the hypocrisy that followed, literally, in his wake, as it had prompted him to flee England eight years earlier. Those who once idolized him abruptly turned their backs when scandalous rumors of incest and homosexuality began circulating after his wife left him in 1816.

Byron's ill-fated marriage to the pious and wealthy Annabella Milbanke had taken place only a year earlier after he halfheartedly proposed in a letter, hoping that a union with her would ease his financial troubles and distract him from the temptations of his half sister, Augusta. He later wrote that it was his sister—whose feelings for Byron were equally passionate—who had urged him to marry "because it was the only chance of redemption for *two* persons."

Although fully aware of the poet's notorious reputation, Lady Byron foolishly succumbed to his charms and believed—like so many women—that she could tame his wild ways. By then Byron was England's most famous poet and most desirable catch, with aristocratic good looks and overpowering sexual charisma. When the first edition of his poem *Childe Harold's Pilgrimage* sold out within three days, the young, Cambridge-educated aristocrat was instantly transformed into the world's first celebrity. The poem went on to be reprinted eight more times in six years, selling an estimated twenty thousand copies at a time when even the most popular novels had sales of only half that number. Byron's overnight stardom was unprecedented and sparked an obsessive fascination with him known as Byronomania.

Byron craved the spotlight and perfectly fit the part of the rebellious, melancholic hero he had created in Childe Harold. His beauty and lameness (he was clubfooted) only added to his aura, and hundreds of women sent him fan letters appealing for a meeting, an autograph, or a lock of his long, flowing hair. The poet's effect was all the more potent in person: one woman reportedly fainted at the sight of him, while many others—regardless of their marital status—threw themselves at him. Like many a lothario, Byron was quick to respond to female advances and just as quick to get bored and move on to the next conquest.

One of his longest and most publicized liaisons was a six-month affair with the mentally unstable Lady Caroline Lamb, niece of the Duchess of Devonshire, who became obsessed with Byron despite being married. Caroline was an enthusiastic cross-dresser and—intuiting Byron's homoerotic attraction to young boys—she titillated him by dressing as a page and making herself look boyish. Despite their sexual chemistry, Byron soon wearied of her attention-seeking theatrics and cruelly broke off their relationship by post.

When Caroline received the letter, she reportedly seized a razor and tried to cut herself but was prevented by her mother. Her repeated threats that she would "revenge herself upon *herself*" did not move Byron, and cringeworthy mementos she sent—such as a lock of her pubic hair tinged with blood—went unreciprocated. Byron's unresponsiveness sent Caroline into hysterics, once leading her to don her page costume as a disguise to gain entrance to his chambers, which she then refused to leave.

It became clear to the poet that the only way to be rid of Caroline was to marry someone else. Byron took no pains to hide his odd proclivities from his new wife, and on their honeymoon he immediately began dropping hints about atrocious sins in his past. Peculiar aspects of his personality also began to emerge. Obsessed with controlling his weight, he dieted as zealously as a runway model, often surviving for days on biscuits and green tea. Other times he would stuff himself and then purge. He also had a bizarre aversion to watching women eat, thus for his wife, mealtimes were lonely affairs.

Over the course of the following year, the stress of his mounting debts, coupled with heavy drinking, made him prone to violent mood swings and fits of rage. He sometimes paced the house brandishing a loaded pistol and threatening suicide, causing his servants to fear for his mental health and the safety of Lady Byron.

Worst of all for Lady Byron was the horrifying realization that there were three people in her marriage. Two years before, Byron had begun an incestuous affair with his half sister, Augusta, and his infatuation with her showed no signs of abating (although it is thought she at least had the decency to refuse him sex after his betrothal). Echoes of incest and forbidden love appear in several of Byron's poems, particularly the autobiographical *Manfred*, in which he writes of the hero's love for a woman who is "like me . . . her eyes, / Her hair, her features, all, to the very tone / Even of her voice . . . were like to mine."

Lady Byron quickly perceived the nature of the illicit love between brother and sister, realizing that "it was hopeless to keep them apart—[however] it was not hopeless, in my opinion, to keep them innocent." She regarded it as her Christian duty to guard them against slipping over "the brink of a precipice."

Byron didn't make it easy for her, openly showing a preference for his sister's company. Despite being married herself, Augusta and her children (one of whom may have been fathered by Byron) resided with the couple for long stretches at a time. Lady Byron was sent to bed alone while Augusta stayed up late with the poet, who would condescendingly tell his wife, "We can amuse ourselves without you, my dear." Other evenings he would lie on a sofa and instigate a competition between the women by instructing them to take turns kissing him.

Meanwhile, Byron was also carrying on with an actress and making drunken references to prior sexual escapades with young boys, causing his wife's horror at "the apprehension of crimes on his part yet more dreadful" than even incest. Byron's interest in boys had been awakened in boarding school and was further stoked during travels in Greece and Turkey, where sex between men was comparatively acceptable.

When the poet threatened "to *do everything wicked*" shortly after Lady Byron gave birth to their daughter, she took it to mean he was planning to return to his earlier homosexual practices. On the morning of January 15, 1816, she took their infant daughter and left London before Byron had risen, seeking refuge with her parents. The poet was never to see either of them again.

Concluding that her husband was mentally deranged, Lady Byron drew up a list of his symptoms to submit to lawyers upon filing for separation. Byron, who felt he was the wronged party, later took revenge on the "virtuous monster" in his satiric poem *Don Juan*, creating an unflattering portrait of his wife in a character who "called some druggists and physicians, / And tried to prove her loving lord was mad."

The separation caused enormous public scandal as details of the marriage leaked out and became ever more sensationalized, transforming Byron from the darling of London society into a pariah.

His embittered ex-mistress, Lady Caroline, is thought to have added fuel to the fire by spreading dangerous rumors of his past acts of sodomy, a crime carrying the death penalty in Regency-era England.

Attacked by the press and ostracized by society, Byron's final weeks at home were spent in seclusion:

"I was advised not to go to the theatres, lest I should be hissed,—nor to my duty in parliament lest I should be insulted . . . even on the day of my departure, my most intimate friend told me afterwards, that he was under apprehensions of violence—from the people who might be assembled at the door of the carriage."

After he reluctantly signed the separation agreement with his wife on April 21, 1816, Byron fled his homeland, never to return alive. Arriving in Europe, a brief liaison he had undertaken with Claire Clairmont, the young stepsister of Mary Shelley, came back to haunt him. The pair's short-lived union had resulted in a pregnancy that gave Claire, then traveling in Europe with the Shelleys, an excuse to meet up with her ex-lover and impart the news.

Byron quickly bonded with the Shelleys—whose own reputations had been blackened after Percy abandoned his pregnant wife to elope with Mary—and spent the summer with the threesome on the shores of Lake Geneva. Even abroad, they could not escape the attentions of nosy English tourists, who spied on them from across the lake, paparazzi-style, using telescopes rented out by an entrepreneurial hotel owner.

Byron later journeyed to Italy, eventually settling in Venice, which he nicknamed "sea-Sodom." There he reached new levels of dissipation, by his own estimation sleeping with around two hundred women.

Many of Byron's assignations were incognito, taking place while masked during the late-night Carnival festivities or at the Ridotto, luxurious private rooms for entertainment and gaming where masks were required. Because of the anonymity it afforded, the Ridotto was a haven for fleeting sexual encounters between strangers. A dark room with couches, titillatingly known as the Chamber of Sighs, provided a convenient setting.

As well as his anonymous flings, Byron commenced a torrid affair with the wife of his landlord, boasting lustily that there was "never a twenty-four hours without giving and receiving from one to three (and an occasional extra or so) pretty unequivocal proofs of mutual good contentment." He took a particular perverse thrill in the riskiness of carrying out such a liaison under his landlord's nose—and roof. Although discreet, adultery was the norm rather than the exception in Venice. As the poet explained in a letter to his sister: "A woman is virtuous here who limits herself to her husband and one lover. Those who have two, three or more are considered a little wild."

Byron's first mistress was replaced by an illiterate baker's wife, who left her husband and moved into his villa, joining his fourteen staff members as a housekeeper. Although he loved her fiery passion and quirky habits —such as crossing herself if she heard a church bell ringing while they were making love—he eventually tired of her jealousy and theatrics, which were reminiscent of Lady Caroline. When asked to leave, she first came at him brandishing a table knife and then proceeded to hurl herself into the Grand Canal. Byron's gondoliers dragged her from the freezing waters, but the poet remained unmoved, sending her packing as soon as she had recovered.

Eventually, his dissipated lifestyle wore on him and by January 1819 he announced that he had "quite given up Concubinage." Yet three months later, he became transfixed with twenty-year-old Teresa Guiccioli, whom he met at the salon of a retired courtesan. Teresa, married to a wealthy count thirty years her senior, was to become Byron's true, enduring, and final love.

Although she resisted his initial overtures, during a later encounter she found that her "strength gave way—for B was not a man to confine himself to sentiment." As for Byron, he wrote that the "*essential* part of the business" of their first liaison occupied them for "*four* continuous days."

When the count took Teresa back to their home in Ravenna, the lovesick Byron followed and at the unwitting count's invitation, took up rooms on the ground floor of the couple's palazzo. Byron and Teresa's liaisons took place in the grand salon during the count's afternoon siesta, and as the doors had no locks, the risk of discovery titillated Byron even further. In one of his amorous missives to Teresa, he wrote, "Think, my love, of those moments—delicious—dangerous . . . not only for the pleasure . . . but for the danger."

Eventually, the count did catch them in flagrante delicto and demanded that the affair cease. Rather than give up Byron, Teresa had her family petition the pope for a separation and thereafter became the poet's constant companion. Their domestic bliss lasted only two years, cut short by the outbreak of the Greek War of Independence, when Byron felt compelled to join the Greeks in their struggle. Although distraught at the prospect of leaving Teresa, the poet had nurtured a powerful attachment to Greece since his travels there as a young man and could not be dissuaded from the cause.

"My dearest Teresa . . . believe that I always *love* you," he assured her in a letter written en route to his beloved country in July 1823. The finality of his statement takes on particular poignancy given that Byron was never to see his great love again. He died of rheumatic fever nine months later at the age of thirty-six, fulfilling his destiny as a doomed romantic hero.

Teresa mourned Byron for the rest of her life. Although she had other relationships, her heart and mind were always with the poet. Forty years after his death, when Teresa was living in France, she traveled to England several times. There, she made pilgrimages to various Byron shrines, including his rooms at Cambridge and his ancestral home, Newstead Abbey. One of her final acts was to publish her own account of the poet's life, writing on her deathbed, "The more Byron is known, the better he will be loved."

❧ NATURAL-BORN LADY-KILLERS ❧

Sometimes, you *can* judge a book by its cover. Any woman eavesdropping on the conversations of these serial seducers didn't need to read between the lines. Match the skirt chasers with their pearls of romantic wisdom.

THE SKIRT CHASERS

___1. Accusations of homosexuality and incest didn't faze hedonistic poet **Lord Byron**, whose feats between the sheets included bedding two hundred women in Venice alone.

___2. **Ian Fleming** had much in common with his fictional alter ego, suave ladies' man James Bond. But even he trumped 007's womanizing ways, playing more slap than tickle in the bedroom by indulging in sadomasochism.

___3. Legendary Italian lover **Giacomo Casanova** didn't discriminate with his affections. Among the objects of his seductions were noblewomen, chambermaids, five sisters (and their mother), a hunchback, and even a nun.

___4. The world has the word "sadism" thanks to the notorious **Marquis de Sade**, a Frenchman whose perverse sexual pleasures included using hot wax in open wounds on an unsuspecting widow he lured home.

___5. Known for writing, fighting, and womanizing, it's no wonder that infamous misogynist **Norman Mailer** went through five wives before he finally found one willing to stick around.

WORDS THEY LIVED BY

A. "Men want a woman whom they can turn on and off like a light switch."

B. "A woman should never be seen eating or drinking, unless it be *lobster salad* and *champagne*, the only truly feminine and becoming viands."

C. "Women think of being a man as a gift. It is a duty. Even making love can be a duty. A man has always got to get it up, and love isn't always enough."

D. "The sweetest pleasures are those which are hardest to be won."

E. "It is always by way of pain one arrives at pleasure."

Answers: 1. B, 2. A, 3. D, 4. E, 5. C

Never Curse Me

GUSTAVE FLAUBERT

What he didn't understand was all this fuss over something as simple as love.

—Gustave Flaubert, *Madame Bovary*

Handsome but hardly an ideal catch, reclusive confirmed bachelor Gustave Flaubert was nonetheless a hit with the ladies—even those he didn't pay for companionship. His longest relationship was a stormy eight-year affair with a poet who unwittingly helped inspire the title character in his controversial novel *Madame Bovary*.

A carriage with the blinds drawn, "tossing about like a boat," slowly makes its way along the streets of Rouen, France, and through the neighboring countryside. Inside the cab, Emma Bovary is having a passionate encounter with a man from her past. The famously lusty scene in Gustave Flaubert's masterpiece *Madame Bovary* was inspired by one of his real-life amorous encounters with the beautiful poet Louise Colet, which took place in her carriage as it circled a park on the outskirts of Paris.

Twelve hours after the lovers parted ways, Flaubert was at his family's home in Croisset, a village in the Normandy countryside, writing passionate letters to Louise. Stoking his ardor was a collection of mementos she had given him, including a pair of slippers, a lock of blonde hair, and a blood-specked handkerchief he wished "were completely red with it." In one missive Flaubert informed his lover he wanted to bite her, while in another he enclosed a rose from his mother's garden and instructed her to "put it quickly to your mouth, and then—you know where."

When the twenty-four-year-old writer met Louise in July 1846 at a sculptor's studio, where she was serving as a model, he had yet to publish a single word. Eleven years his senior, Louise was already well-known in Parisian literary circles and hosted a popular salon. Like Emma Bovary, she had wed partly to escape the boredom of provincial life but was unfulfilled in her marriage. After tying the knot, she and her music professor husband headed to Paris, where she pursued a career as a journalist and poet. While his career foundered, Louise began to achieve a measure of success—no easy feat for a female writer at the time—even garnering a poetry prize awarded by the prestigious Académie française. The Colets' marriage was soon beset by money troubles and jealousy, with Louise's controlling spouse dictating how she should dress and with whom she could associate. The unhappy couple eventually went their separate ways.

Flaubert believed he and the tempestuous Louise were predestined to cross paths, and within days of meeting they were trysting in her carriage. He wasn't Louise's only lover, nor was he scared off by her volatile past. A long-term liaison with the philosopher and historian Victor Cousin, a prominent government figure, brought Louise exposure for her writing along with some unintended notoriety. When she became pregnant following five years of childless marriage, a well-known gossip columnist printed a story suggesting Cousin was the father. Outraged, Louise paid a visit to the reporter's home and unsuccessfully attempted to stab him with a kitchen knife.

Famously reclusive, Flaubert kept himself at arm's length from his lover and her theatrics. At his urging, their affair was conducted primarily through correspondence, with only occasional assignations. He made up for their lack of physical proximity with effusive promises of future attentions. "I want to cover you with love when I next see you. . . . I want to gorge you with all the joys of the flesh, until you faint and die." In spite of his seeming enthusiasm for their relationship, even in his early letters to Louise he sent mixed signals. He professed to miss her terribly and assured her there was a void in his heart when they were apart, while at the same time cruelly alluding to the end of their relationship. "Never curse me! Ah, I shall love you well before loving you no longer," he vowed.

While Flaubert was content to indulge in ardent encounters and then hermetically retreat to the riverside estate where he lived with his mother and niece, Louise pleaded to see him more and implored him to move to Paris. Unyielding, Flaubert forbade her to visit him in Croisset and kept their affair a secret from his overbearing mother. Like Emma Bovary's devoted but dull husband, Charles, he felt torn between the two women. In his first letter to Louise after parting ways in Paris, he drove the point home. "My mother was waiting for me at the station. She wept at seeing me return. You wept to see me leave," he wrote. "In other words, such is our sad fate that we cannot move a league without causing tears on two sides at once!"

Although he was genuinely close to his mother, Flaubert used her as a pretext to keep Louise at bay. "My life is shackled to the life of another, and will be so for as long as she lives," he informed his mistress. In even stronger language, he warned her, "You must never come here." Flaubert saved most of his passion for his writing and, in between corresponding with Louise, obsessively toiled at his craft.

The writer made no secret of his aversion to marrying or siring children, once telling Louise when she expressed a desire to have a baby with him that the very idea turned him cold. To emphasize the point, he declared he would rather launch himself into the river with a cannonball tied to his feet. When his mistress later informed him she was pregnant, he was utterly dismayed and swiftly crushed her happiness by encouraging her to have an abortion. To his relief, she complied, and once the crisis was averted he declared, "All the better if I have no offspring. My humble name will perish with me."

Flaubert's heartless request didn't diminish Louise's infatuation with him, and she even proposed they run away together, something Emma Bovary suggests to her lover. Instead, the couple soon parted ways, and Flaubert took off on an eighteen-month trip to the Middle East. Louise continued to carry a torch for the writer, who did not even bid her farewell before he departed.

While Louise was pining away and near suicidal with longing, Flaubert was gazing at the pyramids, sailing down the Nile, and cavorting with prostitutes. Visiting brothels was not a new pastime for the writer, who brought back an unwanted but well-deserved souvenir from his Middle Eastern jaunt: syphilis. During his travels, no prostitute's haunt was so low that he wouldn't, sometimes literally, stoop to satiate his desires, occasionally crawling into low thatched huts on his hands and knees in search of a good time. Nor did his syphilis deter him (although one prostitute turned him away because of an open sore), and on a particularly lusty occasion he claimed to have availed himself of three women before lunch and another after dessert.

But it was an Egyptian courtesan and exotic dancer, Kuchuk

Hanem, "a regal-looking creature, large-breasted, fleshy, with . . . enormous eyes, and magnificent knees," who truly captivated him. He regaled just about anyone who would listen with the story of their long night of ecstasy, during which, he bragged, they had intercourse five times and oral sex three times. (Years later, when Louise was on assignment to cover the opening of the Suez Canal, she jealously tried to track down her foreign rival but failed.)

On the trip the writer also dabbled with male prostitutes, and one of his letters reports that he finally "consummated that business at the baths" in a sexual encounter with "a pockmarked young rascal wearing a white turban." He noted that it was an experiment worth repeating.

The last leg of Flaubert's journey brought him and a traveling companion through Greece and Italy, where they were joined by the writer's mother. A piece of gossip she brought with her from France, concerning the ill-fated fortunes of a young country doctor and his adulterous wife who took her own life, planted the seed for *Madame Bovary*.

After Flaubert returned to France, the still-bereft (and now widowed) Louise Colet broke his cardinal rule. When he didn't respond to a letter she sent, she showed up at his home in Croisset, where he was dining with guests and refused to see her. Undeterred, she kept strolling by the house until Flaubert emerged and promised to meet her later that night. Despite his seemingly resolute refusal to rekindle their romance, he relented a month later and the two fell back into a familiar pattern. Once again they began exchanging copious, often contentious letters and meeting in person from time to time.

It took the perfectionist writer—who frequently worked twelve-hour days, sometimes producing only a single page of text in a session—five years to complete *Madame Bovary*. The fact that he reignited his relationship with Louise shortly before he began working on the novel is thought to be no coincidence. Not only did he surreptitiously mine details from her life, he also used her as a sounding board and sought advice during the writing process. According to Louise, Flaubert loved her "in a deeply selfish way, to gratify his senses and read me his works."

A year into their renewed affair, Flaubert found out he had competition for Louise's affections in the poet and playwright Alfred de Musset. Uncharacteristically jealous, he suggested some harsh lines she could use to get rid of the other man after she achieved her aim of having him read one of her poems at the Académie française. Also out of character, Flaubert made a loose promise to the long-suffering Louise that they would soon be together permanently. His change of heart was short-lived, and after several blissful weeks together in Paris he returned to Croisset and inexplicably turned against her, claiming he needed to devote himself to his novel.

The pair's fiery, eight-year association came to an abrupt end. The last time they saw each other was at Louise's Paris flat, where she cried and aired her grievances, repeatedly hitting Flaubert in the leg for emphasis. Rather than strike his irritating mistress with a burning log, as he fantasized doing, he simply got up and walked out the door. Flaubert lost interest in Louise for good after that, although she yearned for him and unsuccessfully tried to see him at least once when he was in Paris.

Two years later, in 1856, the thirty-four-year-old writer triumphantly made his literary debut when *Madame Bovary* appeared in installments in the journal *Revue de Paris*. Even without the notorious carriage scene, which was cut for being too salacious, the story still caught the attention of Napoleon III's prudish censors. Flaubert was brought to trial for offending public morality, religion, and decency during a deeply conservative period.

The writer ultimately triumphed in court and dedicated the

book version to his defense attorney. Sales of *Madame Bovary* were spurred by the publicity, which cemented the author's reputation better than any advertising campaign could have done. "Everyone has read it, is reading it, or wants to read it," Flaubert boasted.

Another, more personal, firestorm ensued when Louise read the novel and recognized details from her own life reflected in the story. Not only did she and Emma Bovary share similarities in appearance and attire, including the blue dress she wore at her first meeting with Flaubert, but they also made similar life decisions and shared personality traits. Like Louise, the independent-minded Emma, who quickly became disillusioned with men, used her husband and lovers to advance her social status and achieve her dreams.

Louise was particularly incensed by Flaubert's allusion to a gift she had given him at a time when she could scarcely afford to be so generous, a cigar holder engraved with the words "Amor nel cor" (Love in the heart). Emma Bovary bestows a seal with the same motto on her rakish lover, Rodolphe Boulanger, who later breaks off their relationship in a letter he marks with the romantic insignia. Aptly, one of Louise's acts of literary revenge on Flaubert was a poem titled "Amor nel cor" published in a popular periodical. She also wrote a semiautobiographical novel, *Lui*, based on her love triangle with de Musset and Flaubert, who is depicted as a buffoon and a cad.

Despite eventually losing the youthful good looks that had first attracted Louise Colet, the middle-aged Flaubert didn't lack for female attention. He romanced an actress and also had a lengthy affair with his niece's English governess. But true to his word about forgoing marriage, Flaubert remained a bachelor whose greatest legacy is *Madame Bovary*, the racy novel that sparked a furor and sealed his place in literary history.

SIX DEGREES OF COPULATION

Lord Byron
The English aristocrat famed for his vigorous sex life found true love with a countess, Teresa Guiccioli, but abandoned her to join Greece's struggle for independence.

Teresa Guiccioli
Despite the Italian beauty's enduring feelings for her deceased amour, Lord Byron, she took other lovers, including married professor Hippolyte Colet.

Alfred de Musset
The moody young bard wooed older woman George Sand with poetry composed for her. After their on-again, off-again relationship ended, he complained the sex hadn't been hot enough.

Louise Colet
The fiery French poet juggled relationships simultaneously with Flaubert and Alfred de Musset. She both feared and fantasized that the two men would duel in her honor.

Hippolyte Colet
After the music professor wed provincial girl Louise Révoil, the newlyweds moved to Paris—a path resembling the one taken by the title character in Gustave Flaubert's novel *Madame Bovary*.

George Sand (Aurore Dupin)
As well as courting controversy with her racy novels, Sand scandalously cross-dressed, smoked cigars, and had affairs with younger men. Among the critics of her lifestyle was poet Charles Baudelaire, who vowed to douse her in holy water.

Gustave Flaubert
The novelist had a penchant for prostitutes, as well as older women like Louise Colet and Ludovica Pradier, both of whom were models for the character Emma Bovary.

Alexandre Dumas fils
The lusty Madame Pradier seduced Alexandre Dumas's eighteen-year-old namesake son. A future novelist himself, Dumas fils once said of their first sexual encounter, "She didn't lose any time, I must say, and immediately stood before me totally naked, being equally devoid of physical flaws and modesty."

Ludovica and James Pradier
The sculptor divorced his wife, who brought them to the brink of financial ruin with lavish spending on her paramours. Her spendthrift ways were transposed to Emma Bovary, whose creator, Flaubert, earned a place on her lengthy list of lovers.

Juliette Drouet
The actress, who modeled for James Pradier and had a daughter with him, met Victor Hugo while performing in one of his plays. She abandoned her stage career to become his longtime mistress.

Victor Hugo
When the novelist and playwright fled France for speaking out against the monarchy, Juliette accompanied him into exile. On the isle of Guernsey, he kept house with his family and set her up in a nearby abode.

Go Your Own Way

THE BEATS

The weight of the world
is love.
Under the burden
of solitude
under the burden
of dissatisfaction
the weight
the weight we carry
is love.

—Allen Ginsberg, "Song"

White picket fences were not everyone's idea of the American dream in the postwar 1940s and '50s—least of all Jack Kerouac and the other beat writers who boldly rejected social norms in favor of individuality and a free-love lifestyle. Although their alternative way of life came at a price, the result was groundbreaking books like Kerouac's counterculture masterpiece *On the Road*. Two other works—William Burroughs's sex-and-drug-fueled *Naked Lunch* and Allen Ginsberg's homoerotic *Howl and Other Poems*—instigated notorious obscenity trials that helped end literary censorship in America.

2∽

Edie Parker's wedding gift to Jack Kerouac was bail money. The couple exchanged vows at New York City Hall in August 1944, with the groom handcuffed to a detective during the ceremony. After the nuptials took place, the officer treated the newlyweds to cocktails and accompanied them to a restaurant for a steak dinner before escorting Kerouac back to the slammer until his release could be arranged with funds from Edie's inheritance. The writer had helped a friend conceal a murder weapon, although charges against him were eventually dropped.

While their marriage lasted just six months, Kerouac and Edie had been together in an open relationship for several years. Both were Columbia University dropouts—she was a former art student, and he had abandoned a football scholarship. They met through Edie's boyfriend, who eventually lost her to the handsome, athletic Kerouac after innocently asking him to look after his girl while he shipped out with the merchant marine.

Kerouac also joined up with the merchant marine, both to aid the effort during World War II and to garner fodder for his fiction by sailing the seas like his idol Herman Melville. When he wasn't aboard ship, he shared a Manhattan apartment with Edie and her friend Joan Vollmer, both before and after his wedding. Kerouac had his wife to thank for more than just springing him from jail. It was through Edie that he first came to know the other major personalities of the beat generation: Allen Ginsberg, William Burroughs, and Neal Cassady.

Joan's abode was a popular gathering place for aspiring writers, amateur philosophers, petty criminals, college dropouts, and others living beyond the bounds of traditional 1940s society. Drugs and drink flowed, and free love was practiced in earnest. Nineteen-year-old Ginsberg, the youngest of the bunch, was smitten with Kerouac, who was no stranger to sex with men but preferred to bed women.

Burroughs, the elder statesman of the group at thirty, favored men but began sleeping with their hostess, Joan, a divorcée and Benzedrine addict. Witty and well-versed in philosophy and literature, she often participated in discussions with her housemates while holding court from the bathtub. Burroughs, too, was a divorcé. While traveling in Europe in 1936, he magnanimously married a Jewish woman so she could escape Nazi persecution and had the union dissolved once the bride made it safely to the United States.

Life changed dramatically for Kerouac and Ginsberg after the ruggedly handsome, swaggering Neal Cassady turned up in the Big Apple. Burroughs never got on well with the Denver pool shark and car thief, introduced to the group by an acquaintance from Columbia. Cassady and his sixteen-year-old wife, LuAnne, rumbled into town on a Greyhound bus after their classier mode of transport—a stolen car—had broken down en route. A mass of contradictions, Cassady had been arrested ten times and yet made a serious dent in the offerings at the Denver Public Library.

The madcap adventure-seeker became a muse for both Ginsberg and Kerouac, most famously serving as the model for lively wheelman Dean Moriarty in the latter's tale of wanderlust and youthful rebellion *On the Road*. The semiautobiographical novel incorporated many real-life events, including Kerouac's memorable early encounter with Cassady, during which he arrived at the apartment where the out-of-towner was staying and interrupted a lovemaking session with LuAnne. Rumor has it that Cassady answered the door in the buff, although in *On the Road* Dean is clad in shorts. The randy muse also served as the inspiration for the titular character in Kerouac's *Visions of Cody*, while in Ginsberg's notorious *Howl* he is immortalized as the "secret hero of these poems, cocksman and Adonis of Denver."

Several months after their initial meeting, Kerouac ventured west to look up Cassady but felt like a third wheel when he arrived. Ginsberg had beaten him to Denver and immediately hopped into bed with their mutual friend. In addition to dallying with Ginsberg, Cassady was still seeing LuAnne despite their impending divorce and was also involved with graduate art student Carolyn Robinson. None too pleased at having to compete so heavily for Cassady's affections, Ginsberg wrote bitterly in his journal that he needed to "remind Neal to ditch a few women." No doubt the frustrated Romeo would have been further incensed to know that Cassady had won over Carolyn with love poems Ginsberg had written him, passed off as his own.

While in town, Kerouac became friendly with Carolyn, but when chemistry developed between them he reluctantly told her, "It's too bad, but that's how it is. Neal saw you first." Carolyn wasn't as charmed by Ginsberg, whom she discovered having a ménage à trois with Cassady and LuAnne. She hadn't known about either of her boyfriend's lovers and was aghast at his having sex with a man. And yet she wasn't completely without sympathy for Ginsberg, commenting that "an accident of gender was all that put me where he wanted to be."

Although Cassady was an aspiring writer himself, his only published work, an unfinished autobiography, appeared posthumously. It was his frenetic, rambling personal correspondence that had a lasting literary legacy. Kerouac sought to emulate his friend's spontaneous, discursive letter-writing style and break away from the more conventional prose he'd used in his first novel, *The Town and the City*. Cassady's dispatches, in which he wrote about sexual escapades and his degenerate past, were "all first person, fast, mad, confessional," enthused Kerouac.

Back in New York and unable to interest a publisher in his fiction, Kerouac was consoling himself with casual affairs when Cassady called to report he was the proud owner of a legally obtained, brand-new 1949 Hudson sedan. Leaving Carolyn and their infant daughter behind, he and LuAnne, who was riding shotgun, fetched Kerouac at a relative's house in North Carolina.

Their monthlong, coast-to-coast joy ride, which helped inspire *On the Road*, ended abruptly in San Francisco when Cassady dropped Kerouac and LuAnne at the curb and announced he was heading home to his wife and child. "You see what a bastard he is?" Marylou asks Sal in *On the Road*. "Dean will leave you out in the cold any time it's in his interest." Fiction follows real life when Sal and Marylou, stand-ins for Kerouac and LuAnne, find a hotel room and end up in bed together.

Six years after his hasty city hall nuptials, Kerouac tied the knot once more. This time the bride was Joan Haverty, whose boyfriend had wanted to arrange an assignation between her and his friend Kerouac. Before the tryst took place, the drunken matchmaker was killed trying to climb out the window of a moving subway car. Several weeks later, Kerouac happened to pass by the apartment Joan had shared with her late beau and called up to her window. He proposed to the attractive seamstress within days, and they wed two weeks later. Their whirlwind courtship featured in *On the Road*, in which he recalled the night he met "the girl with the pure and innocent dear eyes that I had always searched for. . . . We agreed to love each other madly."

Despite the ardent vow, this marriage, like his first, lasted a mere six months. Although a dismal time for Kerouac personally, it proved to be a productive stint in his career. After struggling with his "road book," he powered through a three-week marathon typing session fueled by caffeine and drugs. On a continuous piece of scroll-like paper, he turned out 125,000 words, the first draft of *On the Road*.

Kerouac and Joan said good-bye for good when she announced she was pregnant. Forced to choose between her husband, who demanded she have an abortion, and their baby, she opted for motherhood. In a low move, the writer denied paternity, claiming Joan was insane and that she had been unfaithful. He was briefly jailed for failing to pay spousal support and didn't meet his daughter until a decade later. Joan got revenge by airing her grievances publicly in an article, "My Ex-Husband, Jack Kerouac, Is an Ingrate," in *Confidential* magazine, the *National Enquirer* of the day.

After his bitter break with Joan, Kerouac moved into the Cassady's attic in San Francisco for a time. With Neal's approval, his simmering attraction to Carolyn escalated into an affair she instigated. As he did with both of his wives, Kerouac moved in on a woman who had a romantic connection to a friend. The love triangle—reimagined in his novel *Big Sur*—lasted for several months until tensions flared between the two men. The writer then headed to Mexico to visit Burroughs, who was embroiled in a scandal so outlandish it could have been fodder for a film noir crime drama.

Burroughs had moved south of the border with his common-law wife, Joan Vollmer, after fleeing Texas and Louisiana in the wake of drug busts. During a drunken revelry, the pair sought to entertain fellow partiers with a familiar routine. Joan placed a glass on top of her head while Burroughs, a crack shot, took aim with a gun. He fired from six feet away, tragically missing the glass and shooting her instead.

Burroughs insisted Joan's death was an accident but didn't rule out the possibility of darker, subconscious forces at work. Although he was haunted by the terrible incident, in the introduction to his novel *Queer* he confessed that it lit fire to his creativity. "I am forced to the appalling conclusion that I would never have become a writer but for Joan's death," he admitted. Knowing him to be a skilled marksman, an acquaintance suggested that Joan, who suffered debilitating physical symptoms from years of drug use, may have committed suicide by moving at the last minute.

Burroughs escaped jail time with the aid of a local lawyer, some well-placed bribes, and two witnesses prepared to testify that the gun went off inadvertently. The perpetrator fled the country, later learning that he was given a two-year suspended sentence. He set out for Central and South America and then visited New York, bunking with Ginsberg, to whom he declared his love. Although he was once infatuated with Burroughs, Ginsberg was no longer interested and harshly told his houseguest, "I don't want your ugly old cock."

At the time Ginsberg rejected Burroughs's invitation to hit the sack, he was in a straight phase. After intense psychoanalysis, the sexually conflicted poet declared himself heterosexual and began sleeping with women. One of his girlfriends was Alene Lee, an African American woman who later became involved with Kerouac and appears as the main character's love interest in his novel *The Subterraneans*. Ginsberg's vow of heterosexuality lasted until he gazed at a naked portrait of Peter Orlovsky at a San Francisco artist's studio. When he asked about the blond-haired man gracing the canvas, his host obligingly called into the next room and the real thing sauntered into view.

Living a nonconformist life worked out better for some of the beat generation writers than for others. Kerouac achieved overnight celebrity when *On the Road* was finally published, but he then spiraled into alcoholism, eventually unable to write and sometimes walking the streets in a drunken stupor. The writer was married to his third wife and de facto caretaker (she hid his shoes so he couldn't go bar hopping) when he died of internal bleeding, caused by cirrhosis, at age forty-seven. Cassady, too, passed away in his forties, found lifeless in a Mexican ditch after a night of partying. The long-suffering Carolyn had kicked him out for good after he squandered their life savings at the track and bigamously married a model with whom he had a child.

Burroughs lived a hermetic existence, twenty-five years of it abroad, assuaging his loneliness in homosexual affairs and mind-altering drugs while pouring out his experiences on the page (he was one of the first American novelists to write explicitly about gay sex). Guilt and regret over Joan's death perpetually tormented him.

Ginsberg was luckier in love—and life—than his beat counterparts. He took up with Orlovsky, publicly referring to him as his spouse. Neither was monogamous: both slept with other men—including Burroughs, who Ginsberg finally shagged, ugly old cock and all—as well as women. The two maintained a relationship for more than four decades, until Ginsberg's death in 1997. Their daring openness about their liaison, which the poet's celebrity brought into the spotlight, aided in advancing the gay liberation movement.

In a letter to Kerouac, Ginsberg once passed along some wisdom he heard from Burroughs: "I say we are here in human form to learn by the human hieroglyphs of love and suffering. It is a duty to take the risk of love."

❧ IF THESE WALLS COULD TALK ❧

When not toiling at their craft, many writers were living life with abandon. From hotels to a dance hall, these establishments were backdrops for hookups, breakups, and scandalous deeds.

~ **Heartbreak hotel.** Novelist George Sand checked into Venice's swank Hotel Danieli with one man and left with another. She threw over poet Alfred de Musset for the doctor who treated him when he came down with a mysterious ailment (likely contracted during his illicit sexual encounters while Sand was sick herself). The spurned poet left for France alone, while Sand moved in with the Italian physician.

~ **Kiss and yell.** While performing at the famed Moulin Rouge in Paris in 1906, novelist and vaudeville entertainer Colette shocked show-goers when she and her female lover, a cross-dressing aristocrat, kissed onstage as part of their performance. Even at the risqué cabaret-club, the act was so outrageous it incited a riot.

~ **The heat is on.** At London's Thistle Charing Cross Hotel, Edith Wharton and her secret lover, journalist Morton Fullerton, steamed up room 92. Even before getting out of bed the next morning, she immortalized the torrid encounter in the erotic poem "Terminus," recalling "the long secret night . . . lying there hushed in your arms, as the waves of rapture receded."

~ **Sexy sleepover.** The verbal foreplay during a gathering at Fouquet's restaurant in Paris was stimulating enough that playwright Samuel Beckett got lucky. After walking his new acquaintance, art patron Peggy Guggenheim, back to her place, he suggested she join him on the sofa. Their nearly twenty-four-hour sex marathon was interrupted only for a champagne run.

~ **Love shack.** At the villa Fontana Vecchia, the Sicilian love nest where D. H. and Frieda Lawrence had infamous screaming matches in the early 1920s, Truman Capote romanced his new lover thirty years later. His rebound relationship with Broadway dancer-turned-writer Jack Dunphy—who had recently divorced a woman—lasted for fifteen years, until Capote's slide into drug and alcohol addiction.

PART THREE

The Joy of Sex

Sexistentialism

SIMONE DE BEAUVOIR

Love for the woman is a total abdication for the benefit of a master.

—Simone de Beauvoir, *The Second Sex*

French philosopher Simone de Beauvoir once thought about becoming a nun but reconsidered after a crisis of faith. Instead the lapsed Catholic made a scandalous vow to fellow academic Jean-Paul Sartre and boldly embarked on an unconventional lifestyle. Despite her insistence on independence, the resolutely single feminist icon was as much of a fool for love as any married woman.

One of the most infamous relationships in literary history had a surprisingly mundane beginning. Using a mutual friend as an intermediary, Jean-Paul Sartre invited Simone de Beauvoir to hit the books with him at the Sorbonne, the Parisian university where in 1929 they were both studying for an elite graduate degree in philosophy. In two weeks' time, a partnership had been forged that would last half a century and push social and sexual mores to an extreme.

The diminutive, unprepossessing Sartre seemed an unlikely match for beautiful Simone, a blue-eyed brunette who had no shortage of admirers at the university. But what he lacked in physical attributes—he was five feet tall, almost completely blind in one eye, and hardly handsome—Sartre made up for with his brilliant mind and outsize personality. He favored boldly colored shirts, played pranks, generously spent his mother's money on his friends, and became a campus legend for turning up naked at a university event.

At twenty-one, Simone was the youngest student ever to sit for the *agrégation* in philosophy, a competitive exam for a teaching position in the French school system. Although jury members agreed she was the best philosopher (and only the ninth woman to garner the degree), she had to settle for second place. Top honors were awarded to Sartre, presumably because he was male.

Simone didn't hold the slight against him, claiming that they had become "necessary" to each other and continuing to see him nearly every day. To her delight, he turned up out of the blue in southwest France, where she was vacationing with her family. Simone snuck out to meet him in the surrounding fields, where they talked about philosophy and made love for the first time. Concerned their daughter's reckless behavior was becoming fodder for local gossips, her parents confronted the couple and demanded Sartre leave. His refusal, on the grounds that they were working on an important thesis, was a triumphant moment for Simone, emotionally emancipating her from her parents.

After the young lovers were discovered, Sartre asked Simone to marry him. "He felt he had to propose to me after my father accosted us," she later explained. "I told him not to be silly and of course I rejected marriage." Crushed at being rebuffed, her would-be husband admitted that at the time he "was foolish enough to be upset by it: instead of understanding the extraordinary luck I'd had, I fell into a certain melancholy."

Sartre then suggested they make a radical pact that would have been most men's dream scenario: the pair would remain devoted to one another but were free to see other people. "What *we* have is an *essential* love; but it is a good idea for us also to experience *contingent* love affairs," he told Simone. To his surprise, she readily agreed, believing as he did that even their intense relationship "could not make up entirely for the fleeting riches to be had from encounters with different people." They later made a second promise, vowing never to lie to one another the way married couples often do and to share the details of their contingent love affairs.

Although monogamy didn't appeal to Sartre, he had nothing against marriage and came close to tying the knot with other women several times. As for Simone, she had no intention of ever marrying, believing it inevitably led to deceit and cheating and that the female spouse usually drew the short straw. Instead she planned to live her life with the same independence as a man. Making the unconventional choice not to wed and to freely engage in affairs was significantly more courageous for de Beauvoir than it was for Sartre, given society's double standards. Sartre's parents were among her earliest critics, disapproving of her association with their son and refusing to entertain her in their home.

To maintain the independent life she craved, de Beauvoir needed to support herself and didn't balk at being assigned a teaching position in southeastern France, some six hundred miles away from Sartre. Devastated at the separation, he proposed marriage for the second time so they could request a joint assignment. Again Simone turned him down.

At the time Sartre began seeing de Beauvoir, he was also involved with another Simone, Simone Jollivet, a vivacious, intelligent woman he had met at his cousin's funeral. True to their pact, he regaled de Beauvoir with spicy details about his liaisons with the other woman, who received callers in the nude and threw legendary theme parties that included a Roman orgy. Stricken with jealousy, de Beauvoir began to lose focus on her writing. "Watch out," Sartre cautioned her, "that you don't turn into a housewife."

There was no danger of that happening, given the unconventional "trios" the couple began orchestrating. The first was with one of Simone's students, seventeen-year-old Olga Kosakiewicz, the daughter of a Russian émigré. After the two women struck up a friendship, Olga moved into the hotel where de Beauvoir was living and they began an affair, the first of numerous sexual encounters the teacher initiated with female students. Throughout her life, she misled biographers and denied in interviews that she had affairs with women. After Sartre's death, she published his letters to her but claimed the ones she wrote to him were lost. When the missives came to light after her demise, they were published unedited, including passages in which she vividly described her lesbian encounters.

Perpetually on the hunt for fresh conquests (particularly virgins), Sartre relished pursuing the female students that attached themselves to Simone. He fell madly in love with Olga and spent two years futilely trying to seduce her. "As for O., my passion for her burned away my workaday impurities like a Bunsen-flame," Sartre candidly acknowledged. As he and de Beauvoir vied for the young girl's affections, Olga performed her part, vacillating between the two of them and playing them against each other.

No matter how progressive de Beauvoir thought herself when it came to relationships, the green-eyed monster once again had her in its grip when faced with Sartre's unabated desire for another woman. Working through her conflicted feelings, she used the love triangle as the basis for her first novel, She Came to Stay. "The unfortunate episode of the trio did much more than supply me with a subject for a novel," she explained. "It enabled me to deal with it."

Understandably, rage and resentment reverberate throughout She Came to Stay. The emotions de Beauvoir wouldn't allow herself to express in real life were transferred to her fiction. Her novel, the tale of a Parisian couple and the girl who throws their marriage off kilter, remains fairly true to life, with a notable exception. In a grisly act of metaphorical revenge, the character based on Simone coldly and calculatingly murders the stand-in for Olga (to whom, ironically, she dedicated the novel).

Sartre's licentious hopes for a tryst with Olga were crushed when she fell for Jacques-Laurent Bost, one of his pupils. Despite being denied physical gratification, Sartre, too, got literary mileage out of the situation. His novel *The Age of Reason* is the story of a philosophy teacher in a tired relationship with his girlfriend of seven years. He falls in love with a student, the daughter of a Russian aristocrat who bears a striking resemblance to Olga, but as in real life, lust went unfulfilled.

A consolation prize came along for Sartre in the form of Olga's younger sister, Wanda, although another two years passed before he succeeded in bedding the striking sibling. When he finally did, he was titillated as much by the opportunity to brag about it as by the deed. Ever the cad, he left his lover lying in bed while he dashed off to a café to write Simone with the scintillating details.

Sartre and de Beauvoir's association with Olga was the beginning of an extended network they dubbed the "family," made up mostly of their former students. They not only influenced their young acquaintances' careers but also managed their personal lives, paying doctor bills and bankrolling vacations. While Sartre pursued Wanda, Simone took up with another "family member," Olga's boyfriend Jacques-Laurent Bost. Their relationship, kept secret from the other woman, blossomed while they were hiking in the Alps. Sartre gave his nod of approval, and a new trio was formed when he spent several weeks traveling through the Greek islands with Simone and Bost.

Sartre's sexual escapades were curbed for a time while he served in World War II and became a prisoner of war for nine months, although he continued wooing with words, declaring his affection for Simone before telling her he planned to write to Wanda next. When de Beauvoir heard that enemy forces had broken through the area where he was serving, she was consumed with worry and fear. He reassured her and urged her to have faith and patience. "My love, it's our eleventh anniversary and I feel so close to you," he wrote during his internment. "You must never again dream that I don't love you anymore."

After his release, the couple's dangerous liaisons with de Beauvoir's students resumed and eventually almost brought about her ruin. The parents of one pupil lodged a complaint, accusing her of corrupting a minor. The charges would be dropped if she was dismissed from her teaching position and forbidden all contact with underage students. Although she vehemently protested her innocence, in 1943, after more than a decade in the French school system, de Beauvoir was out of a job.

The professional downturn didn't last long for the philosopher, who rebounded almost immediately with the publication of *She Came to Stay*. Also appearing that year was Sartre's *Being and Nothingness*, which he'd begun writing while a prisoner of war. In the weighty philosophical tome, which heralded the rise of existentialism in twentieth-century France, he espouses the belief that there is no God and that individuals are responsible for their own choices.

Existentialism gained popularity during the post–World War II years and launched its two most famous proponents into the media spotlight. De Beauvoir and Sartre traveled together to promote their books and often gave joint interviews. Paparazzi shadowed them, eager to share photos of the trendy philosophers with a public both fascinated and scandalized by their lifestyle.

De Beauvoir's unorthodox life gave rise to *The Second Sex*, her famed treatise on the status and nature of women and the sources of gender inequality. The seeds of the book were sown during a discussion with Sartre in which she confided that she had been considering the ways in which she was typically feminine and the ways in which she was not. He encouraged her to delve more deeply into the idea, and the result was her most well-known work. Published in 1949, the controversial book was an instant best seller and became a cornerstone of the feminist movement, garnering praise while also rousing indignation for questioning traditional notions about women's roles.

While on a lecture tour in the United States, Sartre embarked on an affair that nearly tore asunder his long-standing pact with de Beauvoir. When he became enraptured with Dolorès Vanetti, a French actress married to a wealthy American doctor, Simone correctly perceived the relationship as a serious threat. The lovebirds met in New York and rendezvoused in France before Sartre ultimately bid Dolorès—who had no interest in a romantic relationship that included Simone—a regretful farewell.

The female philosopher had her own stateside liaison with Chicago-based journalist and novelist Nelson Algren. Meeting him, she declared, was one of the most auspicious events of her life. They fell for each other almost instantly and carried on a transatlantic affair for years. De Beauvoir constantly wore a silver ring Algren gave her (which accompanied her to the grave she shares with Sartre) and wrote him letters, referring to him as her husband and only love. She connected on an intellectual as well as physical level with the writer, who in looks—blond, handsome, and six feet tall—was the antithesis of Sartre. More importantly, he was better in the sack than the Frenchman. Despite the innumerable sexual encounters de Beauvoir had before meeting Algren, she claimed she had her first orgasm with him, at age thirty-nine.

Algren desperately wanted to marry Simone, but like Dolorès, he was uninterested in a three-way emotional relationship and resented playing second fiddle to Sartre. Despite her deep love for Algren, Simone stood firm on her antimarriage stance, unwilling to give up either Sartre or her freedom. Even the great sex wasn't enough to entice her to abandon the pact she had made long ago, and the ill-fated lovers eventually parted ways for good. Algren went on to marry and divorce twice but never forgave Simone, whom he cursed to a reporter shortly before he died.

Some of Algren's animosity stemmed from de Beauvoir's vivid, thinly veiled depiction of their private life—in particular their sexual exploits—in her 1954 novel *The Mandarins*, which she dedicated to him. (He was further outraged when she revealed even more in her autobiographies.) De Beauvoir's novel, a fictionalized take on the lives of those in her and Sartre's intellectual circle, centers on an adulterous married woman torn between her inner desires and keeping up appearances. The book garnered the coveted Prix Goncourt, France's highest literary prize, and finally moved de Beauvoir out of Sartre's shadow.

The couple's decades-long partnership eventually began to fray around the edges as they both reneged on aspects of the pact. The closest they had ever come to living together was taking rooms in the same hotel, yet in middle age de Beauvoir relinquished her coveted solitude and invited a much younger lover to move in with her. Having children was also against their creed, and yet fifty-nine-year-old Sartre shocked Simone by adopting his Algerian mistress, who was in her midtwenties. Legally declaring the younger woman his heir and giving her posthumous control of his literary estate seemed an enormous betrayal to his longtime partner. An enraged and humiliated de Beauvoir responded by formally adopting her own female protégé and creating a rival family.

Despite the bitterness that erupted between the former lovers in Sartre's last years, de Beauvoir was devastated by his passing. A half century after they made their notorious pact, he professed his love for her on his deathbed in 1980. She kissed him a final time and kept vigil by his side. When he slipped away, she laid next to his lifeless body, wishing she could go with him.

❧ THE ART OF SEDUCTION ❧

Whether wooing or being wooed, few writers played by the book when it came to seduction. For them, novelty and naughtiness trumped roses, champagne, and candlelight.

~ **Sex education.** "Everything one writes comes to pass," declared French cougar Colette of her salacious novel *Chéri*. The 1920 tale of a young man's carnal awakening at the hands of a retired courtesan precipitated the writer's own seduction of her sixteen-year-old stepson. Foreshadowing her intentions, the forty-seven-year-old gave the boy a signed first edition. Soon afterward she informed him, "It's time for you to become a man," and barged into his bedroom to deflower him. The one-night seduction morphed into a five-year affair.

~ **Spirited away.** During her honeymoon, young bride Georgie Yeats was devastated to learn that her husband, W. B. Yeats, was still in love with someone else. Instead of walking out, she salvaged the marriage by pretending to fall into a trance. As though guided by a spirit, she sent her husband reassuring messages that he had done the right thing in marrying her. The technique worked so well—even curing his impotence—that Georgie used it to her advantage for years, even sending Yeats messages from the spirit world on how to sexually satisfy her.

~ **The world was his oyster.** Legendary Italian seducer Casanova is rumored to have eaten more than fifty oysters a day to boost his sexual prowess. He also used the slippery mollusks in his seduction arsenal, feeding them to his lovers and "accidentally" dropping them down quivering bodices. His ultimate aphrodisiac was the "lascivious and voluptuous game" of exchanging them in a partner's mouth, drenched in saliva: "What a sauce that is which dresses an oyster I suck from the mouth of the woman I love!"

~ **Domestic goddess.** Routine chores were anything but in Raymond Chandler's home, where his wife, Cissy, performed housework in the nude. Contrary to appearances, the striking forty-nine-year-old wasn't attempting to reenact a male porn fantasy. Instead, her au naturel ironing, dusting, and vacuuming helped maintain her svelte figure. The former artist's model was a devoted practitioner of the Mensendieck system, a therapeutic exercise regime that advocated performing functional movements in the buff to facilitate good posture and body mechanics.

~ **Kitchen confidential.** "If we could just have the kitchen and the bedroom, that would be all we need," professed Julia Child after forty-seven years of marriage. No one knew better than the famed cookbook author that the way to a man's heart is through his stomach. Before she met her husband, Paul, the future gourmand never thought twice about what she ate, making do with frozen meals. It was his love of haute cuisine that awakened her own taste buds and inspired her to re-create the romantic dinners à deux they enjoyed in French restaurants.

Web of Lies

ANAÏS NIN

Eroticism is one of the basic means of self-knowledge, as basic as poetry.

—Anaïs Nin

Bored housewife Anaïs Nin found the solution to her discontent between the sheets. The diarist and erotica writer's quest for sexual satisfaction began in novelist Henry Miller's arms and included a second, bigamous marriage she kept secret through an elaborate charade.

When Anaïs Nin wed the much younger Rupert Pole before a justice of the peace in Quartzsite, Arizona, in 1955, she was keeping a momentous secret: she was still married to her first husband. For years, Pole had pleaded with her to marry, until she finally ran out of excuses and led him to believe she had gotten a divorce.

The pair had barely known each other when they set out on a cross-country road trip eight years earlier, a mere two months after meeting in an elevator on the way to a party in New York City. "Part Two of my life. I feel loved. I feel invited to the world. I feel free," forty-four-year-old Nin wrote in her diary shortly before sliding into the passenger seat of Pole's Model A Ford roadster, headed for California. What she thought would be a fling with the former actor, sixteen years her junior, was the beginning of a double life that lasted for decades.

Nin had no qualms about leaving Hugh Guiler, her husband of twenty-four years, behind in New York City while she rode off with another man. Rather than choose between the two men, she traveled back and forth across the continent maintaining relationships with both. Guiler provided Nin with emotional and financial security, while Pole gave her the great sex lacking in her marriage.

In contrast to Nin's luxurious lifestyle with the wealthy Guiler, she led a simpler existence with Pole, who became a park ranger and then a middle school math teacher. Before moving to Los Angeles the duo resided in a rustic cabin in the mountain village of Sierra Madre, where Nin cleaned and kept house herself. Each man accepted, or at least pretended to accept, the excuses she gave about her frequent travels. Pole believed writing assignments took her to New York, while she told Guiler she sought rest and relaxation for health reasons on the West Coast.

Keeping up the deception of the bicoastal marriages, a risky situation she referred to as her "trapeze," was challenging (and no doubt exhausting) for Nin. She made carbon copies of her letters for reference, had prescriptions filled in two different names, and enlisted friends on both coasts to help keep the men from finding out the truth. The web of falsehoods she spun grew so elaborate that she recorded the details, such as which acquaintances she had used as alibis, on index cards and organized them in a "lie box."

More than once Nin's carefully constructed house of cards nearly collapsed, including the time Pole unexpectedly showed up in New York to surprise her while he was en route to a job interview. In another close call, Pole was tipped off by drunken guests at a Holly-wood soiree and given the number to his rival's New York apartment. When the quick-thinking Nin answered the phone, she informed him that she was temporarily keeping watch over Guiler, who had taken a serious fall. Guiler, meanwhile, accepted her story that the caller was a deranged admirer she had met in California.

What compelled Nin to finally confess her trickery to Pole was a long-awaited leap forward in her literary career and a fear of the IRS. After struggling for years to make it as a novelist, Nin eventu-ally found fame with the intimate diaries she had kept for most of her life. Realizing publication could bring unwanted scrutiny to her personal life, and possibly have legal ramifications since both men reported her income on their tax returns, she came clean with Pole and had their marriage annulled.

Instead of parting ways, Pole opted to continue the unortho-dox association. "In a way, I did not care. My idea of marriage is different," he claimed, despite having pressured Nin to make it legal. "We had a wonderful, deep relationship, and that is what counted. I was not interested in conventional women." Nin at first believed Pole would leave her for a younger woman once he found out her real age, but their relationship ended only with her death from cancer in 1977. He cared for her during her final years when, too ill to travel, she settled with him in Los Angeles. (A *Los Angeles Times* obituary identified her as Mrs. Pole, while the *New York Times* referred to her as Mrs. Guiler.)

Even after Nin told Pole they were not legally hitched, she con-tinued to keep up the pretense with Guiler, whom she refused to abandon due to a strong, albeit warped, sense of loyalty. It's thought that while he eventually found out about his wife's relationship with Pole, he didn't know she had married the other man until she passed away. But it was far from Nin's first extramarital affair and certainly not the only time Guiler tolerated her infidelities.

The Paris-born writer met her future husband, Guiler, in New York City, where her mother relocated after Nin's father deserted the family for a younger woman. Introduced at a dance in 1921, Nin and Guiler wed two years later. Both newlyweds were sexually inexperienced, and despite Nin's urging, it was months before they consummated their marriage. When they finally did have sex, she was unimpressed with her husband's prowess as a lover.

Claiming late in life, "I learned how to live from literature," Nin likely had two books in mind: D. H. Lawrence's *Lady Chatterley's Lover*, once banned for obscenity, and the "strange and wonderful" *Women in Love*. Faithful to Guiler for the first nine years of their marriage, she discovered the scandalous works around the time she began seriously thinking about expanding her sexual boundaries. Reading Lawrence's tales, Nin realized she had never experienced the passion and sensations he describes. She wrote the nonfiction book *D. H. Lawrence: An Unprofessional Study*, "out of gratitude, because it was he who awakened me."

Nin's longed-for, real-life sexual awakening happened shortly thereafter when an acquaintance introduced her to Henry Miller in Paris, where she and Guiler were living at the time. She was attracted less to the struggling American novelist's looks (he was short and balding) and more to his literary talent and zest for life. When Guiler expressed concern over Nin's friendship with Miller, pointing out that she had a tendency to fall in love with people's minds, she assured him he was not going to lose her. Although she told her husband, "I am already devoted to Henry's work, but I separate my body from my mind," Guiler's fears were not unfounded. Nin's acquaintance with Miller morphed into a torrid affair several months after they met. Just as her later lover Rupert Pole would do, he pleaded with her to leave Guiler but she refused.

Meeting Nin was a fortuitous turn of events for Miller. For years she gave him money to live on, pilfered from the household allowance Guiler provided, so he could concentrate on his writing. She coerced her husband into financing the publication of *Tropic of Cancer*, Miller's first novel, by threatening to sell her fur coat and other possessions if he didn't supply the cash. Nin penned the preface to Miller's semiautobiographical tale, which follows the bawdy adventures of an aspiring American writer in Paris. The book was published in France but banned for obscenity in the United States for nearly thirty years.

Nin and Miller first slipped between the sheets in 1932, after his femme-fatale wife paid a whirlwind visit to Paris and involved them all in a flirtatious love triangle. When Nin found out the notorious June Mansfield Miller—who had paid her husband's steamship passage to Paris with money from a male admirer—was in town, she invited the couple to dine with her and Guiler. That night, "I saw for the first time the most beautiful woman on earth," Nin recorded in her diary. She was mesmerized by June's "color, brilliance, strangeness," although the illusion was somewhat diminished when the other woman spoke. "She killed my admiration by her talk. Her talk. The enormous ego, false, weak, posturing," said Nin. "She lacks the courage of her personality, which is sensual, heavy with experience."

Nevertheless, Nin became infatuated with June, finding that in comparison to her, "Henry suddenly faded." She lavished clothes, jewelry, and money on the other woman and was intrigued by her reminiscences of lesbian encounters. June, meanwhile, made sure to tell her husband about Nin's passionate displays of affection. Spitefully, she played on Miller's fear of losing Nin's patronage if she threw him over for her. Before the women escalated beyond hand holding, kissing, and touching, June abruptly left Paris for New York.

With one spouse temporarily out of the picture, Nin and Miller began their affair at a Paris hotel and spent their days discussing literature, writing, drinking, and having sex. When they were apart, they penned each other missives that were part racy love letters and part evaluations of each other's work. Miller knew how to pour on the charm, promising Nin, in one graphic note, a "literary fuck fest." In case she didn't get his meaning, he explained, "That means fucking and talking and talking and fucking."

When June heard through the rumor mill that Nin was not only Miller's benefactor but also his mistress, she hastily returned to Paris. She feared her husband was going to take up permanently with Nin, just as he had once left his first wife for her. (The former Mrs. Miller returned home one day to find Henry and June making use of her bed.)

The two women picked up where they had left off, with Nin spending extravagantly on June and both making sexual overtures. Nin acted as mediator between the feuding Millers, but once June's suspicions about the affair were confirmed, she demanded a divorce. The cowardly Miller hid out at Nin's house until his wrathful wife left town. He returned home to find a note from June, scrawled on a piece of toilet paper, instructing him to get a divorce immediately. Their decade-long relationship lasted about the same length of time as Miller's affair with Nin, who eventually broke it off with him as well.

Although Nin was jealous that Miller had used June, and not her, as the model for the narrator's wife in *Tropic of Cancer* and its follow-up, *Tropic of Capricorn*, she also used the seductress for literary inspiration. In Nin's surrealist prose poem *House of Incest*, June is personified as Sabina, a woman who captivates the anonymous female narrator.

When Joaquín Nin learned that his daughter intended to title her first work of fiction *House of Incest*, he was rightly concerned about what she might reveal in the book. Reacquainted after a nearly twenty-year separation, they had become lovers at the urging of

Nin's therapist (whom she also bedded). The therapist had advised her to seduce and then dump her father in retaliation for abandoning her as a child. Following the misguided advice, Nin rendezvoused more than once with Joaquín at a hotel in the south of France and then abruptly cut him off.

Not realizing the word "incest" in the book's title was used metaphorically rather than literally, Joaquín was afraid their inappropriate relationship would become public knowledge. Nin enjoyed the discomfiture she caused her father and reported that he was tearing his hair out over not being able to read the book. "To me it is intensely humorous, my giving the *Incest* title," she confessed, "knowing it will give my Father chills of fear."

In addition to Pole, Miller, and her father, Nin had countless other liaisons. She often juggled numerous affairs simultaneously, sometimes bed-hopping among several men in a single day. Nin believed her sexual escapades strengthened her marriage. By taking action, she was cured of her restlessness and curiosity and was able to find contentment in her life with Guiler. "I am aware of a monstrous paradox: By giving myself I learn to love [my husband] more. By living as I do I am preserving our love from bitterness and death," she penned in her diary.

Nin began keeping a diary at age eleven, after her mother gave her a blank book to help pass the time on an ocean voyage from Spain to New York. The diary, her "best friend," started out as a letter to her absentee father and morphed into a detailed account of her life over the next sixty years. In what eventually totaled some 150 volumes, she wrote copiously and freely about her teen years in New York, her unconventional marriage, her forays into psychoanalysis, and her erotic adventures.

The detailed, intimate diaries eventually brought sixty-three-year-old Nin the recognition that eluded her as a novelist. Despite being heavily edited for legal and personal reasons—much of the salacious material was removed, along with all references to Guiler at his request—the original seven volumes of published diaries turned Nin into a feminist icon. Her pursuit of artistic and sexual freedom and her exploration of the female psyche resonated with many in the women's movement.

Nin referred to her diary as "my drug and my vice" and refused to give it up even when Miller and others advised her to do so, saying it distracted her from novel writing. More than her fiction, her colorful personal tales are what have fascinated readers. When Pole was once asked why he remained with Nin even after finding out he was a duplicate husband, he replied, "Her life was her masterpiece, and I am honored to have been a part of it."

LAWRENCE IN LUST:
D. H. LAWRENCE

Legend has it that Frieda Weekley seduced D. H. Lawrence within twenty minutes of meeting him in 1912. Although the hasty erotic encounter is likely a fanciful rumor, it's a scenario similar to one the writer envisioned in his novel *Mr. Noon*. In real life, the twenty-six-year-old writer rapidly fell for the buxom blonde housewife while paying a call on her husband, his former university professor. Frieda, six years his senior and mother to three children, was no stranger to extramarital encounters and believed Lawrence would be nothing more than a brief distraction. Instead, she and the writer created a scandal when they ran off to her native Germany less than two months later.

The passionate, argumentative pair eventually wed and roamed the world for fifteen years. Even though their sex life was hot and heavy, Lawrence allowed Frieda the freedom to wander. She regularly indulged her libido, once seducing a Sicilian mule driver by stripping off her clothes and running naked through a vineyard. It's no coincidence that Lawrence's reputation as a sex-obsessed writer blossomed during his marriage, with the publication of racy novels like *Women in Love* and *Lady Chatterley's Lover*. Frieda believed she was equally deserving of the credit for her husband's works, as the muse who enabled him to tap into his amorous side.

Lawrence liberally drew on his wife's traits and experiences for his characters, and she is the likely source of inspiration for his most famous creation, Lady Chatterley, a young noblewoman who cheats on her war-wounded husband with a gamekeeper. In many ways the novel paralleled the Lawrences' own domestic situation. At the time it was written, the writer's worsening tuberculosis had rendered him impotent, and Frieda had taken an Italian lover. Controversial for its obscene language and explicit sex scenes, *Lady Chatterley's Lover* was banned, burned, and instigated obscenity trials following its 1928 publication.

Shock and Awe

TENNESSEE WILLIAMS

Love is a very difficult—occupation. You got to work at it, man. It ain't a thing every Tom, Dick and Harry has got a true aptitude for.

—Tennessee Williams, *Period of Adjustment*

Art and life were inseparable for Tennessee Williams, who brazenly gave the theatergoing public a dose of reality in mid-twentieth-century America. Often drawn from firsthand experience, his explosive dramas explored homosexuality, alcoholism, and other taboo topics, garnering him censure from some quarters and accolades from others.

During Tennessee Williams's first visit to Key West, Florida, he spent his time working on the play *Battle of Angels* and trading stories about sexual escapades with new bosom buddy Marion Black Vaccaro. Dubbed the Banana Queen of Coconut Grove for the source of her husband's wealth as well as a more risqué reason, she and the writer became lifelong confidantes and traveling companions. A foray to revel in Havana's "frolicsome nightlife"

even included a visit to a male brothel, where they were entertained in adjoining rooms and compared notes afterward.

The playwright nearly rivaled randy Lord Byron for the number of notches on his bedpost, and anecdotes about his amorous
activities made his racy *Memoirs* a sensation when it was published in
1975, a decade before his death at age eighty-one. In the unabashed
autobiography, which he warned would "offend a lot of people," he
focuses more on his personal affairs than his professional endeavors.
"I could devote this whole book to a discussion of the art of drama,
but wouldn't that be a bore?" he declared.

Even so, the dramatist's memoir sheds insight into his art, since
what transpired in the real world often showed up in his fiction.
Writing was a psychological necessity for Williams, who claimed
the craft was his way of coping with, and keeping in check, his vast
emotional issues. According to Gore Vidal, the playwright "could
not possess his own life until he had written about it."

Williams joked that he was motivated to share his life story by
the hefty advance money and the belief that he would be dead by
the time *Memoirs* came off press. Instead he was alive and kicking,
watching people clamor for his tell-all. One day he turned up at a
New York City bookshop, which ran out of copies for him to sign,
sparking a riot among disgruntled customers. But not every reader
was enthusiastic. Some critics vehemently panned *Memoirs*, including one who blasted, "The love that previously dared not speak its
name has now grown hoarse from screaming it."

The playwright didn't start out dating men. His first love was a
childhood friend, Hazel, whom he once saved from a band of bul-
lies. Their comradeship blossomed into a chaste teenage romance
that garnered his parents' disapproval. Unbeknownst to Williams,
his father, in a bid to end his son's infatuation with a divorcée's
daughter, conspired to break up the young couple by ensuring they
attended different universities. Undeterred, Williams wrote to

Hazel and proposed. She pragmatically turned him down, claiming they were too young to tie the knot, and he moved on.

While in college, Williams struggled with his sexual identity, attracted to men while also responding to girls. A several-month dalliance with a coed he calls Sally in *Memoirs* was his only experience having sex with a woman. Their first lusty romp was a "wild break-through of my virginal status," recalled Williams. "I took to it like a duck to water." He claimed to have no interest in men while he was involved with Sally, who consoled him when his play *Fugitive Kind* was performed by an amateur theater troupe in Saint Louis, his hometown, and flopped. After she dumped him for someone else, the playwright tried dating other girls but couldn't make a go of it.

Influenced by a conservative society and his religious upbringing, it's not entirely surprising that it took Williams until his late twenties to embrace his homosexuality. "I was late coming out, and when I did it was with one hell of a bang," he declared. In 1939 he rang in the New Year in New Orleans by having his first tumble with a man. Despite his dismay that the encounter ended with his bedfellow sneaking out the next morning, he continued his homosexual awakening with gusto.

A vigorous sex life and restless moves from city to city didn't deter Williams from keeping to a strict writing schedule. To support himself, he took temporary gigs like stacking pins in a bowling alley, reciting poetry to patrons at a bar, working a Teletype machine during World War II, and operating a hotel elevator. During a stint as a screenwriter in Hollywood, he spent his off-duty hours at a hilltop park, cruising for servicemen.

While anxiously awaiting word on when his first professionally produced play, *Battle of Angels*, would be staged, Williams headed to Provincetown, Massachusetts, a seaside retreat and liberal haven. He distracted himself in the arms of a string of partners, including

Canadian dancer Kip Kiernan, who sometimes slept on the beach for a respite from the sexually insatiable writer. Although Williams wasn't interested in a permanent relationship or monogamy, he claimed to be shattered when the younger man—his first male companion who was more than a fling—ended the affair over concerns he could be deported for being homosexual.

Once *Battle of Angels* made it to the stage, it was a disappointing box-office failure. The drama, which centers on a married woman who shocks her small-town neighbors by having an affair with a drifter and poet, also attracted the notice of the government censors that monitored entertainment content. Undeterred by the disapproval, Williams continued to keep the censors abuzz. He scandalized and entertained theatergoers in the 1940s and '50s by addressing subjects previously kept under wraps and rarely, if ever, acknowledged in public. Through his dramas, he challenged them to open their eyes to homosexuality, female sexuality, rape, mental illness, alcoholism, and drug use.

The tide turned for the struggling writer four years after the curtain closed on *Battle of Angels*, when *The Glass Menagerie* wowed audiences and became Williams's first critical and financial success. Based on his own family, the play unfolds the story of a young man, Tom (the author's given name); his shy, disabled sister, Laura; and their controlling mother. Intent on playing matchmaker for her daughter, the mother insists Tom bring home a coworker as a possible suitor, only to have the evening end miserably for Laura.

Basking in his newfound renown, Williams returned to New Orleans, a city he embraced for its laid-back attitudes and eccentric inhabitants. There he embarked on his most serious relationship to date, shacking up with Pancho Rodriguez, an attractive, macho hotel clerk he had met in New Mexico. But the relationship was doomed almost from the start. While twenty-five-year-old Pancho, a decade younger than the writer, wanted a stable, committed partnership, Williams wouldn't give up sex with other men. Although he admitted that Pancho alleviated the loneliness that "follows me like a shadow," he couldn't abide his boyfriend's insecurities, which often led to stormy rows. Writing the Big Easy–set *A Streetcar Named Desire* at the time, Williams transferred some of Pancho's volatile tendencies into the brutish, short-tempered Stanley Kowalski.

It wasn't just men whom Pancho perceived as rivals. He was seized with jealousy when Williams developed a close friendship with writer Carson McCullers. The two met after Williams sent her a fan letter praising her novel *A Member of the Wedding*. A mutual acquaintance then arranged for McCullers to join Williams and Pancho for the summer on Nantucket. An aggrieved Pancho was relegated to the sidelines as the writers worked on their respective projects, followed by marathon cocktail hours and long candlelit dinners.

At the end of McCullers's visit, Williams gave her a token of his affection: a jade ring that had belonged to his sister, Rose. In many ways his new writer pal—moody, depressed, and an alcoholic in fragile health—reminded him of his sibling. After Rose suffered from a period of erratic behavior and violent fits, his mother authorized a lobotomy to be performed (one of the first in the United States), which left the twenty-nine-year-old institutionalized for life and in a perpetual childlike state. Kept in the dark about the operation until it was over, Williams never forgave his parents for the barbaric act. His anguish over his sister's tragic fate inspired the play *Suddenly, Last Summer*, in which a woman fears that her niece might reveal embarrassing family secrets and conspires to have her lobotomized.

Although the married McCullers didn't have romantic designs on Williams, other members of the opposite sex thought he would make a great groom. One was theater director Margo Jones, who staged several of the playwright's dramas and wanted to collaborate behind the scenes as well. Williams suspected she had ulterior motives and was terrified the dynamic "Texas tornado" would use her forceful personality to bring about a wedding against his will.

Williams managed to remain a bachelor, much to the dismay of thrice-married actress Diana Barrymore (aunt to Drew), who also wanted to march him down the aisle. The dark-haired beauty, who had a history of substance abuse, attended alcohol- and drug-fueled parties with Williams and helped him dress in drag on occasion. He was writing a play with her in mind when she was found dead in her apartment, apparently having overdosed on pills and booze.

While Diana plotted to convert Williams to heterosexuality, a move supported by his therapist, she had serious competition: Frank Merlo, a strikingly handsome, New Jersey–born Sicilian. During a stay in Provincetown with Pancho, Williams had a single passionate encounter on the dunes with Frank. Suspecting what he had been doing, Pancho tried to run him down in a car, and then chased him on foot after the vehicle got stuck in the mud. The final straw that led Williams to send Pancho packing came when his temperamental lover tossed his typewriter out a hotel window.

The playwright's brief rendezvous with Frank in Provincetown turned out to be the beginning of his most enduring romantic relationship. When the two crossed paths by chance in a New York City delicatessen the next year, Williams asked the other man why he had never called. Frank replied that he didn't want to seem as though he was trying to ride the coattails of Williams's success, which had exploded since their quickie on the dunes. *A Streetcar Named Desire*, which unfolds the tragic downward spiral of southern belle Blanche DuBois, was a resounding success and launched Williams into the pantheon of great American playwrights.

Within weeks of becoming reacquainted, Frank moved into Williams's Manhattan apartment. A truck driver and navy veteran, he had transformed himself from a street kid into a self-educated literary and theater buff. Williams was attracted as much to Frank's upbeat enthusiasm as to his good looks. "He was so close to life!" exclaimed the writer. "He gave me the connection to day-to-day and night-to-night living. To reality. He tied me down to earth. And I had that for fourteen years, until he died. And that was the happy period of my adult life."

Frank brought stability to Williams's chaotic life, encouraging him to curtail his drug and alcohol use and supporting him when he struggled with his writing. During their years together, the playwright added *The Rose Tattoo* to his oeuvre and dedicated it to his lover. Although it was his most lighthearted play, it nonetheless horrified Williams's mother on opening night due to its overt references to sex and lovemaking. His father, meanwhile, threatened to sue over the recently published short story "The Resemblance Between a Violin Case and a Coffin." Reportedly upset at being portrayed as a "devilish" and difficult man, his real grievance was that his son all but admitted his homosexuality in the autobiographical tale.

Williams often chafed at the structured existence Frank imposed and stepped out on the sly, hooking up with other men and taking drugs. At one point he even invited a young paramour to live with them in their Key West home. The relationship was further strained in 1960, when the playwright arrived home to find a furious Frank brandishing a copy of *Newsweek*. In an interview in the magazine, Williams admitted to using barbiturates.

After the two had broken up, Williams received word that Frank was seriously ill and rushed to be at his side. Diagnosed with inoperable lung cancer, Frank passed away the next year. Grief-stricken and feeling guilty about the dismal way he had treated his devoted lover, Williams plunged into a severe depression and self-medicated with mass quantities of drugs and alcohol during a period he later called his "stoned age."

Although Williams went on to have plenty of partners in the ensuing years, losing his longtime companion affected him greatly. In *Memoirs*, written a dozen years after Frank's death, he recalled trying to put on a good front following the memorial service. Seeing his friend Elia Kazan exchange looks with his wife, Williams sadly acknowledged, "They knew that I had lost what had sustained my life."

⤳ TALK DIRTY TO ME: JAMES JOYCE ⤳

Pornographic love letters kept the passion simmering for James Joyce and Nora Barnacle during a rare separation while the Irish writer was traveling. It was Nora who initiated the sexually charged correspondence to keep her partner away from prostitutes, fearing a recurrence of his earlier venereal disease. She let him know she was longing to have sex with him and confided that she couldn't afford to buy undergarments, so wasn't wearing any.

Joyce eagerly took up the gauntlet, penning graphic missives that should have come with an XXX rating. He revealed to his darling convent girl and "dirty little fuckbird" that "the two parts of your body which do dirty things are the loveliest to me." The writer expressed his enthusiasm for anal sex with Nora, while waxing poetic about her blow jobs, the smells of her nether regions, and the eroticism of her flatulence during intercourse. In other correspondence, he offered instructions on how to pleasure herself and informed her that he masturbated while reading her letters.

The statuesque, auburn-haired beauty first caught the young writer's eye five years earlier on a Dublin thoroughfare near the hotel where she worked as a chambermaid and bartender. He fell madly in love with her, and it didn't hurt that she treated him to a happy ending on their first date.

Joyce commemorated the day of their encounter in his novel *Ulysses* and used Nora as the inspiration for the book's spirited, lusty Molly Bloom, the concert-singing wife of an advertising agent. When asked if she had read the tale, Nora answered, "Why would I bother?" She admitted perusing only the last few pages in which her counterpart's inner thoughts about sex, adultery, fetishes, breast milk, and more are poured onto the page. "I guess the man's a genius," she said of Joyce, "but what a dirty mind he has, hasn't he?"

PART FOUR

Unlucky in Love

Sweet Sorrow

KAREN BLIXEN (ISAK DINESEN)

Love, with very young people, is a heartless business. We drink at that age from thirst, or to get drunk; it is only later in life that we occupy ourselves with the individuality of our wine.

—Isak Dinesen, "The Old Chevalier"

Marriage was a means to adventure for plucky Danish-born writer Karen Blixen, who wed a baron and decamped to Africa. She spent seventeen eventful years on the continent, but her dream life unraveled when her marriage fell apart and tragedy struck. Adopting the nom de plume Isak Dinesen, she immortalized her experiences in the memoir *Out of Africa*.

While manning an information-and-supply outpost in British East Africa at the outset of World War I, Karen Blixen had a surprise visitor at the camp. Her husband, Bror, who was serving elsewhere, walked more than eighty miles in two days to see her, a romantic gesture that indirectly shattered her happy marriage.

The Baron von Blixen and his bride had wed less than a year

earlier in Kenya, the day after Karen arrived from Denmark to join him in the exotic land where they had chosen to settle. One of the few guests in attendance at their January 1914 nuptials was Prince Wilhelm of Sweden, who offered a champagne toast during the wedding supper aboard a train bound for Nairobi. The newlyweds were headed to their new abode, a coffee farm situated outside the city at the foot of the Ngong Hills, where Karen immediately felt at home.

The couple honeymooned on safari, during which Bror enthusiastically taught his wife to hunt big game, followed by another memorable expedition several months later. During the adventurous outings, they made love in the woods, bathed in a river, and dined on the day's catch roasted over an open fire. Years later Karen wistfully remarked, "If I should wish anything back of my life, it would be to go on safari once again with Bror."

The baron went on to become a legendary safari guide and a model for professional hunter Robert Wilson in Ernest Hemingway's tale "The Short Happy Life of Francis Macomber." Like the character, Bror was known to tote along a double-size cot on the safaris he guided "to accommodate any windfalls he might receive," wrote Hemingway. "He had hunted for a certain clientele, the international, fast, sporting set, where the women did not feel they were getting their money's worth unless they had shared that cot with the white hunter."

Around the time of her first wedding anniversary, Karen began experiencing insomnia, fatigue, loss of appetite, joint pain, and other symptoms. She was diagnosed with syphilis, which her husband likely contracted during an overnight stopover at a native village while on his marathon trek to see her. The disease and some of the treatments physicians administered—mercury tablets and arsenic-laced remedies among them—took a toll on her health for the rest of her life.

Bror's indiscretion was far from an isolated incident. Shortly before finding out she had syphilis, an acquaintance informed Karen that her husband had cheated on her repeatedly. Among his conquests since arriving on the continent were the wife of a close friend, other European associates, and numerous African women. When she confronted Bror, he nonchalantly replied that she was free to follow suit. "It is as if a claw had grabbed your heart, as if you had been shaken and tumbled by a wild animal," said Karen of the jealousy and shock his blunt statement evoked.

Before marrying Bror, Karen had been infatuated with his twin brother, Hans. The elder of the two by minutes, he was slightly better looking than Bror and their father's favorite. While Karen's ardor went unrequited, her feelings for the dashing Hans motivated his brother and sometime rival to pursue her. The third time Bror asked her to marry him, she agreed on the condition they forgo settling in Denmark or his native Sweden for life abroad. The couple decided on Kenya as the locale where they would set up house, inspired by an uncle who returned from a visit full of praise for the country.

Karen kept her engagement a secret, fearing her family's reaction, even admonishing Bror for sending ardent messages on unsealed postcards that might give away their intentions. When her family did find out, she met, as she had expected, with resistance. They supported her desire to live in Africa; it was her choice of husband they questioned. Although they liked the amiable Bror, who was a year younger than his twenty-eight-year-old fiancée, they thought the rowdy womanizer was a bad match for the intellectual, pensive Karen.

While the relationship was more of a loving friendship than the passionate pairing Karen had envisioned with Hans, she was fully committed to the marriage and devastated when she found out about Bror's dalliances. Embarrassed at the thought of getting a divorce, especially after being married only a year, and unwilling to return to her stifling family, she decided to stay with Bror. "There are two things you can do in such a situation: shoot the man, or accept it," she claimed.

Karen did not immediately let on to Bror that he had given her an unwelcome gift. She planned to seek treatment in Europe and keep the reason for her departure a secret, vengefully leaving his case of syphilis untreated. (She knew her decision would not endanger other women as the disease is no longer contagious after the first several months.) During a fight over his refusal to allow a servant to accompany her, she informed him in a rage about the disease. Without saying a word, he turned on his heel and left the room.

In later years, Karen was more philosophical about the illness, claiming it was a price she paid for aligning herself with a man like Bror. "If it did not sound so beastly I might say that, the world being as it is, it was worth having syphilis in order to become a 'Baroness,'" she admitted. Echoes of the disease worked its way into her fiction. In the short story "The Cardinal's Third Tale," an aloof, virginal noblewoman whose motto is "noli me tangere" (don't touch me) innocently contracts a venereal disease after kissing a statue in St. Peter's Basilica, where a young man had just done the same thing. Rather than diminish Lady Flora's life, it enhances it by making her less reticent to engage with the world.

After a year of treatment in Denmark, Karen was homesick for Africa and even missing Bror, who wrote her caring letters while she was away. He joined her in Europe, where they made the rounds visiting family and friends before heading back to their Kenyan farm. On their return, Bror earnestly resumed his amorous pursuits. True to his word, and abiding by his belief in personal freedom, he afforded his wife the same latitude. With his blessing, she embarked on safari with Swedish military officer Erik von Otter. In between hunting buffalo and rhino, they stargazed and read aloud to each other from *The Three Musketeers*. Although Karen enjoyed spending time with him, she turned down von Otter's marriage proposal, which he offered up to rescue her from the unappreciative Bror.

Von Otter was forgotten by the time Karen met Denys Finch Hatton at a dinner party in 1918. She quickly bonded with the witty, intelligent Englishman over a mutual love of Shakespeare, art, opera, and the ballet, interests Bror didn't share with his wife. Although an avowed bachelor, the handsome Finch Hatton had no shortage of female admirers. Karen's friendship with him morphed into an affair that lasted for more than a decade.

Finch Hatton became fast friends with both of the Blixens, finding common ground with Bror on the subjects of hunting and wine, although the couple sometimes openly competed with each other for his attention. During a gathering at the Blixens' spacious farmhouse, the baron introduced his mistress to Finch Hatton, jokingly describing him as his good friend and his wife's lover.

The dynamics of Karen's marriage shifted dramatically during a visit to London. She spent time with Finch Hatton, who was also in town, and Bror met his future second wife during an outing at the theater. At some point during their stay, Karen and the baron had a blowout severe enough to set her sailing for Denmark without him.

When Karen reached her home country, her mother and other family members encouraged her to divorce the philandering Bror on moral grounds, as well as for his extravagant spending and financial misconduct running the coffee company. While Karen was ill with Spanish influenza, Bror left Europe without her and returned to Africa. When she arrived at the farm, she was greeted by a dismal scene. Not only had furniture been repossessed by creditors, her husband had pawned her silver, used her expensive crystal for target practice, and reportedly held orgies.

Bror moved out a short time later, seeking refuge with friends in an attempt to evade the creditors on his trail. With her pride at stake and so much of her identity wrapped up in being a baroness, Karen was still reluctant to legally part ways with her husband, who was eager for a separation so he could marry his mistress. She finally relented, penning the poem "Au Revoir" the day she received word their divorce was final, concluding the verse with the nostalgic line, "Friend, it was sweet, in any case."

After the dissolution of her eleven-year marriage, Karen's relationship with Finch Hatton offered some consolation, although their association was based on his stringent terms. There were to be no demands and no commitments made on each other's freedom. When Karen suspected she was pregnant, a happy occasion for her, she cabled Finch Hatton in England with the news. She told him Daniel (their code name for an imaginary child) was on the way. In his reply, he strongly urged her to cancel Daniel's visit. She didn't abort the pregnancy, as her lover callously suggested, but is believed to have either miscarried or been mistaken about her condition.

The Englishman moved into Karen's farmhouse but came and went as he pleased, going away for weeks and months at a time on safari or visiting England. She considered making a marriage of convenience to someone else, and even had three candidates in mind, but ultimately decided not to tie the knot. Even a halfhearted relationship with Finch Hatton was apparently better than none. "For all time and eternity I am bound to Denys, to love the ground he walks upon, to be happy beyond words when he is here, and to suffer worse than death many times when he leaves," she confided to her brother.

After a trip to England, Finch Hatton returned with a two-seater plane, telling Karen it was so he could show her what the landscape looked like from the air. She never forgot the experience of seeing her beloved Kenya sprawling below, writing in *Out of Africa*, "To Denys Finch-Hatton I owe what was, I think, the greatest, the most transporting pleasure of my life on the farm: I flew with him over Africa."

For a decade, Karen ran the coffee business with her brother and then solo, until she was forced to sell the property after the business went under. Unable to remain in Africa with no livelihood, Karen confessed to her lover that she thought about shooting her animals and herself rather than leave her home. Finch Hatton lamented her departure but refused to capitulate on his no-strings-attached stance, even though it would have offered Karen a way to remain in Africa. Instead he urged her to be more optimistic about the future.

Before Finch Hatton left to check on a piece of land he owned, he and Karen had a stormy row, possibly over his interest in another woman. Speculation also has it that she may have proposed marriage to him and was rebuffed or that she admonished him for his cavalier attitude about her predicament. Adding insult to injury, he asked her to return a ring he had given her, suspecting she was going to make it a farewell gift to one of her farmhands since she couldn't afford to buy something else.

As it turned out, Karen's despondency over Finch Hatton's refusal to commit was irrelevant. He died in a plane crash shortly before he was due to return to see her. When he didn't show for their lunch date she headed into Nairobi, where numerous acquaintances turned away when they saw her, until someone finally relayed the tragic news. As one of her last tasks before departing the continent, she planned Finch Hatton's funeral and oversaw his burial in the hills above her farm in a scenic spot they had picked out for their graves.

Karen left Kenya by train in 1931, seen off by a small group of friends on her final journey out of Africa. She reluctantly returned to the family fold in Denmark, where she remained for the rest of her life, never remarrying. Writing as Isak Dinesen, she poured her emotions into print, drawing on her belief that "all sorrows can be borne if you put them into a story."

HAPPILY NEVER AFTER: CARSON MCCULLERS

Army soldier and aspiring writer Reeves McCullers knew how to charm a girl. While courting Carson Smith in her Georgia hometown in 1935, he brought flowers for her mother and beer and cigarettes for her. The couple wed two years later, only to find their marriage tainted by alcoholism, sexual jealousy, and professional envy (at twenty-three Carson published her first novel, *The Heart Is a Lonely Hunter*, to great acclaim).

Carson divorced Reeves four years after they wed, cutting him loose not only for abandoning her but for forging checks in her name to finance an extramarital affair. When they decided to tie the knot again several years later, they sought a fresh start in France but couldn't outrun their demons. Reeves threatened to jump out the window of their Paris hotel room, but what he really wanted was for his wife to accompany him to the great beyond.

In a morbidly romantic gesture, Reeves selected a cherry tree for the pair to hang themselves from. He later presented Carson with two sets of rope during a drive through the French countryside and pleaded with her to enter into a suicide pact. She agreed and asked him to stop at a tavern so they could fortify themselves for the grisly deed. While Reeves was inside buying a bottle of wine, Carson made a run for it and then fled stateside without him. It was the last time she saw her spouse before he overdosed on barbiturates and booze in a Paris hotel room.

When Carson received the news of his demise, she didn't say a word and simply downed a bottle of whiskey. She later used her tumultuous, eighteen-year relationship with Reeves as the basis for the dark family drama *The Square Root of Wonderful*.

House of Secrets

DAPHNE DU MAURIER

The house possessed me from that day, even as a mistress holds her lover.

—Daphne du Maurier

From the moment Daphne du Maurier stumbled across a run-down Tudor manor house on the English coast in Cornwall, it ignited her imagination and became Manderley, one of the most memorable characters in her novel *Rebecca*. Much as a real-life place helped inspire the chilling tale, the writer's lesbian infatuations paralleled its gripping storyline of female obsession.

"Seeds began to drop. A beautiful home . . . a first wife . . . jealousy, a wreck, perhaps at sea, near to the house. . . . But something terrible would have to happen, I did not know what."

Many of the haunting "seeds" that inspired Daphne du Maurier's moody psychological thriller *Rebecca* were drawn from elements in her own life. The "beautiful home," fictionalized as Manderley in the novel, was in actuality Menabilly, an isolated mansion on the Cornish coast. As a young woman, Daphne became obsessed with the vacant house and, with the proceeds from *Rebecca*, eventually realized her dream of becoming the mistress of Menabilly.

The jealousies that fueled the gothic tale were as steeped in reality as its haunting setting. Soon into her marriage, Daphne stumbled across a carefully preserved cache of love letters to her husband, Tommy Browning. They had been written by his former fiancée, a glamorous brunette with whom he had been besotted until their engagement mysteriously ended. While reading the hidden letters, Daphne was struck by the stark contrasts between herself and the confident, sophisticated correspondent and she worried that Tommy was still attracted to his ex.

She channeled her fearful feelings into *Rebecca*'s narrator, a timid wife struggling to break free from the shadow of her beautiful predecessor. Tommy became the novel's debonair, inscrutable husband, while his former fiancée was transmuted into the titular Rebecca, who even from the grave exerts control over Manderley.

Despite Daphne's insecurities, it was Tommy, a senior military officer, who had boldly pursued her after becoming an admirer of her debut novel, *The Loving Spirit*. In spectacularly romantic fashion, he had sailed his yacht into the harbor where the du Maurier family had a vacation home, hoping to meet the young author. Daphne was swept off her feet, and in spite of a ten-year age difference their attraction was immediate. "He's the most amazing person to be with, no effort at all, and I feel I've known him for years," she gushed in her diary. After a whirlwind courtship, the couple wed in July 1932.

While the marriage brought them happiness and soon produced three children, their mismatched temperaments became glaringly apparent. Among other differences, Tommy was a gregarious extrovert while the shy, reclusive Daphne spent hours each day writing in isolation. The onset of World War II drove a further wedge between them. Tommy was stationed abroad and during his brief leaves home, he was emotionally distant and would only talk of war. Like many wartime couples, the pair became virtual strangers, leading to a disappointing homecoming after Tommy's five-year deployment.

The awkwardness of their reunion was compounded by the presence of another woman in Tommy's life: his attractive, twenty-three-year-old field secretary, who returned home with him and became his peacetime assistant. Although Daphne's suspicion that they were having an affair proved unfounded, she was disheartened to find that her husband had lost sexual interest in her. The rejection made her feel spurned and unattractive, but she failed to recognize that her own deatachment and inflexibility reinforced the distance between them.

When Tommy won a prestigious appointment as treasurer to the future Queen Elizabeth, Daphne was unwilling to leave her beloved Cornwall and relocate their family to London. The pair established separate lives, with Tommy making the long trip home only on weekends. It was an arrangement that suited the solitude-loving writer just fine. She was possessive of her time at the typewriter, and Tommy's excessive drinking and mood swings often made him unpleasant to be around. Rumors of the couple's marital difficulties began to circulate, heightened by Daphne's frequent absences at the social functions that were a necessary part of her husband's job. She felt insecure and out of her element in large groups, preferring the isolation of Menabilly.

Her fortress of solitude was breeched in 1947 when she was called to New York to defend *Rebecca* against plagiarism allegations. In the face of a distressing court appearance and Tommy's withdrawal, it was hardly surprising that she turned to someone else for comfort. More unexpected was the object of her affections: Ellen Doubleday, the wife of her American publisher.

Upon meeting the elegant socialite, feelings of passion overwhelmed the middle-aged writer, making her feel like "a boy of eighteen . . . with nervous hands and a beating heart, incurably romantic and wanting to throw a cloak before his lady's feet." As Daphne explained in one of the many intimate letters she and Ellen exchanged over the years, growing up she had always felt like a boy trapped in a girl's body. Throughout her life, she secretly struggled to keep the boy "locked up in a box," submerging the masculine side of herself that was attracted to women. But after meeting Ellen on the steamer bound for America, her long-repressed feelings resurfaced. Daphne struggled to contain them, later admitting to Ellen, "I pushed the boy back into his box again and avoided you on the boat like the plague."

During the many weeks she spent stateside giving testimony, she was a guest of the Doubledays at their luxurious Long Island mansion. Although she and Ellen developed a unique bond that endured for several decades, the latter made it clear that it could never be more than a friendship. The point was driven home on a trip they took to Italy after the death of Nelson Doubleday. Much to Daphne's disappointment, being alone with Ellen in a romantic locale wasn't enough to induce the widow to express "Venetian" feelings (Daphne's euphemism for lesbianism).

Unable to consummate their relationship, Daphne sublimated her longing into *September Tide*, a play about forbidden love. The heavily disguised storyline, in which a young man falls in love with his mother-in-law, mirrored the writer's hopeless romantic infatuation. When the play debuted in London in December 1948, it starred the next object of Daphne's sapphic passions: acclaimed English stage actress Gertrude Lawrence.

In performing the role of Ellen's fictional doppelgänger, Gertrude became a stand-in for Daphne's affections. The flamboyant actress, known as much for her sexual dalliances as for her magnetic performances, was no stranger to illicit romance. Among her conquests were actor Yul Brynner (seventeen years her junior when they starred together in *The King and I*) and the Prince of Wales, the future King Edward VIII.

While it is not known for certain if Daphne followed Gertrude's famed bedfellows between the sheets (a supposition denied by the actress's daughter), there is no doubt the two women shared an intimate and wildly flirtatious rapport. Daphne joined Gertrude on vacation in America on two occasions, and the actress spent long weekends at Menabilly, usually when Tommy was in London. When apart, the two would write to each other at least twice a week.

Their radically different personalities made it an unlikely friendship—Gertrude was known for her erratic mood swings, violent temper, and fun-loving nature, while Daphne was a mild-mannered loner. But the real incongruity was that the actress was a former lover of Daphne's father. Gerald du Maurier, a celebrated actor, had had numerous casual affairs with young starlets, which aroused in his adoring teenage daughter a mixture of jealousy and resentment. Daphne had formerly despised Gertrude, referring to her as "that bloody bitch," but twenty years later it seemed as though she was taking on her father's role of seducer.

The surprising friendship between the two women lasted for more than four years until Gertrude's premature and sudden death, an event which left Daphne catatonic from grief and unable to sleep or eat. Her family was taken aback by her extreme and seemingly disproportionate reaction to the death and chalked it up to belated mourning for her father.

Growing up, her father was extremely possessive of her. While there is speculation but no hard evidence that they had a physical relationship, Daphne later told a friend, "We crossed the line and I allowed it. He treated me like all the others—as if I was an actress playing his love interest in one of his plays." A family friend noted, "He couldn't keep his hands off her. It was quite embarrassing at times."

When Daphne wrote to her father about her impending marriage to Tommy, he reportedly broke down and wept. Gerald du Maurier died two years later, though not before he had read Daphne's novel *The Progress of Julius*, featuring a controlling father who drowns his daughter because he can't bear for her to become interested in other men.

Gerald had also despised homosexuals, and while both of the writer's sisters revealed that they were lesbians, Daphne—his favorite—may have felt pressured to conform to a traditional marriage. Echoing her father's sentiments, she expressed great contempt for lesbians and was unable to even bear the word itself. When writing about an adolescent crush on a female tutor, she declared vehemently, "By God and by Christ if anyone should call that sort of love by that unattractive word that begins with 'L,' I'd tear their guts out." On another occasion, she swore she'd jump into New York's Hudson River if Ellen lumped her together with the "L" people.

Rather than identifying herself as bisexual or lesbian, Daphne viewed herself as something vaguely "other": "neither girl nor boy but disembodied spirit." Her father had always wished she was a boy, and as a child she wore boys' clothes and invented a male alter ego. She continued to dress in mannish attire into adulthood and used her alter ego as the narrator in five of her novels.

Daphne often reworked themes from her own life in her fiction and used her writing as a crutch to escape from reality. Her retreat into her fictional world came at the expense of her real one, a fact she was forced to acknowledge when Tommy suddenly collapsed of a nervous breakdown just before their twenty-fifth wedding anniversary. She was further blindsided by a call from a woman claiming to be Tommy's mistress, who told her the strain of his secrecy and double life had spurred the breakdown.

Although her relationship with Tommy had long been devoid of physical intimacy and Daphne herself had been unfaithful, she was stunned when Tommy admitted his infidelity and revealed the magnitude of his feelings for her rival. The guilt-ridden writer blamed her husband's unhappiness on her detachment and confessed to him of her own indiscretions, which included a wartime affair with a married man. As for her intense female friendships, she chalked those up to inner turmoil: "My obsessions—you can only call them that—for poor old Ellen D. and Gertrude—were all part of a nervous breakdown going on *inside myself*, partly to do with my muddled troubles, and writing, and a fear of facing reality."

The couple's mutual affection and their shared history ultimately won out over more prurient passions, and they put the incident behind them. Despite their ups and downs, they remained dedicated to each other until Tommy's death in 1965. Navigating life as a widow after thirty-three years of marriage, Daphne was dealt another devastating blow when the owners of her beloved Menabilly decided to take possession of their ancestral home and would not renew her lease.

She reluctantly accepted their offer to live in a smaller property on the estate, but the ache for her old home never left her. Even catching a glimpse of it through the trees would pain her, and she mourned, "I find myself missing it now in the way one misses anyone who has died and whom one loved."

☙ LONELY HEART: EMILY DICKINSON ❧

If online dating had existed during Emily Dickinson's day, no doubt the introverted writer would have capitalized on the anonymity of the computer to find her soul mate.

SWF SEEKING SWM/F

Reclusive green-thumbed poet seeking fellow sensitive homebody (male or female) who enjoys solitude and quiet nights at home, reading and conversing. Must share a love of gardening and an appreciation for nature. Respondents employed in journalism or publishing will receive special consideration.

Age: Early thirties
Location: Amherst, Massachusetts

Physical Description: "I . . . am small, like the wren; and my hair is bold, like the chestnut burr; and my eyes, like the sherry in the glass that the guest leaves."

I spend my leisure time: Gardening (nothing makes me happier than seeing my spring perennials in bloom) and baking (coconut cake is a family favorite).

My idea of a perfect date is: Taking long walks in the woods and fields, collecting wildflowers with a charming companion and my Newfoundland, Carlo, at my side.

Most surprising thing about me: While I'm known for sending friends and acquaintances poems on special occasions, no one—not even my sister—suspects I write a poem nearly each and every day. I've already written more than a thousand, copied onto sheets of notepaper and stitched into bundles, so who knows how many there will be by the time I die.

Most likely to be spotted: Cultivating my garden by lantern light between midnight and two in the morning. Yes, I know it's unusual, but when you're as shy as I am, it's the only time you can avoid awkward encounters with chatty neighbors and random passersby.

I would describe my style as: Simple. Although my family is wealthy and I could be one of the best-dressed girls in town, I think fashion is frivolous. And since I never leave my home, what would be the point in having an extensive wardrobe? Instead I own seven plain white dresses, one for each day of the week.

Parisian Passion

EDITH WHARTON

❦

I don't know that I should care for a man who made life easy; I should want some one who made it interesting.

—Edith Wharton, *The Fruit of the Tree*

Late bloomer Edith Wharton came into her own in her forties, writing her first best-selling novel, *The House of Mirth*, and seeking a new life in Paris. While abroad, the unhappily married novelist experienced a belated sexual awakening with a roguish journalist she immortalized in print.

❦

"Very intelligent, but slightly mysterious, I think," Edith Wharton said of Morton Fullerton, the dashing American newspaperman she met at a Paris literary salon in 1907. While they were an ideal intellectual match, the forty-five-year-old novelist and her future lover were otherwise opposites. She was an upstanding high-society matron trapped in a dismal, twenty-two-year marriage, while he was a ladies' man with a sordid past.

A Harvard graduate from a distinguished New England family, Fullerton was fluent in French, widely read, and well-connected in

Parisian literary and publishing circles. Behind his distinguished facade, though, the mustached charmer was mired in misdeeds. After a whirlwind marriage to a French opera singer that crumbled after a year, he promptly resumed living with a former mistress and was cohabitating with her during the time he wooed Wharton. Prior to settling in Paris, Fullerton had moved in London's upper-class circles and indulged in affairs with aristocrats of both sexes, a fact that would later come back to haunt him.

Although Wharton and Fullerton's attraction simmered for more than a year before it became sexual, she quickly cozied up to the journalist. She invited him to dinner so they could "talk shop" and asked him to proof the French translation of *The House of Mirth*, the novel that had launched her into the literary limelight two years earlier.

Like the story's ill-fated heroine, Lily Bart, Wharton's life was dictated by the unwritten rules that governed the upper crust at the turn of the twentieth century. Born into a wealthy Gilded Age family that inspired the saying "Keeping up with the Joneses," she struggled with the conflict between her desire to become a writer and the pressure to conform. Making a good match and overseeing the running of a household were the primary pursuits expected of a woman of her standing. Writing was a frowned-upon endeavor. As Wharton put it in her autobiography, *A Backward Glance*, "In the eyes of our provincial society authorship was still regarded as something between a black art and a form of manual labor."

Wharton's "unseemly" literary aspirations were blamed for a broken engagement when she was twenty. Seven poems she published were apparently reason enough for her fiancé's mother to call off the wedding. A gossip magazine reported that the nuptials were nixed because of "an alleged preponderance of intellectuality on the part of the intended bride."

At age twenty-three and facing the prospect of spinsterhood,

Wharton was railroaded into what her family deemed a suitable marriage to a friend of her older brother. Teddy Wharton was a blue-blooded Bostonian thirteen years her senior and fashionably unemployed. Aside from their wealthy backgrounds and mutual love of travel, the pair had little in common. From the beginning, the marriage was marred by the cloud of mental illness that ran in Teddy's family. Although he was jovial and good-hearted, his personality and intellect were no match for his wife's cleverness, creativity, and vivacity, and the two went on to endure a strained and unfulfilling relationship.

Nowhere were they more incompatible than in the bedroom. Wharton entered the marriage knowing nothing about sex, naive and afraid, and it wasn't until weeks after the honeymoon that she and her groom were intimate. By the time they began wintering in Paris in 1907, their union was in dire shape. In addition to their dismal sex life and childlessness, Teddy's infidelity, increasing mental instability, and mismanagement of funds (he later admitted to embezzling fifty thousand dollars from her estate and spending it on a house for his mistress) took a toll on Wharton.

Being in Paris was a tonic for the novelist, who enthusiastically embraced life in the bohemian city. Her relationship with Fullerton became both a respite from her marital woes and a long-awaited introduction to great sex. Even before they slept together, she admitted that his mere presence in a room sent a "ripple of flame" through her.

Wharton's association with the journalist took an intriguing turn several months after they met. Before returning to America at the start of the summer, she let him know he could find her at the Mount, her estate in the Berkshire Mountains of Massachusetts. That fall, he showed up for a two-day stay, joining the other houseguests Wharton was entertaining. After his visit, the novelist began confiding her feelings for him in a journal, "The Life Apart" (also known as the Love Diary), written as an intimate missive to an un-named addressee.

Upon returning to Paris, Wharton sent Fullerton flirtatious notes, inviting him to dinner and tea and asking him to the opera. Tossing aside the last of her inhibitions, she finally acted on her feelings, escaping to a country inn outside Paris with him to consummate their affair. She and Fullerton moved in the same social circles, and Wharton endeavored to keep her acquaintances, as well as her husband, from finding out about the romance. The covert lovers met up at the theater and dined in out-of-the-way restaurants where the food was mediocre but the risk of running into anyone they knew was low.

The conservative, reserved Wharton let her defenses down with Fullerton and experienced romantic and sexual passion for the first time in her life. She credited him with waking her from a "long lethargy, a dull acquiescence in conventional restrictions." In the Love Diary, which she once let him read, she glorified him as the one "who ha[s] given me the only moments of real life I have ever known."

After Wharton again returned to the United States at the start of the summer, she was devastated when Fullerton stopped responding to her letters. Although his out-of-sight, out-of-mind silence was typical, in this instance he was arguably too preoccupied to correspond. A former mistress was demanding cash to keep quiet about his past homosexual affairs. Fullerton eventually confided in Wharton about the blackmail—holding back the details of the same-sex nature of the relationships—and she and their mutual friend Henry James rallied around him. They arranged for their publisher to offer Fullerton a book contract, with Wharton secretly funding the advance so that he would have the money to pay off the extortionist.

But Fullerton's secrets ran even deeper than his homosexual

affairs. Unbeknownst to Wharton, she was involved in a love triangle. During his stateside visit a little over a year earlier, Fullerton had proposed marriage to his half cousin, Katherine, who was raised by his parents from infancy as an adopted daughter. The two-timing rogue simultaneously kept up relationships with both women, who met when Katherine made the transatlantic journey to seek out her absentee fiancé.

Wharton was likely in the dark about Fullerton's relationship with his "sister," who similarly did not know the novelist was his mistress. The two women went on at least one outing together in Paris, with the deceitful Fullerton in tow. Wharton even graciously offered Katherine advice on a poem she had composed.

Ultimately, Fullerton proved that a lothario isn't likely to change his roving ways. Katherine waited around for him but eventually wed someone else. Meanwhile, his devotion to, and ardor for, Wharton predictably gave way to indifference and neglect, leading the heartbroken novelist to complain that after their sexual encounters she felt "like a 'course' served & cleared away!" Yet despite his often callous treatment of her, Wharton continued their liaison, alternately pleading to see him and reprimanding him for his inattentiveness. In moments of weakness, she even blamed herself for her fickle lover's loss of interest, writing mournfully to him, "If I had been younger and prettier, everything might have been different."

With callousness outweighing passion and his silences becoming more frequent, Wharton finally gave up on Fullerton. As their relationship disintegrated, she told him, "My life was better before I knew you." After their tumultuous, two-year affair had waned into a tepid friendship, she entreated him to destroy her letters. Despite leading her to believe that he'd complied, the ever-faithless Fullerton ignored her request. The collection of correspondence only surfaced in 1980, when a European bookseller came forward to announce he had it in his possession. The more than three hundred letters portray a side of Wharton very different from the carefully crafted persona of reserve and aloofness she presented to the outside world. They reveal a modern, complex, and passionate woman. In spite of the intensity of her relationship with Fullerton and the meaningful place it held in her life, she never discussed him and declined to give him even a single mention in her autobiography.

The self-centered Fullerton once informed Wharton that he believed she would benefit from their affair because she would "write better for this experience of loving." The year after they parted ways, she sequestered herself for six weeks and emerged with *Ethan Frome*. The novel unfolds the tale of a New England farmer wed to a sickly, older woman while at the same time smitten with his wife's vivacious cousin. For Ethan, marriage is a prison, and his secret love affair ends tragically. The theme of unrequited love appears in numerous Wharton works and was still on her mind a decade after her liaison with Fullerton. In her 1921 Pulitzer-winning novel, *The Age of Innocence*, Newland Archer chooses familial duties over his passion for Countess Olenska.

Fullerton himself was immortalized in another Wharton novel, *The Reef*, serving as the model for diplomat George Darrow. (He also inspired her to write erotic poetry while they were an item.) *The Reef*, the story of a casual sexual indiscretion and its effects on the lives of four Americans living in France, is one of Wharton's most autobiographical novels. The book debuted to lackluster sales and unfavorable reviews, with the *New York Times* deeming it "a bitter, disheartening, sordid story."

The ever-supportive Henry James gave *The Reef* a nod of approval, telling Wharton it was "quite the finest thing you have done." A decade earlier, James, too, had used Fullerton as the inspiration for a character in his novel *The Wings of the Dove*. The fictional

Merton Densher, a handsome, clever journalist, commits an underhanded act but ultimately does the honorable thing.

After the demise of her marriage in 1913, Wharton sold her home in the Berkshires and settled permanently in Paris. It was there, during her brief romance with Fullerton—whom she called the love of her life—that she once professed to know "what happy women feel."

THE WIT OF A WOUNDED WOMAN: DOROTHY PARKER

"I require only three things of a man. He must be handsome, ruthless, and stupid," quipped Jazz Age satirist Dorothy Parker, the dissolute doyenne of the Algonquin Round Table. No doubt her low standards played into her luckless love life, which was marked by three failed marriages (two to the same man), several doomed affairs, and multiple suicide attempts.

While still married to her first husband, an abusive drunk and morphine addict, she fell in love with a married playwright and became pregnant. Her caddish lover offered her thirty bucks for an abortion and suddenly wanted nothing to do with her. Adding insult to injury, she learned she wasn't his only side dish. "It serves me right for putting all my eggs in one bastard," joked the heartbroken writer, who attempted suicide by slitting her wrists.

Her second marriage, to screenwriter Alan Campbell, fared little better. While the pair was successful at penning screenplays together, their off-the-page collaboration was a failure. Alcohol-fueled blowouts and frequent separations became the norm, and Parker—who publicly accused her husband of being gay—dabbled in extramarital affairs.

The couple finally called it quits in 1947, only to tie the knot again three years later. Of their déjà vu wedding reception, Parker remarked, "The room was filled with people who hadn't talked to each other in years, including the bride and bridegroom." Their second attempt was no less volatile than the first, and they spent much of the marriage on opposite coasts. When they were together, Alan escaped Parker's hectoring by sealing off his bedroom behind a revolving bookcase that could only be opened with a hidden spring. It was there that Parker discovered him, dead from an apparent Seconal overdose, in June 1963.

At the funeral, when a woman Parker disliked inquired if there was anything she could do, the widow sarcastically responded by asking for a new husband and a ham on rye.

PART FIVE

Your Cheating Heart

A Tale of Two Dickenses

CHARLES DICKENS

My father was a wicked man—a very wicked man.

—Katie Dickens

Behind his mask as champion of family values, Victorian novelist Charles Dickens led a secretive double life. After separating from his long-suffering wife, he often kept his whereabouts unknown while traveling to remote love nests for hookups with an actress half his age.

"All London . . . had for some time been rife with legends concerning Dickens and an actress, with whom it was at last affirmed that [he] had eloped to Boulogne," the *New York Times* reported in June 1858. Although *Enquirer*-style revelations of an elopement turned out to be false, gossip continued to swirl around the writer following the collapse of his twenty-two-year marriage.

One rumor claimed he was sleeping with his wife's sister, Georgina Hogarth, who served as ad hoc governess for his nine children. While Dickens *did* have a strong affinity for both her and another of his wife's younger sisters, the attachments were purely platonic. The unseemly insinuation is thought to have been spread by his vindictive mother-in-law after Georgina remained loyal to Dickens following his bitter separation. To silence gossips and safeguard her reputation, thirty-one-year-old Georgina submitted to the indignity of a virginity test.

Dickens could only blame himself for the sea of scandal that engulfed him after he separated from his wife, Catherine. Rather than exercising discretion, he preemptively tried to sugarcoat the situation by announcing that the separation had been amicable. In a lengthy published statement, he cited incompatibility of temperaments as the reason for the breakup—a bizarre excuse after two decades of marriage.

This misguided attempt at spin-doctoring only stirred up more gossip among those who might otherwise have remained ignorant of his marital troubles. The public was shocked to learn that the man they held in such high esteem for his morality tales had separated from his wife, an inconceivable act in Victorian times.

Equally incomprehensible was Dickens's decision to issue a public statement about his personal affairs. He had always played his cards close to his vest, even keeping the central tragedy of his life secret from his own family: at age twelve, he was forced to leave school to work in a blacking (shoe polish) factory when his parents were sent to debtors prison. The humiliation and loneliness he endured during the traumatic period stoked his lifelong need to be loved and adored by the public. Such a man would have to be desperately unhappy to jeopardize the fame that meant so much to him by embroiling himself in a public scandal.

While the cause of the fatal rupture between Dickens and his wife remains unknown, the blame is rumored to lie at the hands of a bumbling jeweler who mistakenly sent Catherine a bracelet intended for young actress Ellen "Nelly" Ternan. The novelist's interest in the eighteen-year-old performer had blossomed the previous summer when they appeared together in *The Frozen Deep*, a play written by his friend Wilkie Collins.

Before his writing career took flight, Dickens had nearly become a professional actor, and he indulged his lifelong passion for the theater by producing and starring in his own amateur theatricals with family and friends. Unlike his prior productions, staged in a custom-built theater in his home, *The Frozen Deep* was performed at a concert hall and required professional actresses.

The Ternans, a well-known family in provincial drama circles, were hired to play the female roles. Nelly Ternan was also cast as the heroine in a preceding one-act comedy, which had a farcical yet prophetic plot involving an older man (played by Dickens) who falls in love with his young ward (Nelly). During rehearsals, the blue-eyed, blonde-haired thespian mesmerized the writer with her wit, charm, and flattery. The bright, vivacious girl no doubt seemed the polar opposite of his wife, who, after thirteen pregnancies (including several miscarriages), had grown heavy and indolent. Catherine had never been a match for Dickens's high spirits or intellect, and her struggles with postpartum depression drove a further wedge between them.

The manically energetic writer, who needed little sleep and continually shrugged off his own illnesses, grew increasingly intolerant of his wife. Even her clumsiness, once a subject of affectionate teasing, became contemptible to him. Dickens complained she was "as near being a Donkey, as one of that sex . . . can be"—a far cry from the cuddly pet names, such as "dearest mouse," he had once bestowed on her.

From the beginning, his passion for Catherine paled in comparison to his feelings for his first love, Maria Beadnell, who rejected him when he was a struggling writer. Nelly's appearance reignited those early romantic stirrings in the forty-five-year-old, proving that even Victorian men were not immune to midlife crises. Dickens pursued his new love interest across England, wooing her with the same dogged persistence that had fueled his rise to best-sellerdom. To absolve his conscience, he convinced himself that his marriage had been doomed from the start. "Poor Catherine and I are not made for each other, and there is no help for it. What is now befalling, I have seen steadily coming," he bemoaned to his best friend and future biographer, John Forster.

For a man revered as a noble champion of the poor, helpless, and downtrodden, the novelist's treatment of his wife was remarkable for its cruelty. Without warning, he barricaded the door between the marital bedroom and his dressing room, which he converted into his sleeping quarters. Catherine was informed of the new sleeping arrangements by her servants.

Soon afterward, Katie Dickens came across her mother in tears. On the heels of the bedroom blockade and the misdelivered bracelet, Catherine was ordered to pay a social call on the Ternans, an attempt to dispel rumors and persuade the public that the women were friends. Resenting her father's harsh treatment of her mother, Katie bitterly complained that the affair "brought out all that was worst—all that was weakest in him. He did not care a damn what happened to any of us."

The situation finally reached a breaking point in the spring of 1858, and Catherine reluctantly agreed to leave their home. Divorces were virtually impossible to obtain at that time, and thus the couple formally separated. Dickens had hoped Catherine would agree to live on her own and continue to act as his wife on social occasions, but she rejected the insulting proposal. In a bid to maintain his appearance as a devoted family man, he insisted on keeping their children in his custody.

As if the separation and loss of her children weren't painful enough for his wife, Dickens publicly accused her of having a mental disorder and being a bad mother. The final blow came for Catherine when her sister remained loyal to her estranged husband and took over the management of his household. In spite of the cruel way she was treated, Catherine retained all the letters Dickens had sent her since their courtship began. On her deathbed she instructed they be published so "the world may know he loved me once."

With the drama of the separation behind him, Dickens was finally able to put his personal problems aside and immerse himself in writing a new novel. *A Tale of Two Cities* was the first full-length work he had undertaken since meeting Nelly two years earlier, and its heroine shared his paramour's physical attributes. This nod to Nelly in print was one of few tangible proofs of her ongoing existence after she made her final stage appearance on August 10, 1859, and virtually vanished from the public eye. Although her relationship with Dickens lasted for more than thirteen years and she was undeniably the love of his life, Nelly was intentionally and systematically edited out of history. As carefully as he plotted the installments of his novels, Dickens meticulously set about creating the narrative of his "bachelor" existence.

At annual bonfires, he sent his secrets up in smoke—burning his correspondence and thus preventing a single word he exchanged with Nelly from enduring. Nor was she mentioned in the seminal biography authored by his friend Forster, who knew her well. It is only through allusions to her in undestroyed letters, coded messages in one of the writer's lost diaries, and anecdotes recorded by those close to him that evidence of the relationship survives.

Dickens's elaborate web of deceit was largely made possible by the extensive public readings he began giving around the time he took up with Nelly. Crisscrossing the country by rail, it was easy to camouflage his visits to his mistress, whom he established in a series of remote love nests. In the early 1860s, the readings were temporarily broken off when the writer began making an unusual number of trips across the Channel. During this time, Nelly is thought to have been sequestered abroad. Rumor has it she went to France to hide the existence of their secret love child, who is believed to have died in infancy.

In the summer of 1865, while Dickens was accompanying Nelly and her mother home from France, the three travelers were involved in a catastrophic and highly publicized train wreck. Shaken but miraculously unharmed, the writer helped his mistress (who suffered a fractured arm) and her mother to safety before tending to the injured and dying in the steep ravine where the train had derailed. He then clambered back into his own precariously dangling carriage to rescue the manuscript of his last completed novel, *Our Mutual Friend*. Even amidst the chaos and the ensuing media frenzy, he was careful to maintain the facade that he had been traveling alone, making sure the names of his companions did not leak out.

Despite his fragile health and fear of rail travel after the accident, Dickens returned to his grueling schedule of sell-out public readings. The intensive and energetic performances are believed to have hastened his premature death from a stroke, five years to the day after the train wreck. While it was originally believed he died at home, recent evidence suggests he may have been with Nelly and then hastily transferred after becoming ill. Although she was by his side during his final hours, Nelly was not among the thousands of mourners who attended his funeral at Westminster Abbey.

When the author's will was made public, many were surprised to learn that long-forgotten actress Ellen Ternan was the first beneficiary. Given the trivial size of the legacy (further covert sums of money were separately funneled to her), this public shout-out from the grave proved a clever way of acknowledging Nelly's significance in Dickens's life without arousing undue suspicion. After living abroad during several years of mourning, the writer's former mistress reemerged for a surprising second act. Rather than settling into solitary spinsterhood, she knocked fourteen years off her age, erased her disreputable past, and became one half of a model Victorian couple. Pushing forty and married to an ordained minister, she finally achieved her long-delayed dream of motherhood.

Nelly's new family remained in the dark about her former life, discovering her secrets from items she left behind after her death. When biographers eventually revealed the truth about Nelly and Dickens more than six decades after the writer's passing, the British public refused to believe its beloved idol was anything less than the "eminently truthful, trustworthy and self-denying" moralist described in his obituary.

✺ COVERT AFFAIRS ✺

Some writers used subterfuge as a titillating turn-on, while others kept secrets for more practical reasons.

~ Hot pursuit. While working at an upscale Manhattan department store, thriller writer Patricia Highsmith fell for a beautiful blonde customer and tracked her down to a New Jersey suburb. Spying on the married woman, the writer experienced a "curious" reaction and felt "quite close to murder." She mused, "Murder is a kind of making love, a kind of possessing." Highsmith's quarry unknowingly inspired her lesbian love story, *The Price of Salt*.

~ Side dish. Duty warred with passion when Arthur Conan Doyle fell in love with mezzo-soprano Jean Leckie. Divorce was out of the question—he wouldn't abandon his tuberculosis-stricken wife, plus it would wreck his reputation—and instead he saw his sweetheart on the sly. Although he claimed the relationship was platonic, some relatives were outraged. Others, including his doting mother, helped conceal the affair.

~ Clothes make the man. Cross-dressing Bloomsbury author Vita Sackville-West donned men's garb and used the alias Julian during getaways with her lover, Violet Trefusis. Leaving their long-suffering husbands behind, the pair checked into hotels as man and wife and posed as a heterosexual couple during nights on the town in Paris.

~ Mommy dearest. Mystery writers were deft hands at subterfuge, as Dorothy L. Sayers proved when details of her secret son emerged after her death in 1957. The child, the product of a brief fling three decades earlier, was entrusted to a relative who fostered children for a living. At the time, illegitimacy was a disgrace and Sayers was loath to shock her aging parents, who never learned they had a grandson. Her son, whom she financially supported, spent much of his life believing she was a beneficent cousin.

~ **Your place or mine?** Essayist Susan Sontag and photographer Annie Leibovitz, who were together for fifteen years, maintained separate apartments in the same Manhattan building. Despite their refusal to publicly acknowledge their relationship, it was nonetheless one of the worst-kept secrets in the city.

Turbulent Times

FREDERICK DOUGLASS

This proves I am impartial. My first wife was the color of my mother and the second, the color of my father.

—Frederick Douglass

After pulling off a daring escape from slavery, Frederick Douglass championed abolition and women's rights, counseled presidents, and penned three autobiographies. He long courted controversy with his choice of female companions and shocked the nation when he crossed the racial divide and married a white woman in 1884.

Betrayed by a fellow slave, eighteen-year-old Frederick Douglass landed in jail after his first attempt to escape lifelong bondage failed in 1836. He successfully tried again two years later, this time with behind-the-scenes help from his fiancée, Anna Murray, a domestic servant and free black woman five years his senior. Traveling with a train ticket she purchased and disguised as a seaman in clothing she sewed for him, the runaway slave slipped away from the port city of Baltimore and traveled north to freedom.

The future abolitionist had been separated from his mother, a slave, as an infant, and the only fact he knew for certain about his father is that he was white. Raised on a plantation until he was seven, Douglass was then sent to a Baltimore family to look after their young son, a move that dramatically changed the direction of his life.

The mistress of the house unknowingly started Douglass on the path to greatness by taking the extraordinary step of teaching him to read and write, until her husband put an end to the lessons. Determined to become the master of his own fate, Douglass continued his self-education and honed his oratory skills at the East Baltimore Mental Improvement Society. His literacy gained him admission to the group, whose members were primarily free black men and women.

After arriving safely in New York City, Douglass sent word to Anna to join him. They married immediately, the bride donning a plum-colored silk dress and the groom a suit he had stashed in his decoy sailor's bag. The newlyweds headed to the coastal town of New Bedford, Massachusetts, a safer destination than Manhattan, where slave catchers were out in full force, looking to cash in on rewards offered for runaways. Having shed his given surname, Bailey, to help evade capture, the fugitive chose the moniker Douglass, inspired by a character in Sir Walter Scott's poem *The Lady of the Lake*.

Douglass found work as a day laborer and, for the first time in his life, pocketed the money he earned. "Though we toiled hard the first winter, we never lived more happily," he recalls in *My Bondage and My Freedom*. Within three years of fleeing Baltimore, Douglass found his calling as a speaker and champion of the abolitionist cause, gaining employment with the Massachusetts Anti-Slavery Society.

A gifted orator, Douglass traversed the Northeast delivering powerful speeches to mostly white audiences, who heard for the first time a personal account of what it was like to be a slave. At the same time, his rising fame and constant traveling began to take a toll on his marriage. The reserved and politically unambitious Anna, unable to read or write and never fully comfortable in white society, seldom accompanied her husband to public events. Douglass hired a tutor for her, to no avail, and she remained almost totally illiterate throughout her life.

Not long after the birth of the couple's third child, Douglass sailed alone for Europe. He undertook the journey partly to drum up backing for abolitionism and partly to avoid capture after the publication of his inaugural autobiography, *Narrative of the Life of Frederick Douglass*. The gutsy book all but painted a bull's-eye on his back. During the nearly two years her husband was abroad, strong, resourceful Anna kept the home fires burning. She raised their kids, supplemented the family income by making shoes, and donated time and money to the abolitionist cause.

When Douglass returned stateside, his life had changed immeasurably. He was now a free man, thanks to overseas supporters who raised enough money to purchase his emancipation from his Maryland owner. While abroad, Douglass was also introduced to British abolitionist Julia Griffiths, an encounter that would have serious consequences for him.

Julia joined Douglass in Rochester, New York, where he had moved his family, to help publish his antislavery newspaper, the *North Star*. She turned around the paper's dire financial situation and, along with offering editorial assistance, coordinated Douglass's lecture schedule. She and her sister Eliza moved into the Douglass family home and often accompanied him to antislavery society gatherings and speaking engagements. Julia and the abolitionist were close companions, even strolling arm in arm through the streets of Rochester, a startling sight in the 1850s. On one occasion, Douglass was attacked and beaten while in public with the Griffiths.

The unconventional relationship between a white woman and a black man was grist for the rumor mill, especially after Eliza married and was no longer the ostensible chaperone for her sister and Douglass. Even other abolitionists pleaded with the high-profile figure to end his association with Julia, believing the scandal undermined the cause and offered ammunition to their opponents. Despite a more tolerant attitude in the North, those who wanted to abolish slavery were usually not in favor of interracial intimacies. Douglass held firm to his conviction that his friendships could transcend color lines, although Julia did move out of his house and eventually returned to England.

Shortly after her departure, another white woman entered the picture. Yet again Anna was expected to share her husband, and occasionally her home, with a rival: German journalist Ottilie Assing, who turned up on the family's doorstep with an agenda. A correspondent for a prestigious newspaper in her home country, she wanted to interview the famed abolitionist for an article. Their initial meeting turned into a professional and personal association that lasted for twenty-eight years.

After relocating to the United States and reading Douglass's second memoir, *My Bondage and My Freedom*, Ottilie learned more about the abolitionist movement and made it her mission to educate the German public about the evils of slavery in America. Not only did she see herself as a freethinking crusader like Douglass, she believed that her minority heritage as a half-Jewish German made her an excellent match for him. To her, he was the embodiment of a romantic hero. In the introduction to the German edition of *My Bondage and My Freedom*, which she translated and helped to get published, she lauds his bravery and eloquence—and rather obviously highlights his good looks, mentioning his "beautifully carved lips" and other pleasing features.

Ottilie kept an apartment in Hoboken, New Jersey, where

Douglass was a frequent visitor, and like Julia Griffiths before her, she often accompanied him on lecture tours. She offered him advice on political matters, helped write his speeches, and introduced him to prominent people she knew. In the years before and after the Civil War, the two writers often aligned their editorial messages about slavery—Douglass in his newspaper and Ottilie in the pieces she wrote for overseas publications.

For nearly twenty years, Ottilie spent summers as a guest in the Douglass home. She insinuated herself into the household, spinning entertaining tales for his children and accompanying Douglass on the piano while he played the violin. While Anna tended to household matters, Ottilie and Douglass conversed and read aloud to each other in the garden. Anna was understandably aloof toward the interloper and no doubt resentful at being treated like a servant—which Ottilie had mistaken her for the first time she visited the Douglass residence.

The love-struck German journalist aspired to more than just a working collaboration with the abolitionist and had designs on becoming the next Mrs. Douglass. She was often contemptuous of Anna, whom she and Douglass secretly referred to by the derisive nickname "border state," a reference to the region that separated slavery from freedom.

Douglass seemed aware of, but largely indifferent to, the pain that his friendship with Ottilie caused his wife. Not long after he took up with the reporter, he confided to a friend that Anna wasn't well. She suffered from various physical maladies, including neuralgia, and Douglass acknowledged that his behavior only made things worse. Still, he didn't change his ways and once flippantly reported that, despite her ailments, Anna was "able to use with great ease and fluency her powers of speech" in order to inform him of the many areas in "need of improvement in my temper and disposition as a husband and father."

While no definitive proof exists that Douglass and Ottilie ever slept together, she alluded to a physical and emotional attachment between them. Long into their friendship, she confided to her sister, "If one stands in so intimate a relationship with a man as I do with Douglass, one comes to know facets of the whole world, men and women, which would otherwise remain closed to one."

Two decades after Anna aided Douglass in his escape from slavery, Ottilie had a chance to help him out in a life-threatening situation. After abolitionist John Brown staged a failed raid on a federal arsenal in Harpers Ferry, West Virginia, intending to arm slaves for an insurrection, it came to light that Douglass had known about the plot. A warrant was issued for his arrest, and friends spirited him out of Philadelphia, where he had been giving a speech. Once he made it to Ottilie's apartment in Hoboken, she sent coded telegrams on his behalf and got him to an out-of-the-way train station so he could travel home unnoticed.

Douglass fled the country and again sought refuge in Europe. He lectured in England and Scotland and visited friends, among them Julia Griffiths and her husband. Ottilie planned to rendezvous with Douglass in France, fulfilling a dream of touring the Continent together. But the sudden death of his youngest child, ten-year-old Annie, sent him back to the States. Three weeks after returning to Rochester, where he kept a low profile to evade the authorities until the charges were dropped, he stunned and upset his family by inviting Ottilie to join them while they were in the midst of mourning.

Ottilie's desire to become the next Mrs. Douglass remained unabated. She continued to meet up with him in Rochester and then followed him to Washington, D.C., where by presidential appointment he became the first African American U.S. marshal. Ottilie's emotional demands on him continued to grow and so did her bitterness when he showed interest in another woman. As her mental state unraveled, he began distancing himself from his long-time companion.

In 1881, Ottilie and Douglass spent four days together before she set sail for Europe to wrap up her late sister's estate. It was the last time they saw each other. Anna passed away the next summer, freeing them to marry, but no word came from Douglass initiating a reunion. Instead, he was busy romancing someone else.

Less than a year and a half after Anna's death, Douglass astounded his family and the public by secretly wedding Helen Pitts, a white woman twenty years his junior. The couple's romance had heated up after Douglass hired the vivacious, well-educated, and politically minded Pitts to work as a clerk in his Washington, D.C., office.

Seven months after Douglass's nuptials, an elegantly dressed Ottilie left a Paris hotel and headed to a park. She took a seat on a secluded bench and then swallowed potassium cyanide from a vial tucked in her handbag. Prior to her death, Ottilie told friends she had been diagnosed with cancer, although the widely held belief is that her suicide was prompted by Douglass's actions. Curiously, she never amended her will, leaving him a sizeable trust fund.

Around the time Ottilie committed suicide, Douglass and Helen were enjoying a belated honeymoon trip through Canada and New England. On returning home, the groom reported to a friend that, remarkably, he and his wife encountered "not a single repulse or insult in all the journey."

This was a pleasant surprise after the firestorm of controversy they had weathered at the time of their nuptials in 1884. His children were kept in the dark about the romance and heard the news from a reporter after Douglass applied for a marriage license. Resentful that he was replacing their mother with a white woman, they encouraged his grandchildren to give Helen the silent treatment. Furthermore, they believed their father's choice signified his rejection of their black heritage—a sentiment also held across the country by others who felt betrayed by the abolitionist leader. One newspaper correspondent didn't mince words, saying, "Goodbye, black blood in that family. We have no further use for him."

Helen's father, a longtime antislavery advocate, refused to allow his son-in-law into his home and disowned his daughter. Her sisters and nieces remained firmly in her camp, as did her mother, who as a widow went to live with the Douglasses. Another supporter of the headline-making marriage was suffragette leader Elizabeth Cady Stanton, who heartily congratulated the groom and wished him happiness with his new bride.

No doubt aware that becoming Douglass's wife would garner societal and possibly familial censure, Helen forged ahead with her decision anyway. She later expressed, eloquently and courageously, a simple reason for proceeding with the nuptials. "Love came to me," she said, "and I was not afraid to marry the man I loved because of his color."

MR. NOT SO NICE GUY:
RICHARD WRIGHT

In 1939 novelist Richard Wright stunned the woman he'd asked to be his wife, Ellen Poplar, by recanting his marriage proposal. She had wanted time to mull over the momentous decision, concerned about her family's reaction to her marrying a black man, and he was angered by the delay. When she told him yes a short time later, he sent her packing and promptly tied the knot with another white woman, ballet dancer Dhimah Meadman.

The faithless writer had carried on relationships with both Ellen and Dhimah at the time he was working on his debut novel, *Native Son*. The 1940 best seller was far more successful than his rebound marriage, which lasted until he and Dhimah spent time in close quarters on a belated honeymoon and realized they didn't like each other all that much.

After Ellen learned Wright was back on the market and living with friends, she dropped by on the pretense of visiting their mutual acquaintances. As soon as she laid eyes on her former flame, any concerns she'd had about other people's reactions vanished. Nonetheless, after she and Wright wed, they did struggle against racial prejudice.

Even in liberal New York City, where they were living at the time, interracial relationships were not widely accepted. The couple was often subjected to racial slurs while walking down the street, and their neighbors were openly hostile, hurling stones at their apartment windows. Fearing for their daughter's safety, Wright and Ellen decamped to Paris, where society was more tolerant.

Although the change of scenery was beneficial for Wright's writing career, the overseas idyll eventually soured. The philandering writer fell hard for one of his lovers and informed Ellen that he wanted a divorce. When she wept that he was ruining her life, he cruelly responded, "It's your life against mine. I choose mine."

Born to Be Wilde

OSCAR WILDE

A man can be happy with any woman as long as he does not love her.

—Oscar Wilde, *The Picture of Dorian Gray*

Brazenly breaking all the rules, Oscar Wilde fell from the heights of Victorian society to the bowels of a London prison, losing his health, career, and family along the way. In spite of it all, the hedonistic playwright remained unrepentant, writing defiantly while imprisoned, "I don't regret for a single moment having lived for pleasure."

"Somehow or other I'll be famous, and if not famous, I'll be notorious," Oscar Wilde boasted after graduating from Oxford in 1878. But even with his oversize ego and knack for courting publicity, he couldn't have imagined how well he had prophesied his own destiny. Two decades later, his name was splashed across headlines from England to America, as newspapers gleefully reported on his spectacular fall from grace. Sparkling reviews of his brilliant social comedies were abruptly replaced by startling revelations of his love affair with Lord Alfred Douglas, known as Bosie. As tawdry details of Wilde's illicit sex life came to light, the former toast of the town became the most reviled man in England.

Wilde's innocent days of penning sweet nothings to his new bride, Constance, seemed like a distant memory. "I feel your fingers in my hair and your cheeks brushing mine," he had rhapsodized just ten years earlier. "The air is full of the music of your voice, my soul and body seem . . . mingled in some exquisite ecstasy with yours." When he presented Constance with a heart-shaped engagement ring in 1883, Oscar did genuinely love her, although he may not have realized his feelings were grounded more in affection than physical desire.

Victorian doctors often recommended marriage as a "cure" for patients with homosexual urges, and Wilde may have been acting under those misguided beliefs when he proposed. At the time he met Constance, his romantic passions appeared decidedly heterosexual. The playwright had previously been in love with an Irish woman, who left him for Bram Stoker, and also proposed to two other women, one of whom later wrote with relief that she "nearly as possible escaped the honor of being Mrs. Oscar Wilde." Instead it was Constance who suffered that fate.

Beautiful, talented, and intelligent, Constance had her choice among suitors, but it was Oscar who enchanted her with his artistic, bohemian nature. When she first met the famous man-about-town she was starstruck and "shaking with fright," but her fears were quickly allayed when she and Wilde hit it off. Their personalities were well-suited, and they established a flirtatious rapport and easy conversational manner. Just over two years later, Constance was writing to her brother: "Prepare yourself for an astounding piece of news! . . . I am engaged to Oscar Wilde and perfectly and insanely happy."

Her brother had coincidentally written to warn her of a rumor he heard circulating about the writer, but Constance turned a deaf ear, as she was to do repeatedly throughout her marriage. "I will not allow anything to come between us and at any rate no one can abuse him to me," she replied.

Constance knew that gossip about Oscar needed to be taken with a grain of salt, as he thrived on courting controversy. His flamboyant attire, infamous witticisms, and outrageous behavior (such as rudely taking a curtain call while holding a lit cigarette) were defiantly aimed at shocking Victorian sensibilities. An apostle of the aesthetic movement, his dandified appearance—long flowing hair, velvet coats, and frilly shirts—fueled speculation about his sexuality, as did the dyed-green carnations (a symbol of men who loved men) he wore in his lapel. The playwright, branded everything from a mama's boy to an "effeminate phrase maker," was a favorite target of conservative commentators.

Due to Wilde's long absences on the lecture circuit, he barely knew Constance when they walked down the aisle, but their similar interests and tastes ensured a promising start to their union. Clever, ambitious, and fashionable, they instantly became a high-profile celebrity couple, their every move written about and dissected in gossip columns.

Unusually for the time, they were true partners, writing children's books together, collaborating on the renowned design of their home, and even advising each other on clothing. Constance had a progressive sense of fashion that rivaled Oscar's, often sporting baggy trousers and corsetless dresses, and he frequently solicited her opinions for the women's magazine he edited. The *InStyle* of its day, *Woman's World* dished on fashion and trends in high society, topics upon which Constance, as the hostess of her own glittering salon, was well placed to advise.

Despite the couple's strong partnership, Wilde did not anticipate the sheer revulsion he would feel for the female body once Constance became pregnant. "How can one desire what is shapeless, deformed, ugly?" he lamented. "Desire is killed by maternity; passion buried in conception." Ruing the dramatic shift in his feelings, he noted sadly: "When I married, my wife was a beautiful girl, white and slim as a lily, with dancing eyes and gay rippling laughter like music. In a year or so the flowerlike grace had all vanished . . . I tried to be kind to her; forced myself to touch and kiss her; but she was sick always, and—oh! I cannot recall it, it is all loathsome."

After the birth of their second son in late 1886, Oscar and Constance were never again physically intimate. Instead he embarked on a reckless series of homosexual adventures, exploring the full range of passions he had apparently been repressing for years. He seemed to be living out the mantra expressed by his alter ego in *The Picture of Dorian Gray*: "The only way to get rid of a temptation is to yield to it."

Constance innocently welcomed Oscar's young male admirers into their home and accepted them as family friends. While she must have found it strange that her husband spent so much time surrounded by men nearly half his age, she seemed oblivious to the implications. Rather than putting Oscar on a tighter leash, she tolerated his late nights out and frequent absences, perhaps thinking that she could save their relationship by giving him freedom.

As Wilde's absences increased over the years, Constance became a blur of perpetual motion, attending lectures, political marches, and cultural events, as well as frequently traveling to visit friends. Her manic schedule may have been a frantic attempt to avoid facing the obvious. She also kept herself busy—and kept loneliness at bay—by having a secret affair with a book publisher she met while editing a collection of Oscar's witticisms.

Despite living increasingly separate lives, Oscar and Constance maintained a semblance of familial togetherness during the early years of his infidelities. But not everyone was fooled. The poet W. B. Yeats visited them one Christmas, noting "that the perfect harmony of [Oscar's] life . . . suggested some deliberate artistic composition." The cracks in their relationship would not become outwardly visible until 1891, the year Wilde took up with the spoiled, self-centered Bosie, who replaced Constance as the primary object of his affection. The two men became inseparable, lodging together at various London hotels and often traveling abroad.

In spite of harsh indecency laws that had been introduced, the playwright made little effort to hide his homosexual activities, instead reveling in the rumors that swirled around him. "I am one of those who are made for exceptions, not for laws," he once scoffed dismissively. No one was more affronted by his public parading about than Bosie's father, the Marquess of Queensberry. He blamed Wilde for corrupting his son and took desperate measures to separate them. Pursuing them around London, he threatened restaurant and hotel managers with bodily harm if the pair was allowed on the premises. As a result of their repeated evictions, Bosie and Oscar were frequently on the move.

In June of 1894, Queensberry showed up unannounced at Wilde's house, accompanied by a boxer. After an angry confrontation, the playwright tartly ordered them to leave, warning, "I do not know what the Queensberry rules are, but the Oscar Wilde rule is to shoot on sight." The final, fatal provocation came when Queensberry left a calling card for Wilde at a gentlemen's club, accusing him of "posing as a somdomite [sic]," an insult that, at the time, packed nearly the same punch as insinuating one was a murderer.

Goaded by the manipulative Bosie, who detested his father and wanted to see him humiliated, Wilde took the reckless step of suing Queensberry for libel. His recent box office hits, *The Importance of Being Earnest* and *An Ideal Husband*, had brought him to the pinnacle of celebrity while dangerously inflating his ego. Convinced of his invulnerability, Wilde barely gave a thought to the possibility that Queensberry's words could be proven.

Certain that none of his prior partners would turn on him for fear of being prosecuted themselves, he woefully underestimated the power of a well-placed bribe. Queensberry's steely determination was a formidable enemy, and his private detectives assembled a motley crew of male "rent boys" and other seedy characters who were coerced into testifying to their amorous encounters with the playwright. Gifts he had lavished upon them, from silver cigarette cases to signed editions of his works, were also brought into evidence. Some of the most damning testimony came from chambermaids at London's posh Savoy Hotel, who revealed they had seen boys in Wilde's bed and found semen, Vaseline, and feces stains on his sheets.

Wilde's literary works were also scrutinized, especially *The Picture of Dorian Gray*. The novel, which centers on an older man's infatuation with a younger man, was the inadvertent matchmaker for him and Bosie. "It had a terrific effect on me," admitted Bosie. "I read it about 14 times running." He urged a mutual acquaintance to introduce him to Wilde, who immediately became infatuated with his young fan, referring to him adoringly as "a slim thing, gold-haired like an angel."

The writer began his libel suit full of arrogant bravado, but by the end, one observer noted that he looked "like a tortured, hunted animal." Even his quips, while keeping the audience entertained, proved no match for the merciless, rapid-fire questioning he endured under cross-examination. Forced to withdraw his lawsuit after only three days of testimony, Wilde subsequently found himself indicted by a grand jury and charged with twenty-five counts of sodomy and gross indecency. "I have ruined the most brilliant man in London," Queensberry's attorney, a former schoolmate of Wilde's, glumly told his wife.

Friends pleaded with Oscar to flee the country before bailiffs arrived to arrest him. While staying at the Cadogan Hotel with Bosie, he wavered back and forth long into the night before finally resigning himself to his fate: "The train is gone—it is too late." At the second trial, more damning evidence was produced against him, including love letters he had written to Bosie. Also presented was a poem Bosie had penned, which concluded with the notorious line, "I am the love that dare not speak its name." When the prosecution called on Wilde to explain the meaning of the statement, he roused spectators into applause by delivering his famous defense of love between men invoking Plato, Michelangelo, and Shakespeare.

Ultimately, Wilde was convicted on seven of the original twenty-five charges and given the maximum sentence of two years hard labor in prison. Despite the severe punishment, he was fortunate that sodomy no longer carried the death penalty, as it had for many centuries before Victorian-era reforms.

Constance and her sons were forced to change their surnames and go abroad to escape public scorn and humiliation. Adding insult to injury were Bosie's defamatory and malicious statements that blamed her for the breakdown of her marriage. Through it all, Constance remained loyal to her disgraced husband, visiting him in prison and continuing to offer emotional and financial support. Incredibly, she was prepared to forgive him and even delayed filing for divorce, only giving up hope when he returned to Bosie after being freed from prison.

Within a few months of Wilde's release, thirty-nine-year-old Constance passed away from complications related to a botched operation. After visiting his wife's grave, Oscar wrote sorrowfully of "the uselessness of all regrets. Nothing could have been otherwise, and life is a terrible thing."

❧ **THE PURSUIT OF PLEASURE** ❧

The world's oldest profession proved useful when it came to scratching a carnal itch, spicing up a sex life, or even bestowing a dubious "gift" on a loved one.

~ **Text for sex.** Unable to afford the services at the up-scale Parisian brothel Le Sphinx, an impoverished Henry Miller bartered instead. In exchange for writing a promotional brochure, he was compensated with a bottle of bubbly and a "free fuck" in one of the Egyptian-themed rooms.

~ **For your eyes only.** Feeling guilty about cheating on her husband, erotica writer Anaïs Nin assuaged her conscience by taking him to a bordello. After deftly negotiating the price, she chose two women who treated them to a sex show in a private room. Although Nin encouraged her shy spouse to join the lusty ladies, he demurely held back.

~ **Return of the screw.** At a house of ill repute, nervous teenager Marcel Proust was too embarrassed to do the deed after accidentally breaking a chamber pot. His father had sent him to the brothel, hoping the experience would discourage his homosexual crushes and turn him into a "normal" man. Desperate to make amends, Proust asked his grandfather for thirteen francs: ten for a return visit and three to replace the chamber pot. He reasoned he would try again because "it can't happen twice in one lifetime that a person's too upset to screw."

~ **Staying power.** Randy Adonis Gustave Flaubert could have almost single-handedly kept France's ladies of the night in business. "I love prostitution," he claimed. "One learns so

many things in a brothel . . . and dreams so longingly of love."
Even contracting a venereal disease didn't tarnish his starry-
eyed view of paying for sex with a stranger.

~ **Size matters.** Struggling writer Alexandre Dumas fils
had to end his affair with Marie Duplessis, one of the most
sought-after courtesans in Paris, because his wallet wasn't
thick enough. Ironically, he later made money off *her* when
his novel based on their relationship, *The Lady of the Camel-
lias*, became a best seller.

PART SIX

Paradise Lost

Runaway Romantics

PERCY BYSSHE SHELLEY AND MARY SHELLEY

Love is free; to promise forever to love the same woman is not less absurd than to promise to believe the same creed.

—Percy Shelley

Love is to me as light to the star; even so long as that is uneclipsed by annihilation, so long shall I love you.

—Mary Shelley, *The Last Man*

After Percy Shelley abandoned his pregnant wife to elope with sixteen-year-old Mary, tragedy—or some might say karma—caught up with the couple. The euphoric start to their relationship gave way to reality, turning a hedonistic, free-loving lifestyle into one filled with jealousy and heartbreak.

"They wish to separate us, my beloved; but Death shall unite us," Percy Shelley exclaimed to his teenage paramour, Mary Godwin, after pushing past her stepmother and forcing his way into their house. In a scene worthy of *Romeo and Juliet*, he thrust a vial of laudanum at her, proclaiming, "By this you can escape from tyranny." Pulling a pistol from his pocket, he added, "And this shall reunite me to you." Although Mary attempted to placate him, the agitated poet departed and took a large dose of laudanum himself, bringing on a near-fatal collapse.

A few days before, the young romantics had avowed their love beside the grave of Mary's mother, renowned feminist Mary Wollstonecraft. The couple's first intimate encounter may have even taken place in the churchyard, where Shelley is said to have seduced Mary on her mother's gravestone. The renegade poet revered the radical-thinking Wollstonecraft, who had died following the birth of her daughter sixteen years earlier, and the allure of this connection may have heightened his attraction to Mary. With her unconventional views, Mary seemed to offer the promise of a more rewarding life than Shelley's stifling existence with his pregnant wife and daughter.

Although Mary's father forbade the illicit lovers to continue seeing each other, they were undeterred and hatched a plan to elope to Switzerland. In July 1814, under the cover of darkness, Mary snuck outside to meet the poet's waiting coach. Along for the ride was her stepsister Claire Clairmont, who had helped the couple smuggle notes and may have been in love with Shelley herself. Once dawn broke, their scandalous flight was discovered and Claire's mother set off after the party in hot pursuit. She caught up with them in the French coastal town of Calais but was unable to persuade them to turn back.

A more formidable obstacle was Shelley's pocketbook, which ran dry six weeks into the trip. They were forced to travel on foot and in cramped public omnibuses for much of the journey, which was especially arduous for the newly pregnant Mary. When the penniless threesome skulked back to England, they paid a call on the first Mrs. Shelley.

The poet went to her, not as a repentant spouse seeking forgiveness, but as a deadbeat hoping for a handout. While the sisters sat outside in the coach, Shelley shamelessly tried to extract money from the wife he had abandoned. Although Harriet Shelley had hoped her wayward husband would return home, she certainly hadn't expected him to have two teenagers in tow when he did. Shelley believed they could continue to live together as friends and had even written to Harriet urging her to join his harem in Switzerland, an offer she unsurprisingly turned down.

As divorce was not a viable option, Shelley remained married in spite of his "elopement." A married man cohabiting with two single women was unthinkable, and his aristocratic father severed ties and cut off funds. Shelley tried to rehabilitate his blackened reputation by justifying his desertion of his wife. "Everyone who knows me must know that the partner of my life should be one who can feel poetry and understand philosophy," he pretentiously exhorted, adding, "Harriet is a noble animal but she can do neither." Mary, however, he felt was his intellectual soul mate: "Among women there is no equal mind to yours," he assured her.

During the bleak autumn months after his elopement, the poet was relentlessly hounded by creditors. He was now also financially responsible for Mary and Claire, who had been exiled from their own family. The stepsisters lived from hand to mouth in grim lodgings, while Shelley went into hiding to avoid being arrested for debt. Mary spent each week counting the hours until Sunday, when the law forbade arrests and the lovers could be reunited.

A proponent of the doctrine of "free love," Shelley envisioned having an open relationship, with Mary shared between himself and a friend from his Oxford school days. He encouraged his friend to make sexual overtures to his pregnant girlfriend and urged her to welcome them. Although Mary shared his progressive beliefs, Claire would later recall her stepsister crying bitterly over the proposed arrangement. The seedy sexual liaison likely never took place, due to Mary's grief over the death of her premature child (born just three months after Harriet's baby by Shelley).

While Claire espoused the same liberal views as the others and blatantly pursued the married poet Lord Byron—who dumped her after a roll in the hay—she converted to Catholicism in old age and wrote a scathing indictment of Byron's and Shelley's morals: "Under the doctrine and belief of free love, I saw the two first poets of England . . . become monsters of lying, meanness, cruelty and treachery." Whether Claire also had a sexual relationship with Shelley has never been determined, but the poet had an unusual attachment to her and, much to Mary's annoyance, she remained a permanent fixture in their household.

Nearly two years after the elopement, Shelley and the stepsisters again departed for Europe. Bound once more for Geneva, they hoped to escape the hostile gossip surrounding them at home, but their unconventional living arrangements continued to attract attention. Rumors of their purported "league of incest" drew binocular-wielding curiosity seekers, who spied on them from afar. Claire, secretly pregnant with Byron's child, engineered the trip to coincide with his upcoming travels, hoping she could lure him into her waiting arms.

The ragtag group rented adjoining villas on the shores of Lake Geneva, where incessant rains kept them indoors for much of the summer and provided the perfect breeding ground for Mary Shelley's *Frankenstein*. During a night of ghostly storytelling beside a flickering fire, Byron challenged the group to write their own spine-tingling tales. Mary rose to the occasion with the story of a monster assembled from dead body parts.

Later, she wistfully referred to her novel as "the offspring of happy days," recalling the blissful period before the tragic consequences of her elopement unfolded. When the group returned to England at the end of the summer, Mary's half sister, Fanny, was found dead in a Welsh lodging house from a fatal dose of laudanum. She had become depressed after her sister's elopement, leading some to believe that Fanny was yet another woman hopelessly in love with Percy Shelley.

Barely two months later, Harriet Shelley's pregnant body was found floating in a pond in London's Hyde Park. She too had committed suicide. Shelley, once more seeking to deflect blame from himself, immediately began tarring Harriet's reputation, claiming she had "descended the steps of prostitution." In actuality, his lonely, spurned wife had taken a lover and become pregnant.

Shelley seemed to feel no guilt over his role in the tragedy, although Harriet's suicide letter pointed an accusing finger: "If you had never left me I might have lived but as it is, I freely forgive you and may you enjoy that happiness which you have deprived me of." Before his wife's body had even grown cold, Shelley was walking her replacement down the aisle. Although he and Mary cared little for the institution of marriage, they legitimized their union to strengthen Shelley's case for obtaining custody of his children. But window dressing alone could not restore his tarnished reputation, and the court awarded the children to Harriet's parents.

It turned out to be a fortuitous decision, given the fate of Shelley's two offspring with Mary. Following the couple's disastrous decision to travel to Italy, their infant daughter died of fever and their three-year-old son fell victim to malaria. Devastated, Mary blamed her husband for the deaths. Shelley had delayed getting their daughter life-saving medical attention because he had been preoccupied with Claire's problems. As Mary bitterly noted, her stepsister was the reason they had come to Italy in the first place. The trip had been prompted by the need to bring Claire's illegitimate daughter to Byron, who could better care for the child with his wealth.

Grieving and resentful, Mary withdrew into herself and sank

into a deep depression, which was made worse by her husband's inability to share her pain. Instead of consoling her, he immersed himself in his writing and turned to Claire for company. When Mary's spirits didn't fully recover after the birth of another baby boy, he was particularly unsympathetic since he believed the cause of her sufferings had "become obsolete" with the replacement child.

Applying the same misguided logic, he may have adopted a foundling to compensate Mary for the loss of their daughter. The dubious parentage of the baby girl born in Naples, whom Shelley claimed as his own on the birth certificate, has never been established. A rumor spread by a former servant claimed the mysterious child was Shelley and Claire's, but Mary vehemently denied the allegations. The poet placed the infant with foster parents and continued to support her until she died.

Faced with the chill in his relations with Mary, Shelley wrote of marriage as "the dreariest and longest journey" in his autobiographical poem *Epipsychidion*. The work, inspired by a young Italian girl named Emilia Viviani, unfavorably compares monogamy to the liberating experience of free love. Tellingly, Shelley concealed the poem from Mary for several months and had it published anonymously.

Mary dismissively referred to the betrothed Emilia Viviani as one of Shelley's "Italian Platonics," unobtainable women with whom he became infatuated. Another "Platonic" was their married friend Jane Williams, who inspired many of Shelley's final poems, written during the time she and her husband shared a villa with the couple in Tuscany.

Mary's foundering relationship with the poet never had a chance to blossom back into what it had been during their happy early years. In June of 1822, she suffered a miscarriage that nearly killed her. Three weeks later, Shelley drowned when his boat capsized during a violent storm off the Tuscan coast. He died a month shy of his thirtieth birthday and was cremated in a theatrical pagan ceremony on the beach where his body had washed up.

Following the cremation, an argument broke out between Mary and one of Shelley's friends over who should keep what they thought was the poet's heart. The organ, which was, in fact, probably his liver, had bizarrely resisted burning. After Mary's death three decades later, it was discovered inside her traveling writing desk. Dried to dust, it had been carefully wrapped in silk and placed between the pages of Shelley's poem *Adonais*. The poem was an elegy Shelley had written for fellow romantic poet John Keats, but Mary always felt the final stanza, which eerily alluded to being at sea in the midst of a storm, was a "prophecy on his own destiny."

〜℃ TRAGIC TURNS ℃〜

Even the most creative authors couldn't rewrite history when death called for the partners they loved—or when they themselves met a gruesome fate.

~ **The blame game.** Novelist John Dos Passos's wife, Katy, died in a car accident while he was at the wheel. While en route from Provincetown to Boston, he became blinded by the setting sun and crashed into a parked truck. The couple had been introduced by Ernest Hemingway, who blamed Dos Passos for Katy's death, believing his friend exercised poor judgment by driving at all with bad eyesight.

~ **Endless love.** Henry Wadsworth Longfellow valiantly tried to put out the flames that engulfed his wife, Fanny, when a candle set her dress ablaze. She passed away the next day from her injuries. The poet—who grew his trademark white beard to cover burn scars—expressed his unrelenting anguish in "The Cross of Snow," mourning that the seasons had remained "changeless since the day she died," eighteen years earlier.

~ **Better late than never.** It wasn't until C. S. Lewis's spouse, Joy Davidman, was diagnosed with bone cancer that he realized he was in love with her. They had married in a civil ceremony so the American bride could remain in England but continued to live apart as friends. In Joy's hospital room, they exchanged vows a second time, with a priest performing the nuptials. When she died three years later, Lewis had a crisis of faith and penned *A Grief Observed* in tribute to his wife.

~ **The tale of poor Potter.** Beatrix Potter didn't hold it against Norman Warne when his family's publishing company initially rejected *The Tale of Peter Rabbit*. She eventually signed on with the firm and worked closely with the editor. When he proposed, Beatrix happily accepted, but they never exchanged vows. Norman died suddenly from leukemia a month after the engagement.

~ **A hopeless romantic.** Alexander Pushkin foreshadowed his own demise in the verse novel *Eugene Onegin*. Just as his fictional hero duels to the death over a woman, so too did Pushkin. He boldly challenged his coquettish wife's unabashed admirer, who fired first when they faced off and mortally wounded the poet in the stomach. Before passing away two days later, Pushkin gallantly assured his spouse, "Don't worry, it isn't your fault."

Eclipse of the Heart

VOLTAIRE

Friendship is the marriage of the soul, and this marriage is liable to divorce.

—Voltaire, *Philosophical Dictionary*

France's renegade philosopher, poet, and playwright Voltaire met his match in amateur scientist and mathematician Emilie du Châtelet. The Enlightenment rebel and the aristocrat forged an unusual partnership that lasted nearly two decades, until the stars no longer aligned for them.

Gazing at the night sky and pondering the inner workings of celestial bodies was Emilie du Châtelet's idea of foreplay. The fiery, ferociously intelligent marquise was a tyrant, joked Voltaire. Being with her meant discussing metaphysics when he'd much rather ruminate on sex and love.

Although the thirty-nine-year-old philosopher had never lacked for female companionship (actresses in particular), he was dazzled by more than just Emilie's looks when they were introduced at a Paris opera in 1733. "I met a young lady who happened to think nearly as I did," he enthused of the slim, doe-eyed brunette who shared his passion for subjects like philosophy, mathematics, and linguistics. The married twenty-seven-year-old was also a lusty companion in bed, and it was these less cerebral attributes he had in mind when he wrote in a racy poem, "The hand of Venus is made to touch the lute of Love."

Unusual for a time when even highborn women were often illiterate, Emilie was educated alongside her brothers at the insistence of her progressive father, who had noticed her keen intellect at an early age. She had an avid interest in Isaac Newton's scientific theories and an impressive aptitude for math, which she put to use at the gaming tables. Fluent in several languages, in a matter of weeks she mastered English under Voltaire's tutelage so they could converse freely without fear of eavesdroppers.

Sleeping with a commoner was almost unheard of in Emilie's aristocratic circle (Voltaire's father, a lawyer and notary, was considered a tradesman) and so was the risky business of displaying her affection for her lover in public and entertaining him overnight. Although it was accepted that married members of the upper classes had affairs, discretion was paramount, since adultery was officially illegal—for wives, anyway, who could be punished with public whippings. Emilie's easygoing husband, Florent-Claude, a marquis and high-ranking military officer, vigorously pursued his own extramarital activities and afforded his wife the same latitude.

While Emilie's affair with Voltaire began passionately, the fire was quickly dampened when the philosopher contracted dysentery and expected his reluctant mistress to play nursemaid. In addition to losing patience with her demanding and bad-tempered patient, Emilie was disillusioned at seeing the great man drained of his power and poise. She wasn't looking merely for a lover but for someone with whom she could advance her scientific research and writing.

With Voltaire sidelined by illness, Emilie began seeing a scientist and explorer but found his company wasn't as stimulating as Voltaire's. After occupying herself with both men for a while, she reunited with the philosopher. They were back together long enough to play matchmaker for the duc de Richelieu, Voltaire's longtime friend and Emilie's former lover. At Richelieu's wedding festivities, word of Voltaire's impending arrest reached the surprised revelers. Emilie sidetracked the authorities while the wanted man slipped away and went into hiding.

Voltaire's powerful pen had once again gotten him into serious trouble. A rogue printer leaked copies of *Letters Concerning the English Nation*, an inflammatory treatise that illuminated the shortcomings of the French government by praising the English way of doing things. Voltaire was no stranger to run-ins with the law and had previously been imprisoned, as well as exiled to England, for criticizing the government in print. His reputation was so notorious that he was often accused even when the seditious works were penned by someone else.

The fugitive philosopher caught up with the newlywed Richelieu at a military encampment, where he proceeded to hide in plain sight. While he was making merry with the officers, drinking, singing, and giving readings, Emilie was beside herself with worry. She leveraged her contacts at court to get his arrest warrant rescinded only to discover he had made things more difficult by his choice of hiding place, which seemed to mock government officials.

Miffed that Voltaire had worsened the situation by his defiant actions, Emilie grudgingly allowed him to seek refuge at an ancestral château where they had once rendezvoused. Soon afterward, she made the radical decision to leave the social world of Paris and the court at Versailles to take up residence with the philosopher in the remote village of Cirey in eastern France.

The soul mates set about renovating the dilapidated château, creating a cultural and intellectual love nest complete with a theater to stage Voltaire's plays and a twenty-one-thousand-volume library that rivaled that of the Academy of Sciences in Paris. Despite minor squabbles that sometimes involved hurling cutlery, the marquise reported that after three months of living together they were content in their earthly paradise and more in love than ever.

In the sumptuous sanctuary, the couple pursued their scholarly endeavors with gusto, putting into practice the fundamentals of the Enlightenment by questioning religious, scientific, and philosophical beliefs that had stood for centuries. The main hall was converted into a physics and chemistry laboratory, and over the years the inquisitive pair performed experiments on heat, fire, light, magnetism, and other topics. It wasn't all work and no play, though, as they also entertained guests at champagne-fueled parties and performed plays and operas, including a musical marathon that lasted forty-eight hours.

With Voltaire's support, the marquise finally had the confidence to let her brainpower flourish. "Since I've met a man of letters who gave me friendship I've started to feel different," she confessed. "I've begun to believe I'm a being with a mind." At her suggestion, the lovers teamed up to produce a groundbreaking book interpreting the breadth of Isaac Newton's scientific work. Eager to please his "divine Emilie," Voltaire saw it as a way to keep the flame burning in their relationship.

Although Emilie was the driving force behind the analysis, their finished volume, *Elements of the Philosophy of Newton*, appeared solely under his name, as was the custom at the time. The book was dedicated to Emilie and included a provocative homage—a sketch showing Newton in the heavens while a goddess representing the marquise (with a breast exposed) holds a mirror to collect light and direct it toward Voltaire, seated at a table with a manuscript.

In the midst of their scholarly reverie, the couple was interrupted by yet another forced parting. A warrant was again issued for
Voltaire's arrest when a copy of his poem parodying Adam and Eve
mysteriously fell into the wrong hands. Once more, he went into
hiding. Months passed before the marquise found out that her cousin
was behind the machinations. The cousin—a devout Catholic who
disapproved of Emilie's association with the blasphemous Voltaire—
sought to coerce her into joining his case against a relative vying for
a share of the family fortune.

Not content just to blacken Voltaire's reputation, the nemesis
decided to interfere with Emilie's marriage. He persuaded her
mother, who rued having such an eccentric daughter, to inform
Emilie's husband about the gossip surrounding his wife and Voltaire. But the plan backfired. Not only did Emilie's husband permit
her affairs, he had spent time with his wife and Voltaire at Cirey and
become friends with the philosopher. Like most aristocratic marriages of the time, the du Châtelet union was essentially a business
arrangement, and a congenial one at that. When the well-respected
marquis stood up to the authorities on Voltaire's behalf, the matter
was quickly laid to rest.

Strict government censors and underhanded relatives weren't
the only villains with whom Voltaire and Emilie had to contend.
An emotional love triangle developed between the pair and an unlikely figure: Frederick of Prussia. The twenty-five-year-old heir to
the Prussian throne, who fancied himself a poet and intellectual,
struck up a correspondence with the philosopher. Even after his
ascension, the monarch wooed Voltaire with flattery, intent on acquiring the celebrated writer as an ornament at his court and possibly in his bed.

The French government granted Voltaire permission to visit
Frederick in Prussia with the understanding that he was on a covert mission to gather evidence about the monarch's military plans.

Emilie had long been wary of Frederick's intentions and advised Voltaire not to go, but the feint of friendship duped the philosopher.

While Frederick's guest, Voltaire entertained his host by lampooning French officials in print and even taking unkind jabs at Emilie. The monarch circulated the writings the philosopher thought were for His Highness's eyes only, making him persona non grata—particularly with his mistress—when he recrossed the border. Emilie was wounded by the personal betrayal and incensed that her lover would so cavalierly jeopardize her years-long efforts to keep him out of harm's way.

Unapologetic, Voltaire penned Emilie a breakup poem, claiming (falsely, as he had recently proved with Frederick's sister) that he was too old to have sex anymore. She saw through the pretense, and though they didn't immediately separate, the couple's arguments steadily increased. He was cold and withdrawn, resentful that Emilie had been right about Frederick, and after a decade together they decided to part ways.

Being without each other suited neither of them. Emilie abandoned science for the thrill of gambling. But with her concentration shot she racked up serious debts, which Voltaire eventually paid off after she failed to secure the funds elsewhere. Meanwhile he made amends at the French court, where he helped to find Louis XV a new mistress (a fishmonger's granddaughter who restyled herself as the infamous Madame de Pompadour) but lost his creative spark and all but ceased writing.

Lamenting that he had been foolish to drive Emilie away, Voltaire successfully pursued the marquise once more. Returning to Cirey together, they resumed their intellectual and literary endeavors but not their amorous activities. Although no longer sleeping together, the two tactfully hid their affairs from one another—Voltaire with his niece and Emilie with a younger man, Jean François de Saint-Lambert, a soldier and poet. The philosopher eventually found out about Emilie's liaison, after walking in on her and her lover in flagrante delicto.

When Emilie became pregnant by Saint-Lambert in her early forties, she was overwhelmed with a foreboding that she wouldn't survive the experience. Voltaire remained at her side, while her absentee lover fled when he found out she was expecting. The companions conspired to conceal the baby's illegitimate paternity by summoning Emilie's husband to Cirey for a conjugal visit, to make it seem plausible that he had fathered the child.

Before she gave birth, Emilie was intent on finishing a French translation of Newton's *Principia*—which would become a significant contribution to the Enlightenment—and she journeyed to Paris to retrieve reference volumes needed for the task. On the return trip to Cirey, the carriage in which she and Voltaire were traveling broke an axle and careened off the icy road. While awaiting rescue, they sat on cushions on a snow bank, indulging in their favored pastime of observing the heavens. The unexpected delay offered the couple a rare tranquil moment together, only a few months before Emilie passed away.

The marquise joyously survived the delivery she had so dreaded, only to die a week later of infection. After his sixteen-year relationship with Emilie was tragically and prematurely brought to a close, Voltaire was heartbroken and wandered through a Parisian apartment they had once shared, calling her name. "My tears will never stop flowing," he professed. "It is not a mistress I have lost but half of myself, a soul for which my soul seems to have been made."

ᏧᏭ **ETERNAL FLAMES** ᏬᏬ

Some lovers couldn't seal the deal with the objects of their affections and were doomed to a purgatory of unrequited love.

~ **No fairytale ending**. More than one woman spurned Hans Christian Andersen's affections, among them soprano and "Swedish Nightingale" Jenny Lind. The songstress inspired his fairy tale "The Nightingale," about a bird that was cast aside by a Chinese emperor but returns to aid him in his hour of need. Andersen worked up the nerve to propose to Lind, only to be told she thought of him as a brother.

~ **Silence is not golden.** "To refuse to reply to me—that will be to tear from me the only joy I have on earth—to deprive me of my last remaining privilege," Charlotte Brontë despaired in an 1845 letter to Constantin Héger, her former professor at a school in Brussels. The married father of three didn't reciprocate her romantic feelings and was shocked to receive the passionate correspondence. Brontë's unrequited affections offered fodder for her novel *Villette*, in which a young teacher and a schoolmaster fall in love.

~ **Like mother, like daughter.** William Butler Yeats fell head over heels as soon as he laid eyes on Maud Gonne, a six-foot-tall redhead who for three decades turned down his repeated marriage proposals. Still unwilling to give up, the poet proposed to her daughter, who also rejected him. Gonne believed she did the world a favor by keeping Yeats lovesick, since his unhappiness inspired many of his lyrical, poignant verses.

~ **Tough love.** The girl-on-girl crushes of bisexual novelist Carson McCullers rarely led to any action. She failed to score with Katherine Anne Porter at a writers' colony, where she followed the other woman around like a lovesick puppy and finally resorted to pounding on Porter's door and pouring out her feelings. When no one answered, she lay across the threshold, determined to wait. At dinnertime, Porter merely opened the door, stepped over the prostrate Carson, and went along her way.

~ **Lonely hearts.** The titular character in Goethe's eighteenth-century novel *The Sorrows of Young Werther* falls in love with a woman engaged to another man and commits suicide in despair after she marries. Partly based on the author's own unrequited love, the best seller inspired a rash of copycat suicides by the lovelorn.

A Marriage of Minds

Virginia Woolf

I want to tell you that you have given me complete happiness. No one could have done more than you have done.

—Virginia Woolf

These words from Virginia Woolf's suicide note to her husband, Leonard, illuminate the profound connection she shared with the man who has alternately been praised as a doting nursemaid and vilified as a jailer. Without Leonard's saintly devotion and willingness to sacrifice himself in service to his wife's genius, it is unlikely the high priestess of Bloomsbury would have remained alive and writing long enough to produce her groundbreaking modernist works.

"If anybody could have saved me it would have been you. . . . I don't think two people could have been happier than we have been," Virginia Woolf wrote to her husband before filling her pockets with stones and wading into the river Ouse. During their three decades of marriage, Leonard had nursed his wife through countless breakdowns, some so severe that four nurses were enlisted to help with her care. Yet even his enduring love and vigilant caretaking were no match for his wife's fatalistic impulses.

Although the couple lived under the constant threat of Virginia's self-described "madness," now believed to be manic depression, she was contented and productive for most of their years together. But her frighteningly lethal mood swings could render her violent, suicidal, and delusional, sometimes leading her to imagine the voice of her dead mother or, once, birds singing in Greek. A typical breakdown would see her vacillate from mania—talking nearly nonstop for days at a time—to periods of profound, suicidal depression.

When Leonard fell in love and proposed in 1912, he was undeterred by Virginia's history of mental illness, although he likely didn't realize the magnitude of her issues. Mental instability ran in her family, and she had suffered the first in a series of breakdowns when she was thirteen, after her mother passed away. The death of her father nine years later provoked another alarming collapse involving a suicide attempt and institutionalization.

Despite her grief at losing her parents, Virginia found herself free to live the bohemian life she had always craved. Together, she and her sister moved from the respectable confines of the family home to London's slightly disreputable Bloomsbury neighborhood. There, Virginia took up smoking, did volunteer work for the women's suffrage movement, and began working on a novel while writing book reviews for the *Times Literary Supplement*. Every Thursday night she and her sister would gather with their brother's friends to discuss the literary, political, and artistic issues of the day, and it was this circle of writers and intellectuals that became known as the Bloomsbury group.

When Leonard appeared on the scene and eventually proposed marriage, Virginia was at first reluctant. Although she knew the presence of a steady partner was critical to her mental stability, she feared making a commitment. When she finally agreed to marry

Leonard, she bluntly informed him: "I feel no physical attraction in you. When you kissed me the other day, I felt no more than a rock." But this was of little importance to her, as she did not consider sexual passion a key ingredient in a happy marriage. As for Leonard, he seemed unfazed by her frank admission.

Their honeymoon did little to ignite her passion. Twenty-nine-year-old Virginia found her first experience with sex distasteful, writing to a friend, "Why do you think people make such a fuss about copulation?" From early on in their unconventional marriage, she and Leonard maintained separate bedrooms. Their relationship was thought to be physically chaste, contrasting starkly with the sexual excesses of others in the Bloomsbury group.

Virginia seemed to find the sex act terrifying, likely because of sexual abuse she had endured at the hands of her stepbrothers as a young girl. Characterizing herself as "sexually cowardly," she noted metaphorically, "My terror of real life has always kept me in a nunnery." Perhaps seeking refuge from the prospect of a marriage with physical intimacy, she had briefly been engaged to a homosexual friend before wedding Leonard. Later, she went on to explore the nuances of a passionless marriage in her novel *Mrs. Dalloway*.

Leonard worried that sex could be a precipitating factor in Virginia's episodes of madness and reconciled himself to the situation, telling a friend he was ready to forgo carnal pleasure "because she was a genius." In spite of his precautions, less than a year into the marriage he was faced with his wife's longest and most acute mental collapse ever. As with future breakdowns, the episode was linked to the pressure she placed on herself to write and to her extreme sensitivity to criticism. The anxiety of finishing and publishing her first novel, *The Voyage Out*, pushed her into a vicious cycle of headaches, sleeplessness, and hallucinations that were to become the all-too-familiar precursors of a full-on manic depressive breakdown.

During the depressive phase of her illness, she required constant supervision to keep from harming herself and had to be coaxed to eat since she found food repulsive. When she attempted suicide by overdosing in September 1913—barely surviving after having her stomach pumped—Leonard was faced with the difficult decision of whether or not to have her institutionalized.

He opted for the more compassionate, and expensive, solution of hiring private nurses to look after her in their home during back-to-back breakdowns. From then on, he assumed the roles of guardian, caretaker, and parent, as well as spouse and literary adviser. He visited doctors and specialists, kept daily notes on her condition, and closely monitored her sleep and diet. Virginia's life was organized with rigorous discipline, with Leonard ensuring that she avoided stressful situations, late nights, and too many social calls, which could trigger her mania. He also insisted they minimize their time in London, as he knew the bustle of the city could often be too much for her.

Although she consistently acknowledged her great debt to Leonard, Virginia lamented her restricted lifestyle, complaining that her husband had turned her into "a comatose invalid." What she most resented was his decision that they not have children. When she originally agreed to marry him, she had enthused, "I want everything—love, children, adventure, intimacy, work." Her letters to friends for the first six months of marriage regularly mentioned her plans to have a baby. But Leonard, ever-vigilant in safeguarding his wife's health, worried motherhood would be dangerous for her, and after consulting with doctors he ruled out the possibility.

Virginia remained anguished by her childlessness, and once when pondering the possible causes of her continued mental illness, she listed "having no children" as the first reason. Even at age forty she was still pining over her loss, writing, "Never pretend that the things you haven't got are not worth having . . . never pretend that children, for instance, can be replaced by other things."

Critics would later blast Leonard as a repressive force that smothered the troubled writer, but Virginia herself acknowledged that the security and encouragement he provided enabled her creativity to flourish. Each time she completed a novel, she would give the first draft to Leonard and anxiously await his validation. He nurtured and advanced her talent and, despite being a writer in his own right, it was as her editor that he made his mark. While he continued to publish works of nonfiction throughout their marriage, he ceased writing fiction after the publication of his second novel, *The Wise Virgins*. He had begun the work while on honeymoon but prudently waited until Virginia was on the mend from her breakdown to show it to her.

Although she only remarked casually upon the novel in her diary, the unflattering roman à clef of their courtship (in which her fictional counterpart was rendered sexually cold and "emasculated") could not have left Virginia unaffected. Indeed, soon after reading it, she spiraled into a second breakdown that was more virulent than the first. This time she was unusually aggressive and hostile toward everyone around her, especially Leonard, whom she refused to see or talk to for nearly two months.

After she recovered, Leonard made good on their dream of owning a small hand-operated printing press, which he purchased and installed in their dining room. The move inaugurated the birth of their joint venture Hogarth Press, named after the house they were living in at the time. Initially, the press was conceived as a form of occupational therapy for Virginia, with the aim of providing a physical outlet for her energies. Leonard worried about her tendency to become all-consumed by her fictional world and hoped that the "manual occupation . . . would take her mind completely off her work."

The press also served the dual purpose of freeing Virginia to publish her work without fear of the judgments and dictates of editors. "I'm the only woman in England free to write what I like," she exulted. While the collaborative endeavor with Leonard started out as a hobby, it soon turned into a profit-making venture that in some ways took the place of the child they never had.

In addition to publishing nearly all of Virginia's oeuvre, Hogarth Press was the original publisher of other groundbreaking works like T. S. Eliot's *The Waste Land* and the English translations of Freud's work. The aristocratic bisexual writer Vita Sackville-West—better known than Virginia in the early 1920s—also published with the press around the time she and Virginia embarked on a short-lived affair.

Virginia described the glamorous and worldly Vita, ten years her junior and the veteran of several tempestuous liaisons, as "all fire and legs and beautiful plunging ways like a young horse." Conversely, Vita was drawn to the plainer, middle-aged Virginia because of her intellect and writing abilities. "I don't know whether to be dejected or encouraged when I read [her] works. Dejected because I shall never be able to write like that, or encouraged because somebody else can?" she mused.

Because of Virginia's distaste for sex and Vita's fear of her mental instability, their relationship was primarily an affair of the heart and reportedly consummated only twice. In many ways, Vita was a maternal figure to the writer, soothing her childlike anxieties and bolstering her self-esteem in much the same way Leonard did. The exhilaration of the relationship released an astonishing burst of creativity in Virginia, and from 1925 to 1930 she published *Mrs. Dalloway*, *To the Lighthouse*, *A Room of One's Own*, and the historical fantasy *Orlando*, which took Vita as the model for its central character.

Vita, flattered by the tribute, wrote, "I feel like one of those

wax figures in a shop window on which you have hung a robe
stitched with jewels." Although Vita eventually turned her fickle
attentions elsewhere and the romance fizzled out, the friendship
endured until Virginia's death more than a decade later. Vita later
opined, "I still think I might have saved her if only I had been there
and had known the state of mind she was getting into." But it is
unlikely that she or anyone else could have mitigated Virginia's obsessive determination to end her own life.

For the troubled writer, the fear of madness was almost worse
than the madness itself. By the mid-1930s, she felt increasingly unable to battle the cycle of mania and depression that began to over-
take her once more. Her anxiety and fatalism were worsened by
the looming specter of England's involvement in another war with
Germany. (She and Leonard, a Jew, had made a suicide pact, agree-
ing to gas themselves in their garage if Hitler won.) Even her writing, long the anchor that kept her afloat, ceased to keep her demons
at bay. Despairingly, she became convinced that her recent works
were failures, while fearing that she was no longer able to write.

Despite her declining condition, Virginia still had many moments of supreme happiness, writing of one blissful afternoon in
London with Leonard: "We walked around the square lovemaking—after 25 years can't bear to be separate. You see it is an
enormous pleasure being wanted: a wife. And our marriage so
complete." But even the deep love she shared with her husband—
her last line of defense—could only hold for so long. Caught in the
grip of hopelessness, she lost the will to keep fighting. On a cold
March day in 1941, she penned a note to Leonard before setting out
for a walk:

I feel certain that I am going mad again. I feel we can't go
through another of those terrible times. And I shan't recover
this time.

Shortly after writing these words, her walking stick was found on the banks of the river Ouse. Her body, weighted by stones, failed to surface for another three weeks. A devastated Leonard, who had no foreboding of the coming catastrophe, wrote mournfully after her disappearance, "I know that V will not come across the garden from the Lodge, and yet I look in that direction for her. I know that she's drowned and yet I listen for her to come in at the door. I know that it is the last page and yet I turn it over."

ROMANCE WITH DEATH:
SYLVIA PLATH

When Sylvia Plath first locked gazes with fellow poet Ted Hughes at a party, their attraction was instant and explosive: he kissed her on the mouth while she responded by biting his cheek, drawing blood. To ensure a second meeting, he helped himself to her headband and earrings as souvenirs. Although Plath sensed the charismatic Casanova would be trouble—infamously describing him as "a breaker of things and people" and predicting their relationship would end in her death—they wed just four months later.

Seven years into their volatile, passionate coupling, Plath was devastated to discover that Hughes was having an affair with a recent dinner guest, thrice-married temptress Assia Wevill. In a jealous rage, she set alight her husband's papers in a backyard bonfire, an act she later immortalized in the poem "Burning the Letters."

When Hughes continued to vacillate between her and his lover, a humiliated Plath ended the marriage. Following their split, she was seized by a fever of creativity and produced many of the fierce, rage-filled poems that would appear in her posthumous collection *Ariel*. Yet her cathartic poetry was not enough to lift her from the grip of despair, and on a bitterly cold winter morning in 1963, Plath took her own life. Placing bread and milk by her children's beds, she carefully sealed their room before walking into the kitchen and asphyxiating herself with the gas oven.

Pilloried for his wife's death, Hughes never emotionally recovered from the tragedy, which permanently tainted his relationship with Assia Wevill and contributed to her copycat suicide six years later. For decades, he maintained a stony silence about his doomed marriage, only opening up the year before he died in *Birthday Letters*, a series of poems exhuming his relationship with Plath.

PART SEVEN

This Side of Paradise

Count the Ways

ROBERT AND ELIZABETH BARRETT BROWNING

Whoso loves believes the impossible.

—Elizabeth Barrett Browning, *Aurora Leigh*

When she met her future husband, Elizabeth Barrett was a thirty-nine-year-old semireclusive invalid who had only ever dreamed of romance. Before she and fellow poet Robert Browning settled blissfully into married life, the risk-taking pair conducted an unusual, twenty-month courtship that culminated in a secret wedding.

Receiving fan mail was no unusual occurrence for popular poet Elizabeth Barrett, who consigned most of the letters from her ardent admirers to the flames. But in January 1845, a beautifully written note arrived that piqued her interest and ultimately changed her life. "I love your verses with all my heart, dear Miss Barrett . . . and I love you too," wrote an audacious Robert Browning.

Although the effusive correspondent had never laid eyes on Elizabeth, he wasn't a complete stranger. Her distant cousin John Kenyon, a friend of Browning's, had often spoken to her of the bard, whose poetry she had read and enjoyed. Following a tradition popular with teenage girls, his portrait, taken from a magazine, hung on her wall, along with the visages of Wordsworth, Tennyson, and other writers.

Elizabeth was in frail health for much of her life, due to a lung ailment doctors treated with morphine. She became even more reclusive after the death of her brother, who drowned in a sailing accident while visiting her in the seaside town of Torquay, England, where she had gone in hopes of improving her health. Despite having little contact with the outside world, it was Elizabeth who set her romance with Robert in motion when she referred to his book *Bells and Pomegranates* in a work of her own, "Lady Geraldine's Courtship." The poem's titular noblewoman and her suitor read "from Browning some 'Pomegranate,' which, if cut deep / down the middle, / Shows a heart within blood-tinctured, of a veined / humanity!"

The enormous compliment Elizabeth paid Robert in print prompted him to write to her. In his introductory letter, he revealed that they had come close to meeting years earlier, when he had dropped by the Barrett residence with John Kenyon. His friend had wanted to introduce him to Elizabeth, but they were told she was unwell. By the time Robert sent his first missive several years later, the celebrated poet rarely ventured out of her room in her family's London home. Her isolation added to her air of mystery, although she did occasionally entertain callers.

By far the better known of the two poets at the time they began corresponding, Elizabeth was nonetheless starstruck by her new pen pal. Rather than being taken aback by his bold declaration of love, she confided to an acquaintance after receiving his note, "I had a letter from Browning, the poet, last night which threw me into ecstasies." In her reply to Robert, she lamented having missed the opportunity of meeting earlier and tantalizingly

THIS SIDE OF PARADISE221

declared that perhaps they would see each other in person in the future. "Winters shut me up as they do dormouse's eyes; in the spring, *we shall see.*"

During their near-daily exchange of letters, Robert frequently reminded Elizabeth of her promise to meet when the weather turned warmer. She continually put him off, stressing their differences. She was a shut-in, while he had a vibrant social life and traveled abroad. Her poor health contrasted with his intense vitality. At age thirty-nine and six years his senior, she was "scarcely to be called young now." Despite claiming she lived in literature and dreams, Elizabeth got her suitor's hopes up by telling him she would willingly "exchange some of this lumbering, ponderous, helpless knowledge of books, for some experience of life and man."

Robert was undeterred in his quest to set eyes on Elizabeth. Four months after he initiated their correspondence, his patience and persistence were rewarded when he finally received the long-awaited invitation to pay her a visit. In her last letter to him before they met, she teased, "Well! But we are friends till Tuesday—and after perhaps." Robert was even more smitten after meeting the dark-haired poet in person, while she, although equally infatuated, remained hesitant to venture beyond friendship and reminded him of her age and precarious health.

Although Elizabeth's controlling father, who sarcastically called his daughter's friend "Pomegranate man," was used to people calling on her, he would likely have barred the door to Robert if he had known what the future held for the couple. The widower had forbidden all of his nine surviving children to marry, threatening them with disinheritance if they defied his demands. Elizabeth attributed her father's behavior to eccentricity until he put his own wishes above her health. In the fall, less than a year after she began exchanging letters with Robert, doctors advised her to escape the harsh winter weather in London and spend time in Italy's warmer climate. Her father refused to let her go, claiming he didn't want the family separated.

"You are in what I should wonder at as the veriest slavery—and I who *could* free you from it," Robert penned to Elizabeth. After he told her, "Now while I dream, let me once dream! I would marry you now," she accepted his proposal. Knowing how her father was likely to react, Elizabeth insisted they keep their engagement a secret. For the next year, they continued to write and rendezvous while outwardly acting as if nothing had changed. Elizabeth told very few acquaintances about their plans, making sure her siblings in particular were kept in the dark so they would not be accountable when her father finally found out his eldest daughter had fled the fold.

Without Robert, Elizabeth would likely have lived out her days a virtual prisoner in her father's house. Instead, with her fiancé's encouragement, she slowly began reclaiming her life. For the first time in years, she left the confines of her bedroom, initially venturing downstairs and later taking carriage rides, dining out, and even doing a practice run to the church of St. Marylebone, where their wedding was to take place.

Despite Elizabeth's periodic offers to release Robert from their engagement—and a rumor floating around that he was going to marry another woman—the couple wed on September 21, 1846, their ninety-first meeting (he kept track). After the clandestine ceremony, the newlyweds had only a few minutes together before they parted ways. Elizabeth hurried home to keep her family from suspecting anything. In a feat of supreme willpower, she kept the secret for a week before slipping out of her father's house to reunite with Robert. Along on the adventure were two coconspirators, her cocker spaniel, Flush, and her maid, Elizabeth Wilson, who had been in on the secret almost from the beginning (even administering smelling salts to her mistress on the way to the covert ceremony when the overexcited bride-to-be nearly fainted). The fugitive group hastily fled London for the Continent.

While the couple honeymooned in France, en route to Italy, word of their elopement made waves across the English Channel. As expected, Elizabeth's father took the news ungraciously. He refused to discuss her ever again or have any communication with her, returning her letters unopened. Mr. Barrett never relented, maintaining his harsh stance even when Elizabeth wrote him about the birth of his grandson several years later.

In a turn of events that surprised and distressed Elizabeth, her brothers sided with their father and expressed disapproval about what she had done. They believed her spouse, a bank clerk's son, was a fortune hunter, wooing her for her fame and the modest yearly allowance she had inherited from a distant relative. Elizabeth's two younger sisters, though, were firmly on her side, especially Henrietta, who had fallen in love with a naval captain. Following her brave sibling's example, she married him several years later. She too was cut off by the possessive Mr. Barrett, as was a son who eventually walked down the aisle.

The Brownings made their way to Florence, where they settled in a fifteenth-century palazzo that became their home for the next fifteen years. Elizabeth embraced life in Italy, and as her health flourished, so did the couple's social life. Among the writers and artists with whom they hobnobbed were Scottish poet Eliza Ogilvy and American sculptor William Wetmore Story.

By the time of the Brownings' third wedding anniversary, they were parents to a son, nicknamed Pen, and still very much in the honeymoon phase. "We live heart to heart all day long and every day the same," Elizabeth happily informed her sisters. The couple's passion inspired their poetry to new heights. While celebrating their anniversary on a getaway, Elizabeth presented Robert with forty-four sonnets she had written throughout their courtship. The last was dated two days before their wedding. He pronounced them the finest since Shakespeare, an opinion the writer John Ruskin seconded in a review of the collection. Among the love poems is number 43, which begins with the now-famous lines "How do I love thee? Let me count the ways."

It took some convincing on Robert's part before Elizabeth agreed to publish the intimate verses, which appeared as *Sonnets from the Portuguese* (Robert's nickname for his wife was "my little Portuguese" on account of her dark complexion). Enormously popular with readers, the collection greatly enhanced Elizabeth's reputation as a poet. She, in turn, was the muse for Robert's *Men and Women*. He addressed her directly in its concluding verses, writing, "The fifty poems finished! / Take them, Love, the book and me together: / Where the heart lies, let the brain lie also." Although the collection received little attention when it appeared in 1855, it has since become one of his most well-regarded works.

At the time, Browning's greatest claim to fame was less his writing than his role as Elizabeth Barrett's husband. While even some modern-day men might feel threatened by a spouse's greater success, playing second fiddle professionally didn't diminish his affection for his wife. The only known sources of discord among the primarily happy pair were Elizabeth's overt enthusiasm for Italian politics (he was less involved); her affinity for the Victorian fad of spiritualism, the belief that the dead communicate with the living (he thought it was charlatanism); and the velvet pants, ruffled shirts, and other romantic-inspired attire in which she dressed their son (he would have preferred less girly garb).

During the twenty months leading up to their marriage, the prolific pair had exchanged 574 letters, which Elizabeth almost didn't pack when she and her husband fled England. "I *tried* to leave them, & I could not," she admitted. Once they married, there were essentially no more letters, as the couple strove never to spend a night apart. In one close call, the resourceful Robert even hitched a ride back to Florence, in a cart with two priests, after his train was canceled during a day trip to Siena.

The Brownings ultimately were separated by Elizabeth's death on June 30, 1861, after the lung ailment that had afflicted her for much of her life recurred. Knowing she was not likely to survive the night, her husband refused to leave her side. "My Robert—my heavens, my beloved," she exclaimed before passionately kissing him over and over. In the early morning hours, as she slipped in and out of consciousness, he asked her how she felt. "Beautiful," she replied. Elizabeth died in his arms a short while later, with her head resting on his cheek.

After Elizabeth's funeral, Robert returned to London and never again set foot in Florence. He became involved with several women, one of whom rejected his marriage proposal, telling him his heart was buried in the Italian city. The poet remained a widower for the twenty-eight years he outlived his wife, wearing on his watch chain a perpetual reminder of their time together—her gold ring adorned with the inscription "AEI," Greek for "always."

❧ HOW DO I LOVE THEE? ❧

These writers and their selfless partners proved gifts that pull at heart strings, rather than purse strings, are the most memorable of all.

~ **All's well that ends well-rested.** When William Shakespeare passed away, he ignited a four-hundred-year controversy by leaving his "second-best" bed to his wife Anne. Contrary to appearances, the bard's bequest—which led to speculation that his marriage was unhappy—was a romantic gesture rather than a slight: Per Tudor custom, the best bed was reserved for guests while the one he left to Anne would have been the bed on which she conceived and gave birth to their children.

~ **Pay it forward.** When struggling writer O. Henry saved up money for his wife to attend the Chicago World's Fair, she took the cash but never boarded the train. Instead she used the gift to spruce up their sparse cottage with muslin curtains and wicker chairs. Later, while her husband was on the lam avoiding embezzlement charges, she made a lace handkerchief and auctioned it for twenty-five dollars in order to send him a Christmas care package. Her generous acts inspired his tale "The Gift of the Magi."

~ **Scarlett fever.** While Margaret Mitchell was housebound recovering from a car accident, her husband did more than offer tea and sympathy. He came home with a second-hand typewriter and sheaf of paper, saying: "Madam, I greet you on the beginning of a great new career." By then Mitchell had read most of the books at the library and her husband insisted she try writing one of her own. She took up his challenge and set to work on her masterpiece *Gone with the Wind*.

~ **The gift that keeps on giving.** Anglo-American poet W. H. Auden only met his bride the day before their 1935 nuptials. Although a homosexual, he married Erika Mann (daughter of Nobel Prize–winning novelist Thomas Mann) so she could obtain British citizenship and flee Nazi Germany. Auden and his bride never lived together and only met up occasionally but remained married for thirty-three years.

~ **A hair-razing breakup.** The stormy liaison between feminist French novelist George Sand and dissolute poet Alfred de Musset lasted less than two years but was filled with enough quarrels, breakups, and tearful reunions to last a lifetime. When their relationship finally fell apart, Sand said farewell with a dramatic parting gesture: she cut off her dark, waist-length hair and sent it to Musset in a skull.

Romantic Suspense

AGATHA CHRISTIE

Women can accept the fact that a man is a rotter, a swindler, a drug-taker, a confirmed liar, and a general swine without batting an eyelash and without its impairing their affection for the brute in the least! Women are wonderful realists.

—Agatha Christie, *Murder in Mesopotamia*

Just as Agatha Christie was hitting her stride as a novelist, her personal life took a downturn. Not long after her husband demanded a divorce, the crime writer found herself at the center of a real-life mystery that made international news. Still, the spirited writer refused to play victim and triumphed over her two-timing spouse with a killer career and a younger man.

"A Woman Novelist Vanishes" and "The Mystery of Mrs. Christie" were two of the headlines trumpeted by newspapers across England in December 1926. In what could have been a plot taken straight from one of her crime novels, Agatha Christie disappeared and sparked a massive nationwide manhunt.

On the day Christie went missing, she had argued with her

husband, Archie, before he brazenly left to keep a rendezvous with his mistress. Close to midnight that evening, the novelist left their manor house, Styles, outside London, without telling anyone her destination. The next morning her car was found abandoned on the side of a country road, several miles away, with an expired driver's license, a fur coat, and a suitcase inside. Christie was nowhere to be found, seeming to have vanished into thin air.

As police began to investigate, Christie meanwhile checked into the ritzy Swan Hydropathic Hotel in northern England, using an interesting alias, Teresa Neele, incorporating the surname of her husband's mistress. During her stay at the Swan, in the Yorkshire spa town of Harrogate, Christie spent her time shopping, dining, and playing cards. "Mrs. Neele" also chatted amiably with fellow guests about the case of the missing writer, whose latest book, *The Murder of Roger Ackroyd*, was a best seller that year.

When a hotel employee finally tipped off police about Christie's whereabouts, Archie headed to Harrogate for a reunion with the wayward writer. According to a witness, she "only seemed to regard him as an acquaintance . . . whose identity she could not quite fix." Eager to get on with his own life, Archie attempted to lay the matter to rest by issuing a statement confirming her identity. "She has suffered from the most complete loss of memory and I do not think she knows who she is," he told the media. "She does not know me and she does not know where she is. I am hoping that rest and quiet will restore her."

To the consternation of Christie's curious fans, her clandestine getaway has never been fully explained. She refused ever to speak publicly about going on the lam and, in the ensuing years, only sparingly granted interviews to the media, which had made a spectacle of her private life during her disappearance.

Leading up to the fateful night Christie left Styles, she was in a fragile emotional state. Not only was her marriage likely coming to an end, she was grief stricken over her mother's sudden death after a bout of pneumonia earlier in the year. Barely eating or sleeping, she had to tie up her mother's affairs and clean out her childhood home almost single-handedly. "A terrible sense of loneliness was coming over me," she admits in *An Autobiography*. "I don't think I realized that for the first time in my life I was really ill. I had always been extremely strong and I had no understanding of how unhappiness, worry and overwork could affect your physical health."

Although Christie makes no reference to the missing eleven days in her memoir, she does allude to a reason for her bizarre behavior. After hearing another woman recount symptoms similar to the ones she experienced prior to her disappearance, Christie replied, "I think you had better be very careful; it is probably the beginning of a nervous breakdown."

In addition to being a deliberate no-show while Christie dealt with her mother's passing, her caddish husband moved out soon afterward. He informed her he was in love with Nancy Neele, an attractive secretary who, unlike his wife, shared his obsessive passion for golf. Archie later returned to Styles in an attempt to repair his marriage, largely for the benefit of the couple's young daughter. Despite initiating the reconciliation, he treated his wife abysmally, barely talking to her or even replying when she spoke to him, and eventually he reiterated his desire for a divorce.

"His coming back was, I think, a mistake, because it brought home to him how keen his feeling was. Again and again he would say to me, 'I can't stand not having what I want, and I can't stand not being happy. Everybody can't be happy—somebody has got to be unhappy,'" Christie recalled. As Archie made abundantly clear, she was to be the unfortunate "somebody."

The shy yet popular future writer first crossed paths with Corporal Archibald Christie at a party when she was twenty-one. She fell for the dashing aviator and soon afterward broke it off with her fiancé (she had already avoided two other "near escapes from getting married"). The couple wed two years later, on Christmas Eve 1914. But married life had to wait, as the groom was serving in World War I with the Royal Flying Corps.

During the war years, Christie volunteered as a nurse at a hospital in Torquay, the seaside town in southern England where she was born and raised by a British mother and an American father. For a time, she worked in the dispensary, where she picked up the knowledge about poisons that would feature in her fiction. To help fill her idle hours, Christie took up her sister's challenge to write a detective story and began working on what would become her debut novel, *The Mysterious Affair at Styles*.

The newlyweds saw each other sporadically when Archie was home on leave and finally set up house together four years after saying "I do." The decorated Colonel Christie landed a job with the Air Ministry in London before embarking on a business career. In 1920, a year after their daughter was born, Christie published *The Mysterious Affair at Styles*, launching her literary career and introducing Belgian sleuth Hercule Poirot.

With Archie's encouragement (and his hunch that there was money to be made), Christie penned a second crime caper, *The Secret Adversary*, featuring detective duo Tommy Beresford and Tuppence Cowley. The tale arrived in stores in January 1922, just as Christie embarked on a ten-month round-the-world excursion with Archie, who had been invited to join a delegation promoting the upcoming British Empire Exhibition. They journeyed to South Africa, Australia, New Zealand, Canada, and Hawaii, where they were among the first Britons to surf standing up. When the couple returned to England, they settled in the country abode from which she later disappeared, naming it Styles in honor of Christie's inaugural novel.

After a dozen years of seeming domestic contentment, Christie was blindsided when her husband, whom she idealized, admitted his adulterous betrayal and announced he was leaving her for Neele. "With those words, that part of my life—my happy, successful, confident life—ended," confessed Christie, who initially believed the situation would blow over. "There had never been any suspicion of anything of that kind in our lives. We had been happy together, and harmonious." Shocked and bewildered, she blamed herself for her husband's defection and thought she "must in some way have been inadequate to fill Archie's life."

When word of Archie's affair became public knowledge during Christie's disappearance, he was suspected of doing away with his wife and pilloried by the press as a philanderer and possible murderer. Others thought the novelist had staged the getaway to embarrass her unfaithful spouse. Some suggested Christie had committed suicide or run away with a lover, while the more outlandish notion arose that she was researching a plot for a new book. Public opinion at the time was largely negative, with many people believing it was a hoax and that she had deliberately orchestrated it as a publicity stunt.

Police organized what was dubbed the "Great Sunday Hunt," mobilizing volunteers—some five thousand to fifteen thousand, depending on reports—to look for Christie near the wooded area where she was last seen. A pond in the area was dragged for her body and, for the first time in British history, airplanes were used in the search for a missing person. A high-profile consultant on the case was Sherlock Holmes creator Sir Arthur Conan Doyle, who enlisted the aid of a psychometrist (someone who can purportedly ascertain facts about an object or a person associated with it). The diviner handled a glove of Christie's and pronounced that the wearer would be found alive. Mystery writer Dorothy L. Sayers also got in on the action, taking part in the "Great Sunday Hunt." In a piece she wrote about the case for a British newspaper, she contradicted police brass by declaring that she didn't believe Christie's body would be found in the woods.

Newspapers offered sizeable sums for information and hired clairvoyants to discern the writer's whereabouts. The mysterious vanishing act made headlines throughout Europe and even across the pond. After Christie was discovered at Harrogate, the *New York Times* announced the news on its front page.

Doctors diagnosed Christie as having amnesia, perhaps caused by a concussion when her car ran off the road the night she undertook her secretive journey from Styles. While undergoing hypnosis, the novelist recalled making her way to London, where she saw a poster touting the healing benefits of the Yorkshire spa-hotel where she eventually resurfaced. After being found, Christie returned to Styles with Archie, although she ultimately agreed to grant him the divorce he was desperately seeking.

Christie's struggles and disappointments on the home front, as well as her happily married early years, are mirrored in *Unfinished Portrait*, one of six novels she wrote under the pseudonym Mary Westmacott. The fictional Celia and Dermott's relationship so closely resembled the author's history with Archie that her second husband, Sir Max Mallowan, claimed in his memoirs, "In Celia we have more nearly than anywhere else a portrait of Agatha."

After her divorce, distraught and being hounded by the press, Christie sought a change of scenery. Striking out solo in 1928, partly to recapture her sense of self and prove her independence, the thirty-eight-year-old writer fulfilled a lifelong dream of traveling aboard the Orient Express. Her destination was Baghdad, an exotic, off-the-beaten path locale popular with well-to-do travelers. While there, she indulged her interest in archaeology by visiting a dig at Ur in southern Iraq.

When Christie returned to Ur two years later, more than just ancient artifacts were on display. There she met Max Mallowan, a tall, dark-haired archaeologist fourteen years her junior, who was drafted to show her around the area. Intrigued by his quiet yet perceptive demeanor, she hit it off with him immediately. The daring duo set out on a tour of Baghdad and the Middle Eastern desert, where they explored ruins and had to be rescued after their car became stuck in the sand.

The antithesis of the self-absorbed, fickle Archie, Mallowan proved steadfast from the start. En route to England, Christie intended to part ways with him midway through their trip. But when she received word during a stopover that her daughter was dangerously ill, the archaeologist changed his plans so he could escort her the entire way home. Their friendship took an unexpected turn several months later when Max popped the question during a weekend at her home. He proposed in her bedroom, knocking on the door under the pretense of returning a book.

Believing their age difference had ruled out a romantic relationship, Christie was caught by surprise and spent two hours trying to talk Max out of his decision. She had vowed that she would never again be at anyone's mercy, like she had been with Archie. "The only person who can really hurt you in life is a husband. Nobody else is close enough," she reasoned. After mulling over Max's proposal for weeks, Christie decided to risk the heartbreak and married the younger man. Her concerns about their age difference proved groundless, and she later quipped, "An archaeologist is the best husband any woman can get. Just consider: the older she gets, the more interested he is in her."

Her accommodating spouse even agreed to her vehement request that he never play golf, while she happily traipsed along on his excavations. On archaeological digs, she often took on the tasks of a junior assistant, cleaning and repairing objects, matching pottery fragments, and cataloging finds. The pair's travels in the Middle East inspired atmospheric tales like *Death on the Nile*, *Death Comes as the End*, and *Murder in Mesopotamia*, set on an archaeological dig.

Mallowan was finalizing his autobiography when Christie passed away in 1976, her death leaving him feeling empty after forty-five loving, merry years together. He reminisced about his wife's creative mind and her capacity for infusing life with zest, finding comfort in the huge volume of condolence letters he received from her fans. Mallowan was touched to see that they recognized the "love and happiness which Agatha radiated both in her person and in her books."

∾ AWAKE YE MUSES NINE ∾

Since the days of the Greek lyric poets, writers have looked to muses—women who exist somewhere between the earthly and the ethereal—to stimulate their creativity and inspire their work to new heights.

Match these writers to the muses who moved them.

___1. In addition to penning this flame-haired siren a book of passionate love sonnets, Chilean poet **Pablo Neruda** built her a hilltop hideaway in Santiago, where they rendezvoused behind his wife's back for five years.

___2. Although he met her only twice, and both were married to others, **Dante Alighieri** wrote about his Florentine muse for decades and used her as the model for an ideal woman in his *Divine Comedy*.

___3. Between crafting serious poetry, romantic poet **John Keats** would compose sonnets to his flirtatious next-door neighbor. His celebrated "Bright Star" is a plea for her everlasting love, which he compares to a steadfast star.

___4. **Edgar Allan Poe** coyly hid the name of this woman in the lines of his poem "A Valentine," published in the New York *Evening Mirror* in 1846.

___5. **Graham Greene's** novel *The End of the Affair* centers on an adulterous liaison between a writer and the wife of a civil servant during World War II, mirroring his own illicit relationship with this married American.

___6. The events in the **James Joyce** masterpiece *Ulysses* unfold over the course of a single day: June 16, 1904, selected to commemorate his first date with his wife, the free-spirited model for the novel's Molly Bloom.

___7. This celebrated Moscow actress, who brought **Anton Chekhov**'s leading ladies to life on stage and later became his wife, inspired the character of Masha in *Three Sisters*.

___8. To salvage a lackluster honeymoon, this newlywed feigned an episode of spirit-guided writing to impress her husband, **W. B. Yeats**, and found herself being used regularly as a medium to prompt his poetry.

___9. The sparkling intellect and charm of this Russian muse stoked the creative fires of no less than philosopher **Friedrich Nietzsche**, poet **Rainer Maria Rilke**, and psychoanalyst **Sigmund Freud**.

A. Nora Barnacle

B. Catherine Walston

C. Georgie Hyde-Lees

D. Fanny Brawne

E. Olga Knipper

F. Matilde Urrutia

G. Lou Andreas-Salomé

H. Beatrice Portinari

I. Fanny Osgood

Answers: 1. F, 2. H, 3. D, 4. I, 5. B, 6. A, 7. E, 8. C, 9. G

Delicious Dish

GERTRUDE STEIN AND ALICE B. TOKLAS

> What is marriage, is marriage protection or religion, is marriage renunciation or abundance, is marriage a stepping-stone or an end. What is marriage.
>
> —Gertrude Stein, *The Mother of Us All*

Before "coming out" became commonplace, Gertrude Stein and Alice B. Toklas lived openly as a couple. Setting up house together in Paris, the American expats fashioned a life for themselves centered on art, literature, and each other. Smitten from the moment they met, the trailblazing pair's relationship was far more successful than many traditional marriages.

"Please Miss Stein and Miss Toklas, don't disappoint us: we do be expecting you!" entreated a *Vanity Fair* editor prior to the pair's much-anticipated U.S. arrival in November 1934. From the time the ship ferrying them from France docked in New York Harbor until they departed six months later, the middle-aged celebrities were front-page news.

Their newfound fame was a result of the best seller *The*

Autobiography of Alice B. Toklas. Written by Gertrude, the irreverent book is told in the voice of her longtime love, Alice, and recalls their life together. An item for almost thirty years by the time they ventured to America, the duo had been brought together by an unlikely matchmaker: Mother Nature.

When an earthquake rumbled through San Francisco on April 18, 1906, it rattled the Toklas residence, where twenty-eight-year-old Alice was living a humdrum existence, keeping house for her widowed father and brother. All that changed after a chance encounter with Gertrude's brother and sister-in-law, who were visiting from Paris to check on the postquake condition of real estate they owned. Intrigued by the Steins' glamorous stories of life abroad, the adventure-craving Alice eventually packed her bags and set sail for Paris.

Her first stop in the French capital was a soiree at the Steins' place, where she barely spared a glance for her hosts or anyone else in attendance. Her attention was focused solely on Gertrude. "She was a golden brown presence, burned by the Tuscan sun and with a golden glint in her warm brown hair," Alice reminisced in her memoir, *What Is Remembered.* She heard a bell chime in her head after they were introduced, a sound signaling she was in the presence of genius (or so Gertrude claimed).

Not wasting any time, Gertrude asked Alice to take a stroll with her the next day in the Luxembourg Gardens. They quickly became constant companions and two years later moved in together. Their legendary salon was attended by the likes of Pablo Picasso, Ernest Hemingway, and Man Ray. Their role at the center of the Parisian avant-garde fascinated their fellow Americans, who reveled in the colorful stories depicted in Gertrude's autobiography.

The sixty-year-old writer relished her late-blooming rise to fame, which saw her and Alice treated like royalty during their coast-to-coast American tour. Along with being invited to tea with Eleanor Roosevelt at the White House, they rode along in a squad car with Chicago police officers, partied in Hollywood with Charlie Chaplin and Dashiell Hammett, and were given the keys to Edgar Allan Poe's dorm room shrine at the University of Virginia. For six months, with Alice at her side, Gertrude traveled across the United States by car, train, and plane, delivering lectures to packed audiences. Meanwhile, Alice attended to the writer's creature comforts, making sure she dined on her preferred foods—honeydew melon and oysters—before appearances.

The puritanical American public seemed unfazed by the fact that the media darlings were a lesbian couple. To Gertrude's surprise, there were no insulting letters, crank calls, or other displays of bigotry while she and Alice crisscrossed the country. The pair's relationship was essentially an open secret; they didn't flaunt that they were lovers, but neither did they try to hide it. They were interviewed together in their shared hotel room, and Alice appeared alongside Gertrude in almost every published photo.

By contrast with other bed-hopping, divorcing couples in their social circle, Gertrude and Alice's devout, monogamous relationship seemed almost old-fashioned. In many ways they resembled a typical heterosexual couple. Gertrude was the more masculine half of the duo and referred to herself as Alice's husband, while Alice tirelessly managed the details of their home life. Since Alice willingly took on the household responsibilities, Gertrude was free to spend her time writing, acquiring paintings, holding court during her salon, befriending and mentoring up-and-coming artists and writers, and ruminating on her genius.

Emphasizing their respective gender roles, each cultivated a dramatically different personal style. Short and stout, Gertrude (who reminded British poet Edith Sitwell of an Easter Island statue) never donned trousers but did favor plain, simply cut or loose-fitting attire in muted, solid colors. When she decided to trade her long hair for a close-cropped, Caesar-style cut, Alice did the shearing.

The more feminine Alice often wore couture dresses in bold colors or floral prints, flashy earrings, and feather-topped hats. She sported her dark hair in a bob with long, fringed bangs (reportedly to cover a cyst that Picasso compared to a unicorn's horn) and refused to remove the fuzzy down on her upper lip. Foodie James Beard described Alice as "nicely ugly," while a magazine editor once noted that other faces seemed nude in comparison. After the couple stayed with Gertrude's family in Baltimore during their U.S. tour, a three-year-old relative candidly remarked that she liked the man but wondered why the lady had a mustache.

Beyond their distinctive appearances and division of household affairs, the couple's adherence to convention played out in other ways. Although they couldn't make it legal, Gertrude proposed to Alice, offering her a ring and suggesting they move in together. Afterward, they honeymooned in Spain. When they bought a Ford during World War I, so they could distribute medical supplies in the French countryside, Gertrude always took the wheel and Alice organized the goods.

At times Gertrude could even be chauvinistic toward other women, such as when, rather than remark on her prose, she informed fellow writer Djuna Barnes that she had gorgeous gams. And when creative types came to converse with Gertrude, who enjoyed the adoring attention of handsome young men like Hemingway, their wives were banned from the conversation and expected to chitchat with Alice about clothes and cooking.

Relishing her role as domestic goddess and gatekeeper, Alice took on the task of vetting the steady stream of callers that came to see Gertrude. She even did the dirty work, like dumping friends who had worn out their welcome, usually accomplished with a terse phone call or note. As playwright Thornton Wilder, a longtime friend of the couple, put it, "Alice was merely the dragon protecting the treasure."

Although Alice excelled at playing the piano and once considered making a career of it, she ultimately decided her talent wasn't up to par. Instead she devoted herself to cultivating Gertrude's literary achievements. She directly contributed to her partner's professional endeavors, acting as typist, sounding board, critic, editor, publicist, and muse. At one point she even launched a publishing company dedicated solely to producing Gertrude's modernist works, which confounded mainstream publishers because of their experimental style.

"What would Alice have been without Gertrude?" an acquaintance of theirs pondered. Likewise, Gertrude might have toiled forever in obscurity if not for Alice, who offered her emotional stability, an abundance of encouragement, and inspiration for the book that made her a celebrity. Early on, even as Gertrude bitterly lamented her growing stack of manuscripts with no hope of publication in sight, Alice's support was steadfast.

When Alice's own autobiography appeared after Gertrude's death, rancorous reviewers maligned the life she had chosen and suggested she was nothing more than her dynamic lover's pale shadow. One went so far as to call her memoir "the sad, slight book of a woman who all her life has looked in a mirror and seen someone else." But there was much more to Alice behind the deliberately crafted persona of helpmate to a talented spouse. A spirit of adventure inspired her to leave the family fold and forge a new existence abroad, and a rebellious streak led to impetuous acts like throwing her cherry-red corset out a train window during a trip through the sweltering Italian countryside. While Alice's modest, subdued public persona complemented Gertrude's domineering personality, she was secure enough to stand up to her partner, even rebuking her in front of salon guests on occasion.

According to some acquaintances, Alice encouraged her partner's dependence on her as a way to drive others out of her life. Rumor has it Gertrude's brother and roommate, Leo, was the first casualty. He initially called Alice's move to their flat a blessing and gave up his study for her to use as a bedroom, but he later had harsh words for the pair. He derided Alice as "a kind of abnormal vampire who gives more than she takes" and maligned his sister's excessive dependence on her helpmate. Leo declared he had "seen trees strangled by vines in this same way." The bickering siblings, who had lived together for many years, were more than ready to go their separate ways by the time Alice moved in.

While Alice might have been blamed unfairly for Gertrude's falling-out with Leo, she did send others packing. One was American patroness Mabel Dodge, who entertained the couple at her Italian villa. When the hostess flirted with Gertrude and received a sultry look in return, Alice stormed away from the luncheon table, signaling the beginning of the end of Dodge's friendship with the writer.

Largely immune to criticisms of their interdependence, Gertrude and Alice even bestowed pet names on each other: the writer was Lovey, while Alice was Pussy. Lovey unabashedly expressed her affection and desire for Pussy in verse, penning lines like "Alice B. is the wife for me" and describing her as a "tiny dish of delicious." After late-night writing sessions, Gertrude would often leave missives—by turns romantic, humorous, sexually charged, or apologetic—for early rising Alice, who responded with notes of her own to her "strong-strong husband."

As Gertrude romanced Alice with words, the latter used her skills in the kitchen to do likewise. In *Aromas and Flavors of Past and Present: A Book of Exquisite Cooking*, one of two culinary-themed books she wrote (the other is *The Alice B. Toklas Cookbook*, with its notorious recipe for hashish fudge), she offered some evocative advice that showed her clever sense of humor. "Consider the menus carefully, that there is a harmony and a suitable progression," she counseled. "In the menu there should be a climax and a culmination. Come to it gently. One will suffice."

During their four decades together, the couple endured both world wars in France, harrowing experiences that only served to strengthen their bond. They garnered controversy for remaining in the country during World War II under the protection of a long-time friend who supported the pro-Nazi Vichy government. While living in the south of France, where they rode out the majority of the war, they endured some of the same shortages and hardships as their neighbors. As Jews, lesbians, and Americans, they were particularly vulnerable to persecution but nonetheless refused to leave their adopted country and ignored warnings to flee to Switzerland.

In 1946, two years after World War II came to a close in Europe, Gertrude, suffering from stomach cancer, didn't make it out of the operating room alive. The grieving Alice survived her partner by nearly two decades. Not long before her own demise at age eighty-nine, she converted to Catholicism, asking the priest if it would allow her to see Gertrude in the afterlife. The soul mates are buried side by side in Paris's Père-Lachaise Cemetery, where Alice does not have a marker of her own. Her name, date of birth, and death date are etched in gold on the back of Gertrude's headstone, right where she wanted them.

❧ FIRST IMPRESSIONS ❧

Cupid's arrow often took swift aim when writers met their mates, even if the targets of their affections were already taken. Occasionally, though, the cherubic archer missed his mark and had to try again.

~ **With friends like these.** When John Steinbeck invited an actress to spend the weekend with him in northern California, she unwittingly turned into a third wheel by bringing along a married pal as chaperone. The novelist fell hard and fast for his date's friend, Elaine Scott, with whom he tied the knot a year later.

~ **He's just not that into you.** When future culinary icon Julia Child first met the man who became her husband, sparks didn't exactly fly. "It wasn't like lightning striking the barn on fire," admitted Paul Child of the pair's early encounter while they were stationed abroad during World War II. He initially deemed Julia unsophisticated, while she thought his looks were lacking. But by the time the war ended, Paul was reciting love poems to Julia while she told a friend, "He loves good food, so I've got to learn to cook."

~ **A picture is worth a thousand words.** Mark Twain's crush on his future wife began before he even met her. When a fellow steamship passenger showed him a miniature portrait of his sister, Twain was immediately intrigued and accepted an invitation to dine with the family when he returned home. Olivia Langdon did not disappoint in person, and when Twain called on her a second time, his visit lasted a marathon twelve hours.

~ **Sibling rivalry.** The sickly, reclusive Sophia Peabody was an unlikely femme fatale but nonetheless managed to steal her sister's fiancé. When Nathaniel Hawthorne finally met the frail beauty, he couldn't take his eyes off her, ultimately jilting Sophia's sister and marrying her instead.

~ **Pickup artist.** Despite being worse for wear after a five-day bender, celebrity mystery writer Dashiell Hammett charmed aspiring screenwriter Lillian Hellman at a 1930 Hollywood soiree. Although both were married, they left the party together and spent the night in Hammett's car, talking about T. S. Eliot until dawn. Their meeting marked the start of a rocky, thirty-year affair that lasted until Hammett's death.

Come Sail Away

ROBERT LOUIS STEVENSON

❧

What woman would ever be lured into marriage, so much more dangerous than the wildest sea?

—Robert Louis Stevenson, "Aes Triplex"

Scottish writer Robert Louis Stevenson threw caution to the wind after falling for a sharp-shooting American frontier woman and pursuing her across two continents. Their globe-trotting life together was as adventurous as his swashbuckling fictional tales, taking them from an abandoned California mining town to a voyage through the South Pacific.

❧

When Robert Louis Stevenson received a telegram from Fanny Van de Grift Osbourne in July 1879, his response was decisive and dramatic. He set out from his native Scotland, bound for California, crossing an ocean and a continent to be with her. The contents of the mysterious missive were never revealed, thought to be either word that Fanny was finally divorcing her faithless husband or an attempt to break off her relationship with Stevenson. Either way, he wasted no time in reuniting with the object of his affections.

Legend has it that it was love at first sight when twenty-five-year-old Stevenson, then a fledgling writer, met Fanny at an artists' colony in Grez-sur-Loing, France, three years before his transcontinental voyage. Respectable women were a rare sight in the traditionally male environment, and the married American caused a stir when she showed up. Taken with her good looks, intelligence, and outspokenness, the group of painters and writers quickly accepted Fanny into their midst, and she and her two children, eighteen-year-old Belle and eight-year-old Lloyd, were popular from the start.

The amiable, eccentric Stevenson also made a memorable impression when he appeared, vaulting through an open window at a hotel where the guests were dining and taking a seat next to Fanny. He swiftly fell "damnably in love," but she was more interested in his cousin, Bob, an aspiring artist who, in turn, was infatuated with Belle. Charmed by Stevenson's wit and silver tongue, it wasn't long, though, before Fanny's relationship with the "tall, gaunt Scotsman, with a face like Raphael" took a romantic turn.

Although Stevenson surprised some at Grez by pursuing Fanny, a decade his senior, instead of her teenage daughter, his infatuation with the married mother followed a familiar pattern. Prior to meeting her, he had been besotted with a beautiful friend of the family who was also ten years older. Stevenson later dedicated *A Child's Garden of Verses* to another mature female figure who helped shape his childhood and adolescence, governess Alison Cunningham, whom he peculiarly referred to as "My second Mother, my first Wife."

Fanny's marriage was all but over by the time she met Stevenson. She had given her philandering husband, Sam, ample opportunities to change his ways during their nearly two-decade marriage. When his infidelity became excessively flagrant, she thumbed her nose at Victorian mores, leaving him behind while she headed to

Europe with her children. After a stay in Antwerp, Belgium, the avid amateur painter and her daughter both enrolled in a Parisian art school. Tragedy followed when her youngest son, four-year-old Hervey, died of scrofulous tuberculosis, a painful illness that primarily affects the lymph nodes in the throat. Devastated, Fanny sought solace and a change of scenery in Grez.

Years earlier, while seventeen-year-old Fanny was embarking on marriage and motherhood, Stevenson lived a sheltered childhood in Edinburgh, where chronic illness frequently kept him housebound. An only child, he later rebelled against his middle-class upbringing, refusing to continue the family tradition of becoming a lighthouse engineer and denouncing his parents' Calvinism. Dependent upon his father's financial largesse for his survival, Stevenson consented to a fallback career in law but never practiced.

In contrast to Stevenson's cloistered life, Fanny, who was born and raised in Indiana, led a rough-and-tumble existence after her marriage to the erratic Sam Osbourne, who often left her behind while he sought out adventure and get-rich-quick schemes. In remote Nevada mining camps, where her husband prospected for silver, she toted a gun and learned how to use it, rolled and smoked cigarettes, and made her own clothes. When her husband and his traveling party disappeared and were mistakenly presumed to have been killed by Indians, Fanny thought she was a widow and for two years supported her family by working as a seamstress.

When Stevenson first met Fanny, her colorful past inspired him to give her the nickname "Wild Woman of the West." The feisty American embodied the adventurous spirit he later came to imbue in his novels, and her experiences, unlike those of the more proper women in his social circle, gave her "an atmosphere of thrilling New World romance" that irresistibly appealed to the writer.

After his "Wild Woman" left Europe and returned to America, the long-distance separation did nothing to diminish Stevenson's passion. Her telegram a year later spurred him into action. Against the wishes of his parents, and ignoring the advice of friends, he set out for America. Not only did the lengthy journey by ship and rail take a serious toll on his already precarious health, but he arrived in the seaside town of Monterey, California, to a crushing blow. Despite a failed attempt at patching things up with her husband, Fanny was undecided about continuing her relationship with Stevenson.

It was only after he nearly died during a camping trip in the mountains outside Monterey, where he collapsed and was rescued by two ranchers, that Fanny changed her mind. She formally separated from Sam Osbourne, but out of consideration for him, and for Stevenson's parents, the couple waited a respectable five months after the divorce was finalized before marrying. During that time, the writer's parents and friends waged a relentless battle to persuade him to change his mind. But Stevenson stood firm, believing the delays and challenges he and Fanny had weathered only proved the strength of their relationship. "I am now engaged to be married to the woman whom I have loved for three years and a half," he told to a friend. "At least I will boast myself so far; I do not think many wives are better loved than mine will be."

The nuptials took place on May 19, 1880, after Fanny helped nurse Stevenson—who was ultimately diagnosed with tuberculosis—back to health. From the start, the couple's life together was focused on his well-being; frequent and violent lung hemorrhages would often leave him spitting up blood and at death's door. When the San Francisco fog proved damaging to his sensitive lungs, the newlyweds headed north to the Napa Valley. Strained finances forced them to abandon the hotel cottage they were renting, and instead they spent two months living in a ramshackle bunkhouse in Silverado, an abandoned mining town. After departing California, they roamed around Europe for several years, from Scotland and the coast of England to the Swiss Alps and the south of France, ever in search of a climate that would benefit the writer's fragile health.

Stevenson's parents, who initially opposed his marriage to a divorcée and foreigner, embraced their new daughter-in-law after the couple arrived in Scotland. His father in particular developed a close relationship with Fanny, and as a show of his affection he bought the couple a house and footed the bill for the interior design. Stevenson's friends, however, were divided in their opinions of his wife. The writer Sidney Colvin described her as "a character as strong, as interesting, and romantic as his own; an inseparable sharer of all his thoughts, and staunch companion of all his adventures." Others thought she was overbearing, selfish, and stifled Stevenson's creativity. Protective of her husband's health, Fanny refused to allow anyone with a cold—which, she noticed, her husband was particularly susceptible to contracting—to see him. Some acquaintances perceived this as a snub.

During their fourteen-year marriage, Stevenson—who had published two travelogues and an essay collection at the time they wed—produced his most memorable and enduring works, *Treasure Island* and *Kidnapped* among them. A staunch supporter of her husband's writing, Fanny was often the first to read a novel or story in progress. The duo even collaborated on *The Dynamiter*, a collection of tales based on ones Fanny had spun to pass the time during a stay in the south of France. Before Stevenson's father passed away, he extracted a promise from his son that he would never publish anything without Fanny's approval.

Stevenson's riveting psychological drama *The Strange Case of Dr. Jekyll and Mr. Hyde*, which set readers abuzz on both sides of the Atlantic, owed its success in large part to Fanny. After inspiration for the tale about the dark side of man's dual nature came to Stevenson in a dream, he presented her with an early draft, along with the assertion that it was the best thing he had ever written. She thought it was the worst. "I wrote pages of criticism pointing out that he had here a great moral allegory that the dream was obscuring," explained Fanny, who got into heated arguments with her husband over the tale. The original manuscript was consigned to the flames by Stevenson, it was believed, until a letter surfaced in 2000 in which Fanny alludes to having made the dramatic move to burn it.

When Stevenson returned to the United States in 1887, soon after *Dr. Jekyll and Mr. Hyde* reached its shores, his reputation preceded him. The book's publication had catapulted him to fame, and when the ship carrying the writer and his family docked in New York, he was besieged by reporters. After being feted by friends and fans, the couple headed for the Adirondack Mountains to seek out a doctor pioneering an open-air cure for tuberculosis. The bracing climate was a boon to Stevenson's health, but the frigid winter temperatures got the adventurer thinking about a sojourn to the South Seas.

Less enamored of an itinerant lifestyle than Stevenson, Fanny nevertheless put her husband's health first and made his dream of touring the South Pacific a reality. Ever resourceful, she found them a yacht to rent and arranged supplies. During the three years they sailed the high seas on several different voyages, she endured continual seasickness and occasional danger, including treacherous storms, a near-shipwreck, and an onboard fire, from which she bravely rescued a trunk of Stevenson's manuscripts.

Enchanted with the South Pacific, the Stevensons settled on the Samoan island of Upolu, where they spent their final four years together. The idyllic setting agreed with the writer, who was generally in good physical form and in the midst of one of his most productive periods ever. However, it was Fanny's health that gave the couple cause for concern as she began to suffer from breakdowns, refused to eat, and was seized by violent outbursts and hallucinations. Accounts vary widely as to what ailed her, among them the suggestion that she had Bright's disease (a kidney ailment) or that she simply snapped after years of emotional strain brought on by her disastrous first marriage, the death of her youngest son, and the constant vigil she kept over her husband's health.

Despite his anxiety about Fanny, Stevenson professed, "If I could die just now, or say in half a year, I should have had a splendid time of it on the whole." Less than ten months later, he passed away from a cerebral hemorrhage. Among the outpouring of condolence letters the bereaved widow received was one from Henry James, a longtime friend of the couple. "You are nearest to the pain, because you were nearest to the joy and the pride," the novelist consoled her.

Fanny thought to live out the rest of her life in Samoa, where she had strong memories of Stevenson, but circumstances forced her to relinquish their island retreat. After her death, her daughter brought her ashes back to Samoa, where they were interred alongside Stevenson's in a hilltop grave overlooking the sea. Inscribed on her headstone is the concluding stanza from his poem "My Wife":

Teacher, tender, comrade, wife,
A fellow-farer true through life,
Heart-whole and soul free
The august father
Gave to me.

❧ YOU'VE GOT MAIL ❧

Writers didn't just use their way with words in poetry and prose—their love letters benefited as well. In eloquent missives, they declared their everlasting affection, admitted to illicit feelings, and even confessed the occasional shortcoming.

~ **Anonymously yours.** "In spite of myself, my imagination carries me to you. I grasp you, I kiss you, I caress you," novelist Honoré de Balzac professed to Ewelina Hańska, a married Polish noblewoman. Their epistolary romance began after he received an anonymous 1832 letter signed "The Foreigner," which both praised and criticized his work. The correspondent, Ewelina, revealed herself soon after. The Frenchman and his pen pal finally tied the knot after eighteen years, only to be parted five months later when Balzac passed away.

~ **Poetry in motion.** "I almost wish we were butterflies and liv'd but three summer days—three such days with you I could fill with more delight than fifty common years could ever contain," proclaimed romantic poet John Keats to his fiancée, Fanny Brawne. Although Fanny was the proverbial girl next door and they lived in adjoining houses, their contact was restricted by the poet's ill health. They relied on letters to communicate throughout much of their courtship, until tuberculosis finally claimed the twenty-five-year-old poet.

~ **Cold feet.** "I have often thought that the best mode of life for me would be to sit in the innermost room of a spacious locked cellar with my writing things and a lamp," melancholic writer Franz Kafka lamented to girlfriend Felice Bauer. He wrote her hundreds of angst-filled letters during their long-distance romance, stringing her along for five years and proposing twice before finally acknowledging he wasn't husband material.

~ **What she said.** "It's my love that will make me immortal. When I am dead, I will love you still. My body and my life will be used up before one single particle of my love disappears," avowed Juliette Drouet to Victor Hugo in one of some twenty thousand letters she wrote him during their fifty-year affair. Many were lavish love notes that stoked the novelist's ego. Unbeknownst to Juliette, Hugo surreptitiously cribbed from them to use in letters he sent to another mistress.

~ **Language of love.** "My heart is full of you, none other than you in my thoughts, yet when I seek to say to you something not for the world, words fail me. If you were here—and Oh that you were, my Susie, we need not talk at all, our eyes would whisper for us, and your hand fast in mine, we would not ask for language." The recipient of Emily Dickinson's impassioned letter was her former classmate and sister-in-law, Susan Gilbert, who may have been one of the poet's secret crushes.

ACKNOWLEDGMENTS

If Charles Dickens, Anaïs Nin, and the other writers we feature hadn't been two-timers, bigamists, risk takers, and unabashed romantics—resulting in love lives that make for great reading—*Writers Between the Covers* wouldn't exist. We owe a huge thanks to three people who aided us in bringing their stories into print: our agent, Dan Lazar, for his unwavering support and enthusiasm; Becky Cole, whose editorial vision created a livelier (and more salacious) book; and assistant editor Kate Napolitano, who turned grace under pressure into an art form as she shepherded the book to completion.

Notes

Some Like It Hot: Arthur Miller

3 **A suicide kills two people:** Arthur Miller, *Miller Plays,* vol. 2 (London: A&C Black, 2009), 231.

3 **It was like running into a tree!:** Christopher Bigsby, *Arthur Miller* (London: Phoenix, 2009), 4.

4 **he was starved for sexual relief:** Ibid., 373.

4 **She was a whirling light to me then:** Arthur Miller, *Timebends: A Life* (London: Methuen, 1987), 359.

5 **the Great American Brain . . . the Great American Body:** Norman Mailer, *Marilyn: A Biography* (New York: Grosset and Dunlap, 1973), 157.

5 **Egghead Weds Hourglass:** Jeffrey Meyers, *The Genius and the Goddess* (London: Arrow, 2010), 155.

6 **It is a beautiful thing when it is intact:** Ibid., 164.

6 **I'm in a fucking prison:** Ibid., 183.

7 **the most talented slave in the world:** Ibid., 168.

7 **By the time we got to make the film:** Bigsby, *Arthur Miller*, 631.

8 **What's very sad is that I had written it:** Ibid., 629.

8 **I think we believed we'd complement each other:** John Mortimer, "Mortimer Meets Miller," *The Courier Mail* (Australia), October 24, 1987.

9 **I thought Arthur would be a sad person:** United Press International, "Beautiful Isn't Necessarily Pretty," February 6, 1987.

9 **Inge was a great relief:** Bigsby, *Arthur Miller*, 663.

9 **neither more nor less autobiographical:** Miller, *Timebends*, 521.

9 **the best of my life:** Susan C. W. Abbotson, *Critical Companion to Arthur Miller: A Literary Reference to His Life and Work* (New York: Infobase, 2007), 439.

Three's a Crowd

10 **pent up with two women:** Anne Conover, *Olga Rudge and Ezra Pound: "What Thou Lovest Well—"* (New Haven, CT: Yale University Press, 2001), 155.

11 **1 fat Englishman:** Zachary Leader, *The Life of Kingsley Amis* (New York: Pantheon Books, 2007), 510.

The Love Song of T. S. Eliot

12 **What we call the beginning:** T. S. Eliot, *Collected Poems:1909–1962* (Orlando, FL: Harcourt, 1991), 207.

12 **The truth will all come out:** Carole Seymour-Jones, *Painted Shadow: The Life of Vivienne Eliot* (New York: Doubleday, 2001), 514.

13 **It was only when I saw Vivie:** Carole Seymour-Jones, "Not Crazy After All These Years," *The Times Higher Education Supplement*, October 26, 2001.

13 **I shall rush out as I am:** T. S. Eliot, *Collected Poems*, 57.

13 **full of the most fantastic suspicions:** Blake Morrison, "The Two Mrs. Eliots," *The Independent*, April 24, 1994.

13 **fruitless and unnecessary:** Seymour-Jones, *Painted Shadow*, 503.

14 **Will T. S. Eliot please return to his home:** Ibid., 515.

14 **I cannot talk to you now:** Peter Ackroyd, *T. S. Eliot* (Harmondsworth: Penguin, 1984), 232.

14 **Oh God, oh God:** Ibid., 284.

15 **Vivienne ruined him as a man:** Harold Bloom, *T. S. Eliot* (New York: Chelsea House, 1999), 36.

15 **To her the marriage brought no happiness:** T. S. Eliot, *The Letters of T. S. Eliot, vol. 2 (1923–1925)*, ed. Valerie Eliot (New Haven, CT: Yale University Press, 2011), xix.

15 **bag of ferrets . . . biting, wriggling:** Virginia Woolf, *Diary of Virginia Woolf*, vol. 5 (Boston: Mariner Books, 1985), 32.

17 **Who think the same thoughts:** Eliot, *Collected Poems*, 221.

17 **He obviously needed to have:** Ackroyd, *T. S. Eliot*, 320.

Breaking Up Is Hard to Do

18 **For quite awhile before you left:** Andrew Carroll, *Letters of a Nation: A Collection of Extraordinary American Letters* (New York: Broadway Books, 1999), 298.

19 **Irving, when we were at the Essex House:** Barbara Seaman, *Lovely Me* (New York: Seven Stories Press, 2003), 135.

19 **My answer to your proposal:** Charlotte Brontë, *The Letters of Charlotte Brontë*, vol. 1 (Oxford: Oxford University Press, 1995), 185.

20 **Go ahead and get a divorce:** Anna Holmes, ed., *Hell Hath No Fury: Women's Letters from the End of the Affair* (London: Chrysalis, 2005), 151.

Beautiful and Damned: F. Scott and Zelda Fitzgerald

21 **Nobody has ever measured:** Nancy Milford, *Zelda: A Biography* (New York: Harper Perennial Modern Classics, 2011), 367.

22 **I married the heroine of my stories:** Matthew J. Bruccoli and Judith S. Baughman, eds., *Conversations with F. Scott Fitzgerald* (Jackson: University Press of Mississippi, 2004), 7.

23 **Marrying you would be a failure:** F. Scott Fitzgerald, *This Side of Paradise* (New York: Scribner, 1998), 111–12.

23 **I like the ones that are like me:** Milford, *Zelda*, 100.

24 **On one page I recognized a portion:** Zelda Fitzgerald, *The Collected Writings of Zelda Fitzgerald*, ed. Matthew J. Bruccoli (Tuscaloosa: The University of Alabama Press, 1997), 388.

24 **I must say everyone knew about it but Scott:** Milford, *Zelda*, 110.

25 **That September 1924:** Ibid., 112.

25 **it never occurred to me:** Kendall Taylor, *Sometimes Madness Is Wisdom: Zelda and Scott Fitzgerald—A Marriage* (New York: Ballantine Books, 2003), 139.

26 **I did not know Zelda yet:** Ernest Hemingway, *A Moveable Feast: The Restored Edition* (New York: Scribner, 2009), 151.

26 **As soon as he was working well:** Ibid., 155.

26 **She said it was a matter of measurements:** Ibid., 162.

27 **Her fine forehead sloped gently:** F. Scott Fitzgerald, *Tender Is the Night* (New York: Scribner, 1996), 18.

29 **You are the finest:** Jackson R. Bryer and Cathy W. Barks, eds., *Dear Scott, Dearest Zelda: The Love Letters of F. Scott and Zelda Fitzgerald* (New York: St. Martin's Griffin, 2003), 283.

29 **So we beat on:** F. Scott Fitzgerald, *The Great Gatsby* (New York: Scribner, 2004), 180.

Cougars and Cradle Robbers

31 **I honestly didn't know:** Hugh Davies, "At 89, Arthur Miller Grows Old Romantically," *The Daily Telegraph*, December 11, 2004.

All War, No Peace: Leo Tolstoy

32 **Nobody will ever understand me:** Leo Tolstoy, *Tolstoy's Diaries*, vol. 1, ed. Reginald F. Christian (London: Faber and Faber, 2010), 63.

32 **He has never taken the trouble:** Sophia Tolstoy, *The Diaries of Sophia Tolstoy*, trans. Cathy Porter (New York, Random House, 1985), 259.

32 **Happy families are all alike:** Leo Tolstoy, *Anna Karenina* (Oxford: Oxford University Press, 1998), 1.

32 **They wouldn't let me take leave:** Sophia Tolstoy, *The Diaries of Sofia Tolstoy*, trans. Cathy Porter (London: Alma, 2010), 420.

32 **I've lived to the age:** Leo Tolstoy, *Tolstoy's Letters*, vol. 1, ed. Reginald F. Christian (London: Athlone, 1978), 169.

33 **I wept when I saw what his:** William Shirer, *Love and Hatred: The Tormented Marriage of Leo and Sonya Tolstoy* (New York: Simon and Schuster, 1994), 58.

33 **How torturesome it was:** Sophia Tolstoy, *My Life* (Ottawa: University of Ottawa Press, 2011), 59.

33 **Could any marriage be more happy:** Sophia Tolstoy, *Diaries* (Alma), 36.

33 **There probably isn't more than one person:** Leo Tolstoy, *Diaries*, 184.

34 **repulsive, pathetic and degrading to listen to:** Ibid., 207.

34 **it would have been better:** Henry Troyat, *Tolstoy*, trans. Nancy Amphoux (New York: Grove Press, 2001), 466.

35 **He disgusts me with his talk:** Sophia Tolstoy, *Diaries* (Alma), 7.

36 **He and I are amazingly one:** Shirer, *Love and Hatred*, 117.

37 **a struggle to the death:** Lady Cynthia Asquith, *Married to Tolstoy* (New York: Greenwood, 1960), 125.

37 **I burst out crying:** Sophia Tolstoy, *Diaries* (Alma), 365.

37 **I cannot go on living:** Troyat, *Tolstoy*, 669.

38 **Telegraph Father at once:** Alexandra Tolstoy, *The Tragedy of Tolstoy* (New Haven, CT: Yale University Press, 1960), 255.

38 To escape. . . . It is necessary to escape!: Sophia Tolstoy, *The Final Struggle: Being Countess Tolstoy's Diary for 1910* (New York: Octagon, 1980), 362.

Fight Club

39 We love each other like tigers!: Graham Robb, *Rimbaud* (London: Picador, 2000), 178.

39 Ours was a drink story, not a love story: Caitlin Thomas, *Double Drink Story: My Life with Dylan Thomas* (London: Little Brown, 2000), 180.

39 I am the master!: Jeffrey Meyers, *D. H. Lawrence: A Biography* (Lanham, MD: Cooper Square Press, 2000), 298.

40 I long for you to whip me: Robert A. Caplen, *Shaken and Stirred: The Feminism of James Bond* (Bloomington, IN: Xlibris, 2010), 375.

Hell Hath No Fury: Ernest Hemingway

43 No matter how being in love: Ernest Hemingway, *Ernest Hemingway: Selected Letters 1917–1961*, ed. Carlos Baker (New York: Scribner, 2003), 87.

45 They aren't built that way: Ernest Hemingway, *To Have and Have Not* (New York: Scribner, 1996), 162.

45 I think living in sin: Jeffrey Meyers, *Hemingway: A Biography* (Boston: Da Capo Press, 1985), 349.

46 Ernest needs a new woman: Morley Callaghan, *That Summer in Paris* (Holstein, ON: Exile Editions, 2006), 137.

47 Are you a war correspondent: Bernice Kert, *The Hemingway Women: Those Who Loved Him—The Wives and Others* (New York: W. W. Norton, 1986), 391.

47 My crime really was: Ibid., 391–92.

48 Hell hath no fury like E.H. scorned: Martha Gellhorn, *Selected Letters of Martha Gellhorn*, ed. Caroline Moorehead (New York: Henry Holt, 2006), 488.

48 I don't know you: Mary Welsh Hemingway, *How It Was* (New York: Knopf, 1976), 95.

48 an unexpected slap in the face: Ibid., 116.

49 a goddamn, smirking: Ibid., 116.

49 a part which I would play: Ibid., 117.

49 Although I was entirely enthralled: Ibid., 121.

49 such a complicated: Ibid., 142.

50 Good night, my lamb: Ibid., 502.

The Alpha Mailer: Norman Mailer

53 **You know nothing about a woman:** Alice Steinbach, "The Experts on Women, Sex, Marriage," *The Baltimore Sun*, January 26, 1992.

53 **Why had I been so consumed:** Norris Church Mailer, *A Ticket to the Circus: A Memoir* (New York: Random House, 2010), 330.

54 **the search for an orgasm more apocalyptic:** Norman Mailer, *Advertisements for Myself* (Cambridge, MA: Harvard University Press, 1993), 347.

58 **At different times, I had to deal with God:** Adele Mailer, *The Last Party: Scenes from My Life with Norman Mailer* (Fort Lee, NJ: Barricade Books, 1997), 188.

58 **needed a three ring circus to get it up:** Ibid., 374.

58 **We would arrive at a party:** Rosemary Mahoney, "Powerful Attractions," *The New York Times*, December 30, 2007.

58 **should be kept in cages:** Mary Dearborn, *Mailer: A Biography* (New York: Houghton Mifflin, 2001), 286.

59 **You might try reading your books:** Sydney Ladensohn Stern, *Gloria Steinem: Her Passions, Politics, and Mystique* (Secaucus, NJ: Carol, 1997), 174.

59 **Norman has never opposed feminism:** Julia Llewellyn Smith, "It's Unfair That I'm Asked to Defend Norman for Things He Did before I Met Him," *The New York Post*, November 19, 2007.

59 **Which wife are you?:** Martin Weil, "Author and Painter Was Novelist Norman Mailer's Last Wife," *The Washington Post*, November 23, 2010.

60 **In the end, I have no complaints:** Sue Fox, "The Model Wife," *The Times* (London), October 13, 2007.

Mad, Bad, and Dangerous to Know: Lord Byron

63 **I have been all my life trying:** George Gordon Byron, *Lord Byron's Correspondence*, part 1, ed. John Murray (Whitefish, MT: Kessinger, 2005), 251.

63 **Mad, bad and dangerous to know:** Jerome McGann, *Byron and Romanticism* (Cambridge: Cambridge University Press, 2002), 114.

63 **Thus has perished, in the flower:** Abraham John Valpy, *The Pamphleteer*, vol. 24 (London: Valpy, 1825), 213.

63 **the most remarkable Englishman:** Ibid., 211.

64 **because it was the only chance:** Leslie A. Marchand, *Byron: A Portrait* (New York: Knopf, 1970), 173.

65 **revenge herself upon *herself*:** Byron, *Correspondence*, 104.

66 **like me ... her eyes, / Her hair, her features:** George Gordon Byron, *The Poetical Works of Lord Byron* (London: John Dicks, 1869), 167.

66 **it was hopeless to keep them apart:** Fiona MacCarthy, *Byron: Life and Legend* (London: Faber and Faber, 2003), 244.

66 **brink of a precipice:** Ibid., 244.

67 **We can amuse ourselves without you, my dear:** Ibid., 242.

67 **the apprehension of crimes on his part:** Ibid., 259.

67 **to *do everything wicked*:** Ibid., 261.

67 **virtuous monster:** George Gordon Byron, *Lord Byron: Selected Letters and Journals*, ed. Leslie A. Marchand (Cambridge, MA: Harvard University Press, 1982), 144.

67 **called some druggists and physicians:** George Clinton, *Memoirs of the Life and Writings of Lord Byron* (London: James Robins, 1825), 430.

68 **I was advised not to go to the theatres:** MacCarthy, *Life and Legend*, 276.

69 **never a twenty-four hours without:** Byron, *Selected Letters and Journals*, 152.

69 **A woman is virtuous here who limits:** Ibid.

69 **quite given up Concubinage:** Benita Eisler, *Byron: Child of Passion, Fool of Fame* (New York: Knopf, 1999), 606.

70 **strength gave way—for B was not a man:** Teresa Guiccioli, *Lord Byron's Life in Italy*, trans. Michael Rees, ed. Peter Cochran (Newark: University of Delaware Press, 2005), 125.

70 **essential part of the business:** MacCarthy, *Life and Legend*, 355.

70 **Think, my love, of those moments:** Iris Origo, ed., *The Last Attachment: The Story of Byron and Teresa Guiccioli* (New York: Scribner, 1949), 99.

70 **My dearest Teresa ... believe that I always *love* you:** MacCarthy, *Life and Legend*, 461.

71 **The more Byron is known:** Edna O'Brien, *Byron in Love: A Short Daring Life* (New York: W. W. Norton, 2010), vi.

Natural-Born Lady-Killers

73 **Men want a woman whom:** Caplen, *Shaken and Stirred*, 31.

73 **A woman should never be seen:** George Gordon Byron, *Lord Byron's Correspondence*, part 1, ed. John Murray (Whitefish, MT: Kessinger, 2005), 84.

73 **Women think of being a man as a gift:** Robert Andrews, *Routledge Dictionary of Quotations* (London: Routledge, 1987), 169.

73 **The sweetest pleasures are those:** Giacomo Casanova, *The Memoirs of Casanova*, vol. 2 (Middlesex: Echo Library, 2007), 281.

73 **It is always by way of pain:** Marquis de Sade, *The Bedroom Philosophers: Marquis de Sade* (Paris: Olympia Press, 2004), 94.

Never Curse Me: Gustave Flaubert

74 **What he didn't understand:** Gustave Flaubert, *Madame Bovary* (New York: Signet Classics, 2001), 184.

74 **tossing about like a boat:** Ibid., 234.

75 **were completely red with it:** Gustave Flaubert, *The Letters of Gustave Flaubert 1830–1857*, ed. and trans. Francis Steegmuller (Cambridge, MA: Belknap Press of Harvard University Press, 1980), 45.

75 **put it quickly to your mouth:** Ibid., 55.

76 **I want to cover you with love:** Ibid., 64.

76 **Never curse me!:** Ibid., 48.

76 **My mother was waiting for me:** Ibid., 45.

76 **My life is shackled:** Geoffrey Wall, *Flaubert: A Life* (New York: Farrar, Straus and Giroux, 2001), 109.

76 **You must never come here:** Ibid., 112.

77 **All the better:** Ibid.

78 **a regal-looking creature:** Flaubert, *Letters* (Belknap), 116.

78 **consummated that business:** Gustave Flaubert, *Flaubert in Egypt*, ed. Francis Steegmuller (New York: Penguin Classics, 1996), 203.

79 **in a deeply selfish way:** Wall, *Flaubert*, 201.

80 **Everyone has read it:** Elisabeth Ladenson, *Dirt for Art's Sake: Books on Trial from Madame Bovary to Lolita* (Ithaca, NY: Cornell University Press, 2007), 18.

Six Degrees of Copulation

81 **She didn't lose any time:** Francine du Plessix Gray, *Rage and Fire: A Life of Louise Colet* (New York: Touchstone, 1994), 114.

Go Your Own Way: The Beats

82 **The weight of the world:** Allen Ginsberg, *Selected Poems 1947–1995* (New York: Harper Perennial, 1997), 39.

85 **secret hero of these poems:** Allen Ginsberg, *Howl and Other Poems* (San Francisco: City Lights, 2006), 14.

85 **remind Neal to ditch a few women:** Bill Morgan, *I Celebrate Myself: The Somewhat Private Life of Allen Ginsberg* (New York: Viking, 2006), 91.

85 **It's too bad:** Carolyn Cassady, *Off the Road: Twenty Years with Cassady, Kerouac, and Ginsberg* (New York: The Overlook Press, 2008), 30.

85 **an accident of gender:** Ibid., 44.

86 **all first person:** Kevin J. Hayes, ed., *Conversations with Jack Kerouac* (Jackson: University Press of Mississippi, 2005), 54.

86 **You see what a bastard he is:** Jack Kerouac, *Road Novels 1957–1960*, ed. Douglas Brinkley (New York: The Library of America, 2007), 153.

86 **the girl with the pure and innocent:** Ibid., 274.

87 **I am forced to the appalling conclusion:** William Burroughs, *Queer* (New York: Penguin Books, 1987), xxii.

88 **I don't want your ugly old cock:** Ted Morgan, *Literary Outlaw: The Life and Times of William S. Burroughs* (New York: W. W. Norton, 2012), 247.

89 **I say we are here:** Allen Ginsberg, *The Letters of Allen Ginsberg*, ed. Bill Morgan (New York: Da Capo Press, 2008), 96.

If These Walls Could Talk

90 **the long secret night:** Robert Hass and John Hollander, eds., *American Poetry: The Twentieth Century* (New York: The Library of America, 2000), 19–20.

Sexistentialism: Simone de Beauvoir

95 **Love for the woman:** Simone de Beauvoir, *The Second Sex* (New York: Vintage, 2011), 683.

96 **He felt he had to propose to me:** Deirdre Bair, *Simone de Beauvoir: A Biography* (New York: Touchstone, 1991), 155.

96 **was foolish enough to be upset by it:** Jean-Paul Sartre, *War Diaries: Notebooks from a Phoney War, 1939–40*, trans. Quintin Hoare (Brooklyn: Verso Books, 1999), 75.

97 **What *we* have is an *essential* love:** Simone de Beauvoir, *The Prime of Life* (New York: Harper and Row, 1976), 24.

97 **could not make up entirely:** Simone de Beauvoir, *The Prime of Life* (New York: Harper and Row, 1976), 24.

98 **Watch out:** Claude Francis and Fernande Gontier, *Simone de Beauvoir: A Life, A Love Story* (New York: St. Martin's Press, 1987), 110.

98 **As for O., my passion for her:** Sartre, *War Diaries*, 78.

98 **The unfortunate episode of the trio:** De Beauvoir, *Prime of Life*, 365.

100 **My love, it's our eleventh anniversary:** Francis and Gontier, *Simone de Beauvoir*, 190.

The Art of Seduction

104 **Everything one writes comes:** Toni Bentley, *Sisters of Salome* (Lincoln: University of Nebraska Press, 2005), 193.

104 **It's time for you to become:** Judith Thurman, *Secrets of the Flesh: A Life of Colette* (New York: Ballantine, 1999), 296.

105 **lascivious and voluptuous . . . What a sauce:** Giacomo Casanova, *History of My Life*, vol. 3 (New York: Knopf, 2007), 68.

105 **If we could just have the kitchen:** Ruth Reichl, "Julia Child's Recipe for a Thoroughly Modern Marriage," *Smithsonian Magazine*, June 2012.

Web of Lies: Anaïs Nin

106 **Eroticism is one:** Wendy M. DuBow, ed., *Conversations with Anaïs Nin* (Jackson: University Press of Mississippi, 1994), 94.

106 **Part Two of my life:** Deirdre Bair, *Anaïs Nin: A Biography* (New York: Penguin Books, 1996), 327.

108 **In a way, I did not care:** Margalit Fox, "Rupert Pole, 87, Diarist's Duplicate Spouse, Dies," *The New York Times*, July 30, 2006.

109 **I learned how to live from literature:** DuBow, *Conversations*, 176.

109 **strange and wonderful:** Anaïs Nin, *The Early Diary of Anaïs Nin*, vol. 4 (1927–1931) (New York: Harcourt Brace Jovanovich, 1985), 266.

109 **out of gratitude:** Anaïs Nin, *The Diary of Anaïs Nin*, vol. 1 (1931–1934), ed. Gunther Stuhlmann (Harcourt, Brace and World, 1966), 7.

109 **I am already devoted to Henry's work:** Anaïs Nin, *Henry and June: From "A Journal of Love"—The Unexpurgated Diary of Anaïs Nin* (1931–1932) (New York: Harvest/Harcourt, 1989), 10.

110 **I saw for the first time:** Ibid., 14.

110 **color, brilliance, strangeness:** Ibid.

110 **She killed my admiration:** Nin, *Diary*, vol. 1, 20.

110 **Henry suddenly faded:** Ibid., 20.

111 **literary fuck fest:** Gunther Stuhlmann, ed., *A Literate Passion: Letters of Anaïs Nin & Henry Miller, 1932–1953* (New York: Harcourt Brace, 1989), 82.

112 **To me it is intensely humorous:** Anaïs Nin, *Fire: From "A Journal of Love"*—
     The Unexpurgated Diary of Anaïs Nin (1934–1937) (New York: Harvest/
     Harcourt, 1993), 406.

112 **I am aware of a monstrous paradox:** Nin, *Henry and June*, 60.

113 **my drug and my vice:** Anaïs Nin, *Diary of Anaïs Nin*, vol. 2 (1934–1939),
     ed. Gunther Stuhlmann (Harcourt, Brace and World, 1967), 310.

113 **Her life was her masterpiece:** Elaine Woo, "The Ranger Who Told All
     About Anais Nin's Wild Life," *Los Angeles Times*, July 26, 2006.

Shock and Awe: Tennessee Williams

116 **Love is a very difficult—occupation:** Tennessee Williams, *Period of Ad-
     justment, Or, High Point Is Built on a Cavern: A Serious Comedy* (New York:
     Dramatists Play Service, 1961), 47.

116 **frolicsome nightlife:** Tennessee Williams, *Memoirs* (New York: New Di-
     rections, 2006), 67.

117 **offend a lot of people:** Mel Gussow, "Tennessee Williams on Art and
     Sex," *The New York Times*, November 3, 1975.

117 **I could devote this whole book:** Williams, *Memoirs*, 144.

117 **could not possess his own life:** Gore Vidal, *Palimpsest: A Memoir* (New
     York: Penguin Books, 1996), 154.

117 **The love that previously:** Williams, *Memoirs*, xi.

118 **wild break-through:** Ibid., 43.

118 **I was late coming out:** Ibid., 87.

120 **follows me like a shadow:** Ibid., 99.

122 **He was so close to life:** Albert J. Devlin, ed., *Conversations with Tennessee
     Williams* (Jackson: University Press of Mississippi, 1986), 340.

123 **They knew that I had lost:** Williams, *Memoirs*, 195.

Talk Dirty to Me: James Joyce

124 **dirty little fuckbird:** Richard Ellmann, ed., *Selected Letters of James Joyce*,
     (London: Faber and Faber 1992), 185–86.

125 **Why would I bother:** Robert McAlmon, *Being Geniuses Together 1920–
     1930*, rev. ed. with supplementary chapters by Kay Boyle (Baltimore:
     Johns Hopkins University Press, 1997), 167.

Sweet Sorrow: Karen Blixen (Isak Dinesen)

129 **Love, with very young people:** Isak Dinesen, *Seven Gothic Tales* (New York: The Modern Library, 1961), 83.

130 **If I should wish anything back:** Judith Thurman, *Isak Dinesen: The Life of a Storyteller* (New York: St. Martin's Press, 1982), 144.

130 **to accommodate any windfalls:** Ernest Hemingway, *The Complete Short Stories of Ernest Hemingway: The Finca Vigia Edition* (New York: Scribner, 1998), 21.

131 **It is as if a claw:** Thurman, *Isak Dinesen*, 151.

132 **There are two things you can do:** Ibid.

132 **If it did not sound so beastly:** Isak Dinesen, *Letters from Africa: 1914–1931*, ed. Frans Lasson, trans. Anne Born (Chicago: University of Chicago Press, 1981), 281.

134 **Friend, it was sweet:** Thurman, *Isak Dinesen*, 226.

134 **For all time and eternity:** Dinesen, *Letters from Africa*, 224.

135 **To Denys Finch-Hatton I owe:** Isak Dinesen, *Out of Africa* (New York: Vintage International, 1989), 229.

136 **all sorrows can be borne:** Isak Dinesen, *Daguerreotypes and Other Essays* (Chicago: University of Chicago Press, 1984), xix.

House of Secrets: Daphne du Maurier

139 **The house possessed me:** Daphne du Maurier, *The Rebecca Notebook and Other Memories* (London: Victor Gollancz, 1981), 135.

139 **Seeds began to drop:** Ibid., 13.

140 **He's the most amazing person:** Daphne du Maurier, *Myself When Young: The Shaping of a Writer* (London: Virago, 2004), 192.

142 **a boy of eighteen . . . with nervous hands:** Margaret Forster, *Daphne du Maurier* (London: Arrow, 2007), 220.

142 **locked up in a box:** Ibid., 221.

142 **I pushed the boy back into his box:** Ibid., 222.

143 **that bloody bitch:** Michael Thornton, "Daphne's Terrible Secret," *The Daily Mail*, May 11, 2007.

143 **We crossed the line and I allowed it:** Thornton, "Daphne's Terrible Secret."

143 **He couldn't keep his hands off her:** Ibid.

144 **By God and by Christ:** Forster, *Daphne du Maurier*, 222.

144 **neither girl nor boy but disembodied spirit:** Ibid.

145 **My obsessions—you can only call them that:** Forster, *Daphne du Maurier*, 421.

145 **I find myself missing it now:** Ibid, 369.

Lonely Heart: Emily Dickinson

146 **I . . . am small, like the wren:** Harold Bloom, *Emily Dickinson* (New York: Infobase, 2008), 206.

Parisian Passion: Edith Wharton

148 **I don't know that I should care:** Edith Wharton, *The Fruit of the Tree* (Amherst, NY: Prometheus Books, 2004), 226.

148 **Very intelligent:** Edith Wharton, *The Letters of Edith Wharton*, ed. R. W. B. Lewis and Nancy Lewis, (New York: Collier Books/Macmillan, 1989), 113.

149 **In the eyes:** Edith Wharton, *A Backward Glance* (New York: Touchstone, 1998), 68–69.

149 **an alleged preponderance:** Shari Benstock, *No Gifts from Chance: A Biography of Edith Wharton* (Austin: University of Texas Press, 2004), 46.

150 **ripple of flame:** Wharton, *Letters*, 135.

151 **long lethargy:** Ibid., 161.

151 **who ha[s] given me:** Kenneth M. Price and Phyllis McBride, " 'The Life Apart': Text and Contexts of Edith Wharton's Love Diary," *American Literature* 66, no. 4 (December 1994): 683.

152 **like a "course" served & cleared away:** Wharton, *Letters*, 145.

152 **if I had been younger:** Ibid., 161.

152 **My life was better:** Ibid., 208.

153 **write better for this experience of loving:** Ibid., 162.

153 **a bitter, disheartening, sordid story:** Clara Elizabeth Fanning, ed., *The Book Review Digest: Eighth Annual Cumulation—Book Reviews of 1912 in One Alphabet* (Minneapolis: H. W. Wilson Company, 1912), 479

153 **quite the finest thing:** Henry James, *The Letters of Henry James*, vol. 2, ed. Percy Lubbock (New York: Charles Scribner's Sons, 1920), 282.

154 **what happy women feel:** Price and McBride, " 'The Life Apart,' " 673.

The Wit of a Wounded Woman: Dorothy Parker

155 **I require only three things of a man:** Dorothy Parker, *The Uncollected Dorothy Parker*, ed. Stuart Y. Silverstein (London: Duckworth, 1999), 17.

155 **It serves me right for:** Elizabeth M. Knowles, ed., *Oxford Dictionary of Quotations* (Oxford: Oxford University Press, 1999), 567.

155 **The room was filled with people:** Rhonda S. Pettit, ed., *The Critical Waltz: Essays on the Work of Dorothy Parker* (Madison, NJ: Fairleigh Dickinson University Press, 2005), 130.

A Tale of Two Dickenses: Charles Dickens

159 **My father was a wicked man:** Michael Slater, *Dickens and Women* (London: J. M. Dent, 1983), 200.

159 **All London . . . had for some time been rife:** Ada Nisbet, *Dickens and Ellen Ternan* (Berkeley: University of California Press, 1952), 20.

161 **as near being a Donkey:** Charles Dickens, *The Letters of Charles Dickens*, vol. 3 (1842–1843), ed. Madeline House, Graham Storey, and Kathleen Tillotson (Oxford: Oxford University Press, 1974), 271.

162 **Poor Catherine and I are not made:** John Forster, *Life of Charles Dickens*, vol. 3 (Cambridge: Cambridge University Press, 2011), 162.

162 **brought out all that was worst:** Nisbet, *Dickens and Ellen Ternan*, 36.

163 **the world may know:** Slater, *Dickens and Women*, 159.

165 **eminently truthful, trustworthy and self-denying:** Claire Tomalin, *The Invisible Woman: The Story of Nelly Ternan and Charles Dickens* (London: Penguin Books, 2004), 275.

Covert Affairs

166 **curious . . . quite close to murder:** Joan Schenkar, *The Talented Miss Highsmith: The Secret Life and Serious Art of Patricia Highsmith* (New York: St. Martin's Press, 2009), 282.

Turbulent Times: Frederick Douglass

168 **This proves I am impartial:** Mike F. Molaire, *African-American Who's Who, Past and Present, Greater Rochester Area* (Rochester, NY: Norex Publications, 1998), 87.

169 **Though we toiled hard:** Frederick Douglass, *Autobiographies*, ed. Henry Louis Gates Jr. (New York: The Library of America, 1994), 415.

171 **beautifully carved lips:** Maria Diedrich, *Love Across Color Lines: Ottilie Assing and Frederick Douglass* (New York: Hill and Wang, 1999), 139.

172 **able to use with great ease:** Philip S. Foner, ed., *Frederick Douglass on Women's Rights* (Boston: Da Capo Press, 1992), 22.

173 **If one stands:** William S. McFeely, *Frederick Douglass* (New York: W. W. Norton, 1991), 287.

174 **not a single repulse:** Ibid., 322.

175 **Goodbye, black blood in that family:** Ibid., 320.

175 **Love came to me:** Philip S. Foner, ed., *Frederick Douglass: Selected Speeches and Writings*, abridged and adapted by Yuval Taylor (Chicago: Lawrence Hill Books, 2000), 693.

Mr. Not So Nice Guy: Richard Wright

177 **It's your life:** Hazel Rowley, *Richard Wright: The Life and Times* (Chicago: University of Chicago Press, 2008), 388.

Born to Be Wilde: Oscar Wilde

178 **A man can be happy:** Oscar Wilde, *The Picture of Dorian Gray* (Hertfordshire, UK: Wordsworth, 1992), 139.

178 **I don't regret for a single:** Oscar Wilde, *De Profundis, The Ballad of Reading Gaol and Other Writings* (Hertfordshire, UK: Wordsworth, 1999), 68.

178 **Somehow or other I'll be famous:** Wilde, *Dorian Gray*, vi.

179 **I feel your fingers in my hair. . . . The air is full of the music:** Harford Montgomery Hyde, *The Trials of Oscar Wilde* (New York: Dover, 1962), 55.

179 **nearly as possible escaped the honor:** Barbara Belford, *Oscar Wilde: A Certain Genius* (New York: Random House, 2001), 78.

179 **shaking with fright:** Richard Ellmann, *Oscar Wilde* (New York: Vintage, 1988), 235.

179 **Prepare yourself for an astounding:** Oscar Wilde, *The Complete Letters of Oscar Wilde*, ed. Merlin Holland and Rupert Hart-Davis (New York: Henry Holt, 2000), 153.

180 **I will not allow anything:** Neil McKenna, *The Secret Life of Oscar Wilde* (New York: Random House, 2011), 65.

180 **effeminate phrase maker:** Ibid., 106.

181 **How can one desire . . . ? Desire is killed by:** Frank Harris, *Oscar Wilde* (Hertfordshire, UK: Wordsworth, 2007), 266.

181 **When I married, my wife:** Ibid., 266.

181 **The only way to get rid of:** Wilde, *Dorian Gray*, 14.

182 **that the perfect harmony of:** Michael Steinman, *Yeats's Heroic Figures: Wilde, Parnell, Swift, Casement* (Albany: SUNY Press, 1984), 17.

182 **I am one of those:** Wilde, *De Profundis and Other*, 59.

182 **I do not know what the Queensberry:** Vincent Powell, *The Legal Companion* (London: Robson Books, 2005), 13.

182 **posing as a somdomite [sic]:** Wilde, *Dorian Gray*, xxvi.

183 **It had a terrific effect on me:** McKenna, *Secret Life*, 201.

183 **a slim thing, gold-haired like an angel:** Ibid.

183 **like a tortured, hunted animal:** Ibid., 501.

183 **I have ruined the most brilliant man in London:** Richard Pine, *Oscar Wilde* (Dublin: Gill and Macmillan, 1983), 105.

184 **The train is gone—it is too late:** Ellmann, *Oscar Wilde*, 455.

184 **I am the love that dare:** Harris, *Oscar Wilde*, 301.

184 **the uselessness of all regrets:** Franny Moyle, *Constance: The Tragic and Scandalous Life of Mrs Oscar Wilde* (London: Murray, 2011), xxx.

The Pursuit of Pleasure

185 **it can't happen twice:** William C. Carter, *Marcel Proust: A Life* (New Haven, CT: Yale University Press, 2002), 70.

185 **I love prostitution. . . . One learns:** Flaubert, *Flaubert in Egypt*, 9–10.

Runaway Romantics: Percy Bysshe Shelley and Mary Shelley

189 **Love is free; to promise forever to love:** Percy Bysshe Shelley, *The Poetical Works of Percy Bysshe Shelley*, vol. 1, ed. Mary W. Shelley (London: Moxon, 1870), 64.

189 **Love is to me as light to the star:** Mary W. Shelley, *The Last Man*, vol. 1 (Philadelphia: Carey, Lea and Blanchard, 1833), 74.

189 **They wish to separate us:** Richard Holmes, *The Pursuit* (New York: Harper, 2005), 233.

189 **By this you can escape . . . and this shall reunite me:** Ibid., 233.

191 **Everyone who knows me must know:** Rosalie Glynn Grylls, *Mary Shelley* (New York: Haskell House, 1938), 29.

191 **Among women there is no equal mind to yours:** Miranda Seymour, *Mary Shelley* (New York: Grove Press, 2000), 123.

192 **Under the doctrine and belief of free love:** Daisy Hay, *Young Romantics: The Shelleys, Byron and Other Tangled Lives* (London: Bloomsbury, 2010), 308.

192 **the offspring of happy days:** Mary W. Shelley, *Frankenstein, or, The Modern Prometheus* (Boston, MA: Sever, Francis and Co. 1869), 13.

193 **descended the steps of prostitution:** Harry B. Forman, *The Shelley Library: An Essay in Bibliography* (New York: Haskell House, 1971), 5.

193 **If you had never left me:** Walter Edwin Peck, *Shelley: His Life and Work 1792–1817* (Cambridge, MA: Riverside Press, 1927), 502.

194 **become obsolete:** Hay, *Young Romantics*, 183.

194 **the dreariest and longest journey:** Percy Bysshe Shelley, *The Major Works*, ed. Zachary Leader and Michael O'Neill (Oxford: Oxford University Press, 2009), 517.

194 **Italian Platonics:** Grylls, *Mary Shelley*, 139.

195 **prophecy on his own destiny:** Percy Bysshe Shelley, *The Poetical Works of Percy Bysshe Shelley*, vol. 2, ed. Mary W. Shelley (London: Moxon, 1847), 30.

Tragic Turns

196 **changeless since the day she died:** Henry Wadsworth Longfellow, *Poems and Other Writings*, ed. J. D. McClatchy (New York: The Library of America, 2000), 671.

197 **Don't worry, it isn't your fault:** T. J. Binyon, *Pushkin: A Biography* (New York: Vintage, 2004), 600.

Eclipse of the Heart: Voltaire

198 **Friendship is:** Francois-Marie Arouet (Voltaire), *Philosophical Dictionary*, part 1 (Whitefish, MT: Kessinger Publishing, 2003), 355.

198 **I met a young lady:** Samuel Edwards, *The Divine Mistress: A Biography of Emilie du Châtelet—The Beloved of Voltaire* (Philadelphia: David McKay, 1970), 85.

199 **The hand of Venus:** Judith P. Zinsser, *Emilie du Châtelet: Daring Genius of the Enlightenment* (New York: Penguin Books, 2007), 79.

201 **Since I've met a man of letters:** David Bodanis, *Passionate Minds: Emilie du Châtelet, Voltaire, and the Great Love Affair of the Enlightenment* (New York: Three Rivers Press, 2007), 111.

201 **divine Emilie:** Zinsser, *Emilie du Châtelet*, 6.

204 **My tears will never stop flowing:** Nancy Mitford, *Voltaire in Love* (New York: Dutton, 1985), 271.

Eternal Flames

205 **To refuse to reply to me:** Charlotte Brontë, *Selected Letters of Charlotte Brontë*, ed. Margaret Smith (New York: Oxford University Press, 2007), 68.

A Marriage of Minds: Virginia Woolf

207 **I want to tell you that you:** Hermione Lee, *Virginia Woolf* (New York: Random House, 2010), 759.

207 **If anybody could have:** Ibid., 757.

209 **I feel no physical attraction:** Roger Poole, *The Unknown Virginia Woolf* (Cambridge: Cambridge University Press, 1995), 96.

209 **Why do you think people:** Panthea Reid, *Art and Affection: A Life of Virginia Woolf* (Oxford: Oxford University Press, 1996), 137.

209 **sexually cowardly:** Lee, *Virginia Woolf*, 243.

209 **because she was a genius:** Peter Alexander, *Leonard and Virginia Woolf: A Literary Partnership* (New York: St. Martin's Press, 1992), 77.

210 **a comatose invalid:** Julia Briggs, *Virginia Woolf: An Inner Life* (Boston: Houghton Mifflin, 2005), 35.

210 **I want everything—love, children:** Poole, *Unknown Virginia Woolf*, 95.

210 **Never pretend that the things:** Lee, *Virginia Woolf*, 261.

211 **manual occupation . . . would take:** Ibid., 362.

212 **I'm the only woman in England:** Virginia Woolf, *A Writer's Diary*, ed. Leonard Woolf (Boston: Houghton Mifflin Harcourt, 2003), 81.

212 **all fire and legs and beautiful plunging:** Virginia Woolf, *A Change of Perspective: The Letters of Virginia Woolf*, vol. 3 (1923–1928), ed. Nigel Nicolson (London: Hogarth Press, 1977), 479.

212 **I don't know whether:** Victoria Glendinning, *Vita: The Life of V. Sackville-West* (New York: Quill, 1985), 155.

212 **I feel like one of those wax figures:** Virginia Woolf, *Orlando* (New York: Random House, 2005), xx.

213 **I still think I might have saved her:** Victoria Sackville-West, Harold G. Nicolson, and Nigel Nicolson, eds., *Vita and Harold: The Letters of Vita Sackville-West and Harold Nicolson* (New York: Putnam, 1992), 392.

213 **We walked around the square:** Lyndall Gordon, *Virginia Woolf: A Writer's Life* (New York: W. W. Norton, 2001), 250.

213 **I feel certain that I am going mad again:** Reid, *Art and Affection*, 449.

214 **I know that V will not come across:** Victoria Glendinning, *Leonard Woolf: A Biography* (New York: Simon and Schuster, 2006), 332.

Romance with Death: Sylvia Plath

215 **a breaker of things and people:** Paul Alexander, *Rough Magic* (New York: Penguin Books, 1992), 194.

Count the Ways: Robert and Elizabeth Barrett Browning

219 **Whoso loves believes the impossible:** Elizabeth Barrett Browning, *Aurora Leigh and Other Poems* (New York: Penguin Classics, 1995), 149.

219 **I love your verses:** *The Letters of Robert Browning and Elizabeth Barrett Barrett, 1845–1846* (London: Smith, Elder,1899), 1–2.

220 **from Browning some "Pomegranate":** Barrett Browning, *Aurora Leigh and Other Poems*, 330.

220 **I had a letter from Browning:** Frances Winwar, *The Immortal Lovers: Elizabeth Barrett and Robert Browning* (New York: Harper and Brothers, 1950), 126.

221 **Winters shut me up:** Browning and Barrett, *Letters, 1845–1846*, 4.

221 **scarcely to be called young now:** Ibid., 43.

221 **exchange some of this:** Ibid., 44.

221 **Well! But we are friends:** Ibid., 72.

222 **You are in what I should wonder:** Ibid., 222.

223 **We live heart to heart:** Winwar, *Immortal Lovers*, 217.

224 **How do I love thee?:** Barrett Browning, *Aurora Leigh and Other Poems*, 398.

224 **The fifty poems finished:** Robert Browning, *The Poetical Works of Robert Browning*, vol. 4 (London: Smith, Elder, 1912), 173.

224 **I *tried* to leave them:** Julia Markus, *Dared and Done: The Marriage of Elizabeth Barrett and Robert Browning* (New York: Knopf, 1995), 74.

225 **My Robert:** Winwar, *Immortal Lovers*, 280–81.

How Do I Love Thee?

226 **Madam, I greet you:** Marianne Walker, *Margaret Mitchell and John Marsh: The Love Story Behind Gone with the Wind* (Atlanta: Peachtree Publishers, 2011), 162.

Romantic Suspense: Agatha Christie

228 **Women can accept the fact:** Agatha Christie, *Murder in Mesopotamia* (New York: Berkley Books, 1984), 131.

229 **only seemed to regard him:** Janet Morgan, *Agatha Christie: A Biography* (New York: Harper Collins, 1986), 147.

229 **She has suffered:** Michael Rhodes, "Mrs. Christie Found at Harrogate Hotel," *Yorkshire Post*, December 15, 1926; published online December 15, 2006.

230 **A terrible sense of loneliness:** Agatha Christie, *An Autobiography* (New York: William Morrow, 2011), 349.

230 **I think you had better:** Ibid., 349.

230 **His coming back:** Ibid., 352.

231 **near escapes from getting married:** Ibid., 199.

232 **With those words, that part of my life:** Ibid., 351.

232 **must in some way:** Ibid., 352.

233 **In Celia we have:** Max Mallowan, *Mallowan's Memoirs* (New York: Dodd, Mead, 1977), 195.

234 **The only person:** Christie, *An Autobiography*, 411.

234 **An archaeologist is the best:** Bennett Cerf, *The Life of the Party* (New York: Doubleday, 1956), 146.

235 **love and happiness which:** Mallowan, *Memoirs*, 311.

Delicious Dish: Gertrude Stein and Alice B. Toklas

238 **What is marriage:** Gertrude Stein, *Last Operas and Plays* (New York: Taylor and Francis, 1995), 74.

238 **Please Miss Stein:** "The Editor's Uneasy Chair," *Vanity Fair*, September 1934.

239 **She was a golden brown presence:** Alice B. Toklas, *What Is Remembered* (New York: Holt, Rinehart and Winston, 1963), 23.

241 **nicely ugly:** "Alice Toklas, 89, Is Dead in Paris," *The New York Times*, March 8, 1967.

242 **Alice was merely:** "World: Together Again," *Time*, March 17, 1967.

242 **What would Alice have been without Gertrude?:** "Alice Toklas, 89, Is Dead in Paris."

242 **the sad, slight book:** Anna Linzie, *The True Story of Alice B. Toklas: A Study of Three Autobiographies* (Iowa City: University of Iowa Press, 2006), 110.

243 **a kind of abnormal vampire:** Brenda Wineapple, *Sister Brother: Gertrude and Leo Stein* (Lincoln: University of Nebraska Press, 2008), 297.

243 **seen trees strangled:** James R. Mellow, *Charmed Circle: Gertrude Stein and Company* (New York: Henry Holt, 2003), 179.

243 **Alice B. is the wife for me:** Gertrude Stein, "A Sonatina Followed by Another," in *Bee Time Vine and Other Pieces, 1913–1927* (New Haven, CT: Yale University Press, 1953), 12.

243 **tiny dish of delicious:** Gertrude Stein, "The Present," in *Bee Time Vine and Other Pieces*, 212.

243 **strong-strong husband:** Kay Turner, ed., *Baby Precious Always Shines: Selected Love Notes Between Gertrude Stein and Alice B. Toklas* (New York: Stonewall Inn Editions, 2000), 10.

244 **Consider the menus carefully:** Alice B. Toklas, *Aromas and Flavors of the Past and Present: A Book of Exquisite Cooking* (New York: Lyons Press, 1996), xxvi.

First Impressions

245 **It wasn't like lightning:** Nöel Riley Fitch, *Appetite for Life: The Biography of Julia Child* (New York: Anchor, 2012), 5.

245 **He loves good food:** Nöel Riley Fitch, "The Crisco Kid," *Los Angeles Magazine*, August 1996.

Come Sail Away: Robert Louis Stevenson

247 **What woman would ever:** Robert Louis Stevenson, *Essays of Robert Louis Stevenson* (New York: C. Scribner, 1906), 45.

248 **damnably in love:** Robert Louis Stevenson, *RLS: Stevenson's Letters to Charles Baxter*, ed. DeLancey Ferguson (Port Washington, NY: Kennikat Press, 1973), 63.

248 **tall, gaunt Scotsman:** Ian Bell, *Dreams of Exile: Robert Louis Stevenson, A Biography* (New York: Henry Holt, 1993), 105.

248 **My second mother, my first wife:** Robert Louis Stevenson, *A Child's Garden of Verses* (Boston: Mobile Reference, 2009), dedication.

249 **an atmosphere of thrilling:** Nellie Van de Grift Sanchez, *The Life of Mrs. Robert Louis Stevenson* (New York: C. Scribner's Sons, 1920), 1–2.

250 **I am now engaged:** Robert Louis Stevenson, *The Letters of Robert Louis Stevenson*, vol. 1, ed. Sidney Colvin (New York: Scribner, 1917), 318.

251 **a character as strong:** Van de Grift Sanchez, *Life of Mrs. Robert Louis Stevenson*, 82.

252 **I wrote pages of criticism:** Claire Harman, *Myself and the Other Fellow: A Life of Robert Louis Stevenson* (New York: Harper Collins, 2005), 296.

253 **If I could die just now:** Robert Louis Stevenson, *The Letters of Robert Louis Stevenson*, vol. 4, ed. Sidney Colvin (New York: Scribner, 1917), 288.

253 **You are nearest to the pain:** Henry James, *Letters*, vol. 3 *(1883–1895)*, ed. Leon Edel (Boston: Harvard University Press, 1980), 498.

253 **Teacher, tender:** Robert Louis Stevenson, *The Works of Robert Louis Stevenson: The Master of Ballantrae, Weir of Hermiston, Poems* (New York: Jefferson Press, 1922), 624.

You've Got Mail

254 **In spite of myself:** David Lowenherz, ed., *The 50 Greatest Love Letters of All Time* (New York: Crown, 2002), 91.

254 **I almost wish:** John Keats, *Selected Letters*, ed. Robert Gittings (New York: Oxford University Press, 2004), 245.

254 **I have often thought:** Nicholas Murray, *Kafka: A Biography* (New Haven, CT: Yale University Press, 2002), 155.

255 **It's my love:** Evelyn Blewer, ed., *My Beloved Toto: Letters from Juliette Drouet to Victor Hugo, 1833–1882*, trans. Victoria Tietze Larson (Albany: SUNY Press, 2005), 1.

255 **My heart is full of you:,** Emily Dickinson, *Selected Letters*, ed. Thomas H. Johnson (Cambridge, MA: Harvard University Press, 1986), 90.

Select Bibliography

Some Like It Hot: Arthur Miller

Bigsby, Christopher. *Arthur Miller*. London: Phoenix, 2009.

Meyers, Jeffrey. *The Genius and the Goddess: Arthur Miller and Marilyn Monroe*. London: Arrow, 2010.

Miller, Arthur. *Timebends: A Life*. London: Methuen, 1987.

The Love Song of T. S. Eliot

Ackroyd, Peter. *T. S. Eliot*. Harmondsworth: Penguin, 1984.

Bloom, Harold. *T. S. Eliot*. New York: Chelsea House, 1999.

Gordon, Lyndall. *T. S. Eliot: An Imperfect Life*. New York: W. W. Norton, 2000.

Seymour-Jones, Carole. *Painted Shadow: The Life of Vivienne Eliot, First Wife of T. S. Eliot, and the Long-Suppressed Truth About Her Influence on His Genius*. New York: Doubleday, 2001.

Beautiful and Damned: F. Scott and Zelda Fitzgerald

Bruccoli, Matthew J. *Some Sort of Epic Grandeur: The Life of F. Scott Fitzgerald*. 2nd ed. Columbia: University of South Carolina Press, 2002.

Bryer, Jackson R., and Cathy W. Barks, eds. *Dear Scott, Dearest Zelda: The Love Letters of F. Scott and Zelda Fitzgerald*. New York: St. Martin's Griffin, 2003.

Milford, Nancy. *Zelda: A Biography*. New York: Harper Perennial Modern Classics, 2011.

Taylor, Kendall. *Sometimes Madness Is Wisdom: Zelda and Scott Fitzgerald—A Marriage*. New York: Ballantine Books, 2003.

All War, No Peace: Leo Tolstoy

Shirer, William. *Love and Hatred: The Tormented Marriage of Leo and Sonya Tolstoy*. New York: Simon and Schuster, 1994.

Smoluchowski, Louise. *Lev and Sonya: The Story of the Tolstoy Marriage*. New York: Putnam, 1987.

Tolstoy, Sophia. *The Diaries of Sofia Tolstoy*. Translated by Cathy Porter. London: Alma, 2010.

Hell Hath No Fury: Ernest Hemingway

Hemingway, Mary Welsh. *How It Was*. New York: Knopf, 1976.

Kert, Bernice. *The Hemingway Women: Those Who Loved Him—The Wives and Others*. New York: W. W. Norton, 1986.

Meyers, Jeffrey. *Hemingway: A Biography*. Boston: Da Capo Press, 1999.

Moorehead, Caroline. *Gellhorn: A Twentieth-Century Life*. New York: Henry Holt, 2004.

The Alpha Mailer: Norman Mailer

Dearborn, Mary. *Mailer: A Biography*. New York: Houghton Mifflin, 2001.

Mailer, Adele. *The Last Party: Scenes from My Life with Norman Mailer*. Fort Lee, NJ: Barricade Books, 1997.

Mailer, Norris Church. *A Ticket to the Circus: A Memoir*. New York: Random House, 2010.

Rollyson, Carl. *Norman Mailer: The Last Romantic*. New York: iUniverse, 2008.

Mad, Bad, and Dangerous to Know: Lord Byron

Hay, Daisy. *Young Romantics: The Shelleys, Byron and Other Tangled Lives*. London: Bloomsbury, 2010.

MacCarthy, Fiona. *Byron: Life and Legend*. London: Faber and Faber, 2003.

O'Brien, Edna. *Byron in Love: A Short Daring Life*. New York: W. W. Norton, 2010.

Never Curse Me: Gustave Flaubert

Brown, Frederick. *Flaubert: A Biography*. Cambridge, MA: Harvard University Press, 2007.

Gray, Francine du Plessix. *Rage and Fire: A Life of Louise Colet*. New York: Touchstone, 1995.

Wall, Geoffrey. *Flaubert: A Life*. New York: Farrar, Straus and Giroux, 2001.

Go Your Own Way: The Beats

Campbell, James. *This Is the Beat Generation: New York, San Francisco, Paris*. Berkeley: University of California Press, 2001.

Knight, Brenda. *Women of the Beat Generation: The Writers, Artists and Muses at the Heart of a Revolution*. Berkeley, CA: Conari Press, 1996.

Marler, Regina, ed. *Queer Beats: How the Beats Turned America On to Sex: Selected Writings*. San Francisco: Cleis Press, 2004.

Morgan, Bill. *I Celebrate Myself: The Somewhat Private Life of Allen Ginsberg*. New York: Viking, 2006.

Sexistentialism: Simone de Beauvoir

Bair, Deirdre. *Simone de Beauvoir: A Biography*. New York: Touchstone, 1991.

Francis, Claude, and Fernande Gontier. *Simone de Beauvoir: A Life, a Love Story*. New York: St. Martin's Press, 1987.

Web of Lies: Anaïs Nin

Bair, Deirdre. *Anaïs Nin: A Biography*. New York: Penguin Books, 1996.

Ferguson, Robert. *Henry Miller: A Life*. New York: W. W. Norton, 1991.

Fitch, Noël Riley. *Anaïs: The Erotic Life of Anaïs Nin*. New York: Little, Brown, 1993.

Nin, Anaïs, and Henry Miller. *A Literate Passion: Letters of Anaïs Nin and Henry Miller, 1932–1953*. Edited by Gunther Stuhlmann. New York: Harcourt Brace, 1989.

Shock and Awe: Tennessee Williams

Spoto, Donald. *The Kindness of Strangers: The Life of Tennessee Williams*. Boston: Da Capo Press, 1997.

Williams, Tennessee. *Memoirs*. New York: New Directions, 2006.

Sweet Sorrow: Karen Blixen (Isak Dinesen)

Donelson, Linda. *Out of Isak Dinesen in Africa: The Untold Story.* Iowa City: Coulsong List, 1995.
Thurman, Judith. *Isak Dinesen: The Life of a Storyteller.* New York: St. Martin's Press, 1982.

House of Secrets: Daphne du Maurier

Auerbach, Nina. *Daphne du Maurier: Haunted Heiress.* Philadelphia: University of Pennsylvania Press, 2002.
Du Maurier, Daphne. *The Daphne du Maurier Companion.* Edited by Helen Taylor. London: Virago, 2007.
———. *Myself When Young: The Shaping of a Writer.* London: Virago, 2004.
———. *The Rebecca Notebook and Other Memories.* London: Virago, 2005.
Forster, Margaret. *Daphne du Maurier.* London: Arrow, 1993.

Parisian Passion: Edith Wharton

Benstock, Shari. *No Gifts from Chance: A Biography of Edith Wharton.* Austin: University of Texas Press, 2004.
Lee, Hermione. *Edith Wharton.* New York: New York: Vintage, 2008.
Wharton, Edith. *The Letters of Edith Wharton.* Edited by R. W. B. Lewis and Nancy Lewis. New York: Collier Books/Macmillan, 1989.

A Tale of Two Dickenses: Charles Dickens

Ackroyd, Peter. *Dickens.* London: Vintage, 2002.
Slater, Michael. *Dickens and Women.* London: Dent, 1983.
Tomalin, Claire. *The Invisible Woman: The Story of Nelly Ternan and Charles Dickens.* London: Penguin, 2004.

Turbulent Times: Frederick Douglass

Diedrich, Maria. *Love Across Color Lines: Ottilie Assing and Frederick Douglass.* New York: Hill and Wang, 1999.
McFeely, William S. *Frederick Douglass.* New York: W. W. Norton, 1991.

Born to Be Wilde: Oscar Wilde

Ellmann, Richard. *Oscar Wilde*. New York: Vintage, 1988.

McKenna, Neil. *The Secret Life of Oscar Wilde*. New York: Random House, 2011.

Moyle, Franny. *Constance: The Tragic and Scandalous Life of Mrs Oscar Wilde*. London: John Murray, 2011.

Runaway Romantics: Percy Bysshe Shelley and Mary Shelley

Hay, Daisy. *Young Romantics: The Shelleys, Byron and Other Tangled Lives*. London: Bloomsbury, 2010.

Holmes, Richard. *Shelley: The Pursuit*. New York: Harper, 2005.

Seymour, Miranda. *Mary Shelley*. New York: Grove Press, 2000.

Eclipse of the Heart: Voltaire

Andrews, Wayne. *Voltaire*. New York: New Directions, 1981.

Bodanis, David. *Passionate Minds: Emilie du Châtelet, Voltaire, and the Great Love Affair of the Enlightenment*. New York: Three Rivers Press, 2007.

Mitford, Nancy. *Voltaire in Love*. New York: Dutton, 1985.

Zinsser, Judith P. *Emilie du Châtelet: Daring Genius of the Enlightenment*. New York: Penguin Books, 2007.

A Marriage of Minds: Virginia Woolf

Alexander, Peter. *Leonard and Virginia Woolf: A Literary Partnership*. New York: St. Martin's Press, 1992.

Bell, Quentin. *Virginia Woolf: A Biography*. London: Pimlico, 1996.

Gordon, Lyndall. *Virginia Woolf: A Writer's Life*. New York: W. W. Norton, 2001.

Lee, Hermione. *Virginia Woolf*. New York: Random House, 1996.

Poole, Roger. *The Unknown Virginia Woolf*. Cambridge: Cambridge University Press, 1995.

Rosenfeld, Natania. *Outsiders Together: Virginia and Leonard Woolf*. Princeton, NJ: Princeton University Press, 2001.

Count the Ways: Robert and Elizabeth Barrett Browning

Markus, Julia. *Dared and Done: The Marriage of Elizabeth Barrett and Robert Browning*. New York: Knopf, 1995.

Winwar, Frances. *The Immortal Lovers: Elizabeth Barrett and Robert Browning*. New York: Harper and Brothers, 1950.

Romantic Suspense: Agatha Christie

Christie, Agatha. *An Autobiography*. New York: William Morrow, 2011.
Hack, Richard. *Duchess of Death: The Unauthorized Biography of Agatha Christie*. Beverly Hills, CA: Phoenix Books, 2009.
Morgan, Janet. *Agatha Christie: A Biography*. New York: Harper Collins, 1986.

Delicious Dish: Gertrude Stein and Alice B. Toklas

Mellow, James R. *Charmed Circle: Gertrude Stein and Company*. New York: Henry Holt, 2003.
Souhami, Diana. *Gertrude and Alice*. New York: I. B. Tauris, 2009.
Stein, Gertrude. *The Autobiography of Alice B. Toklas*. New York: Vintage, 1990.

Come Sail Away: Robert Louis Stevenson

Balfour, Sir Graham. *The Life of Robert Louis Stevenson*. New York: C. Scribner's Sons, 1915.
Bell, Ian. *Robert Louis Stevenson: Dreams of Exile*. New York: Henry Holt, 1993.
Sanchez, Nellie Van de Grift. *The Life of Mrs. Robert Louis Stevenson*. New York: C. Scribner's Sons, 1920.